Richard Jones

Richard Jones

This book provides a stimulating introduction to the world between AD600 and 1914 for readers with little previous knowledge of history. In our increasingly interdependent world, an understanding of other people and their history is becoming vitally important, but many people find it difficult to acquire an overall view of world history because they never have attractive enough starting points. This book provides these in short visual chapters, describing, in simple terms, the major developments in the history of the world.

It is, of course, an immensely difficult task to produce a world history, especially when aiming at young readers, and controversial selections have inevitably had to be made. We have not attempted, however, to give a comprehensive account of the 13 centuries spanned by this book. A vast amount of detail has had to be omitted, but there are suggestions for finding out more and every library, bookshop and museum contains a wide variety of material which can take children beyond the starting points this book provides.

First published in 1979 by Usborne Publishing Ltd, Usborne House, 83-85 Saffron Hill, London EC1N 8RT, England.

Printed in Belgium

CHILDREN'S ENCYCLOPEDIA OF
HISTORY
Dark Ages to 1914

Dr Anne Millard

Illustrated by Joseph McEwan
Designed by Graham Round
Edited by Robyn Gee and Jenny Tyler

The material in this book is also published as three separate titles in the
Usborne Picture World History series: *Crusaders, Aztecs, Samurai,
Exploration and Discovery* and *The Age of Revolutions*.

Contents

Consultant Editors: Brian Adams, Verulamium Museum, St Albans, England; D. Barrass, University of East Anglia, England; Professor Edmund Bosworth, Dept of Near Eastern Studies, University of Manchester, England; Ben Burt, Museum of Mankind, London, England; Elizabeth Carter, Institute of Archaeology, London, England; Dr M. C. Chapman, University of Hull, England; T. R. Clayton, University of Cambridge, England; Dr M. Falkus, London School of Economics, England; Professor Norman Hampson, University of York, England; George Hart, British Museum, London, England; Dr C. J. Heywood, University of London, England; Peter Johnston, Commonwealth Institute, London, England; Dr Michael Loewe, University of Cambridge, England; Dr M. McCauley, University of London, England; Dr J. A. Sharpe, University of York, England; Dr C. D. Sheldon, University of Cambridge, England; R. W. Skelton, Victoria & Albert Museum, London, England; Dr R. Waller, University of Cambridge, England.

Picture research by Penni O'Grady

About this Book

This book begins at a time when a new religion, Islam, was beginning in the Middle East. Europe was in chaos. The Romans' well-ordered government had been ended around AD400 by invading hordes of barbarians. The time that followed is often know as the European "Dark Ages".

This book describes some of the main developments in Europe from the end of the Dark Ages to the outbreak of World War I. It also tells about the civilisations of Africa, America, India and the Far East and what happened when European explorers found them.

When the barbarians invaded Europe they brought their own religions with them, but the Christians who were left tried to convert them. This picture illustrates one of the stories from this time. It tells of St Coifi, a Christian, who lived in the north of England.

He wanted to show the heathens how powerless their gods were, so he rode into one of their holy places and hurled his spear at the statues there. When the heathens saw that nothing dreadful happened, many decided that he was right and became Christians.

The Beginning of a New Religion

Soon after AD600,* in the land of Arabia, a man called Muhammad was preaching a new religion. He believed in Allah, the "One God". By the time of his death, most people in Arabia followed his religion and called him the Prophet.

In Europe, most people in the Roman Empire were Christians. But when the Empire was invaded, many of them began worshipping other gods. The eastern part of the Roman Empire (called the Byzantine Empire) was not invaded and stayed Christian.

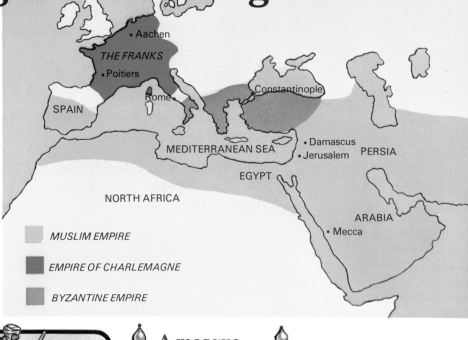

MUSLIM EMPIRE

EMPIRE OF CHARLEMAGNE

BYZANTINE EMPIRE

1 Islam Page from Koran.

The teachings of Muhammad were collected and written down in a book called the Koran. His faith became known as Islam and his followers were called Muslims.

2

The caliphs, who were Muhammad's successors, believed that everyone should become Muslims. They fought many wars to spread their faith and conquered a great empire.

3

These Muslims are making a pilgrimage to Mecca, the home of Muhammad. All Muslims are meant to visit Mecca at least once in their lives.

Muslims eat and drink only at night during the month they call Ramadan. Good Muslims also give money to the poor.

A mosque

Tower called a minaret. People are called to prayer from here by a man called a muezzin.

Recess, called the Mihrab, which shows the direction of Mecca.

Fountain where people must wash before praying.

Muslims should pray five times every day, facing towards Mecca. On Fridays, prayers are said in buildings, like this, called mosques.

2   *AD stands for two Latin words. Dates with AD next to them are that number of years after the birth of Christ.*

Christians in Europe

1 The Christian Church in western Europe was led by the Pope, seen here with one of his priests. Many popes sent out missionaries to persuade people to become Christians.

2 Some missionaries were killed by the people they tried to convert. It was several hundred years before people in Europe accepted Christianity as their religion.

3 The Muslims began to invade southern Europe. In AD732, Charles Martel, king of a people called the Franks, stopped their advance by defeating them at the Battle of Poitiers.

4 This is Roderigo of Bivar, who was known as El Cid, which means "The Lord". He helped to keep the Muslims out of northern Spain and became a great Christian hero.

5 In AD768, Charlemagne (Charles the Great) became King of the Franks. He conquered a lot of Europe and became its first great leader since the fall of the Roman Empire.

6 Charlemagne forced the people he conquered to become Christians, and fought the Muslims in Spain. On Christmas Day AD800, Pope Leo III crowned him Holy Roman Emperor.

7 This gold image of Charlemagne was made to put his skull in.

After Charlemagne's death his empire was divided. The Holy Roman Emperors ruled only the German-speaking peoples of Europe from then on, but were still very powerful.

8 Emperors and popes often quarrelled over power. After one quarrel, Pope Gregory VII kept Henry IV waiting in the snow outside Canossa Castle for three days before he would forgive him. Quarrels between other emperors and popes resulted in long, bitter wars in Germany and Italy.

Key dates

AD570/632	Life of **Muhammad.**
AD622	First year of the Muslim calendar.
AD630	Mecca surrendered to Muhammad.
AD635	Muslims captured Damascus.
AD637/642	Muslims conquered Persia.
AD638	Muslims captured Jerusalem.
AD641/642	Muslims conquered Egypt.
By AD700	All North Africa conquered by Muslims.
AD732	Battle of Poitiers.
AD768/814	Reign of **Charlemagne.**
AD800	**Charlemagne** crowned Holy Roman Emperor.
AD1077	Meeting at Canossa between **Henry IV** and **Gregory VII.**
AD1043/1099	Life of **El Cid.**

Life in Viking Times

In Denmark, Norway and Sweden there lived a people called the North or Norsemen. They were farmers, fishermen and traders. Norsemen who sailed abroad were called Vikings. Some Vikings settled in France and became known as Normans.

Burial mounds

Wooden rampart

Wooden houses

Wooden cart

Fishermen returning home.

Chief's hall

A few animals spend the winter in their owner's house. The rest were killed in the autumn and the meat salted to make it keep.

Carving a walrus tusk.

Sledge

Bed

Wooden bucket

Vikings lived in settlements like this one. The wall and part of the roof of the chief's house have been cut away so that you can see inside.

Carvings

The Vikings were skilled wood-carvers and metal-workers. This carved wooden head is from a wagon.

Runes

Memorial stones to the dead were sometimes set up. These usually had letters called runes carved on them.

A burial

This is the grave of a Viking warrior. Later it will be covered with earth. His possessions, including his animals and sometimes even a slave, were buried with him. The Vikings believed that dead warriors went to "Valhalla", the hall of the gods.

Viking raiders

The men row when they are setting off and landing and when there is not enough wind for sailing.

When they are out of sight of land they steer by the Pole Star and the sun.

Steering oar

Ropes at bottom corners turn sail to catch the wind.

The Vikings were sailors, warriors and adventurers. At first they robbed and plundered other lands. Later they settled in many parts of Europe, including Iceland.

From Iceland they went to Greenland and from there they are thought to have reached America. Long poems, called sagas, were written about brave Viking heroes.

The Vikings in France (Normans) were great soldiers. In AD1066, William, Duke of Normandy conquered England. Another group set out and conquered Sicily and part of Italy.

Where the Vikings went

GREENLAND

ICELAND

NORWAY SWEDEN

BALTIC SEA • Novgorod

NORTH SEA

DENMARK

IRELAND • Dublin

• London

NORTH AMERICA

NORMANDY

• Kiev

ALANTIC OCEAN

ITALY
Rome

Constantinople

SICILY

MEDITERRANEAN SEA

····· Viking raids and voyages

—— Norman invasions

Key dates

AD793/900	Great Viking raids on British Isles and northern France.
AD862	Viking settlers in Kiev and Novgorod in Russia.
AD870/930	Iceland colonized by Vikings.
AD900/911	Normandy settled by Vikings.
AD960	**Harald Bluetooth**, King of Denmark, converted to Christianity.
AD1000	Vikings reached America.
AD1016	**Knut** became King of England.
AD1066	**William of Normandy** (William the Conqueror), descendant of Viking settlers, conquered England. Other Normans conquered part of Italy.

Kings, Knights and Castles

All the countries of Europe were organized in roughly the same way in the Middle Ages. A king or emperor ruled a whole country and owned all the land.

The king sometimes needed support or money for a particular plan. So he called a meeting of his nobles, bishops and specially chosen knights and townsmen to discuss it with him. This was the beginning of parliaments.

The king divided his land amongst his most important men. In return, they did "homage" to him. This meant that they knelt in front of him and promised to serve him and fight for him, whenever they were needed. These men were the nobles.

Each noble divided his land among knights who did homage to him. Peasants served a noble or knight and, in return, were allowed to live on his land. This arrangement of exchanging land for services is called the "feudal system".

Castles were uncomfortable places to live. They were damp, cold and draughty. Early castles had no glass in the windows and there was no running water. They were lit by torches made of twigs or rushes.

Kings and nobles built castles to protect themselves against enemies. These might be foreign invaders, other nobles or even rebellious peasants. We have taken away two walls so you can see inside.

Travelling bringing

Archers practising

Stables

Armour makers

1 Becoming a knight

A boy who wanted to be a knight was sent to a noble's house as a page. He was taught to fight and to behave properly.

2 When he was older he became a squire. It was his job to serve a knight and to follow him into battle. Here is a squire with his knight.

3 If he proved himself to be worthy of the honour, a noble, perhaps even the king, would "knight" the young man.

4 The new knight's father or another noble usually gave him some land with peasants and villages. This was called a manor.

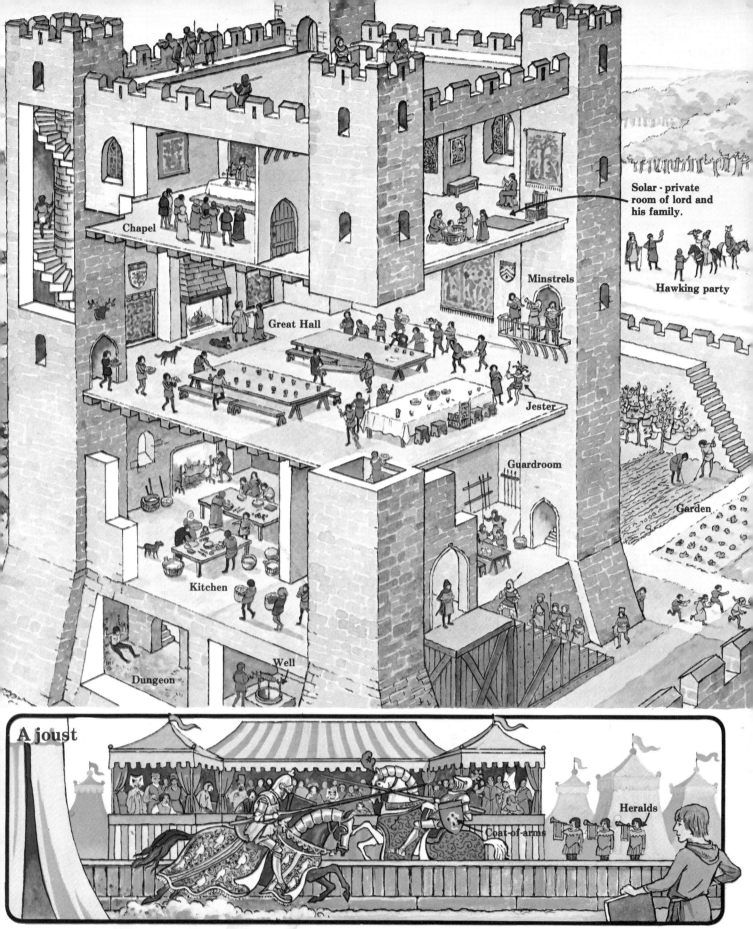

Solar - private room of lord and his family.

Hawking party

Chapel

Minstrels

Great Hall

Jester

Guardroom

Kitchen

Garden

Dungeon

Well

A joust

Coat-of-arms

Heralds

To keep in practice for battle, knights took part in specially organized fights. These were called tournaments or jousts. At a joust, two knights on horseback charged at each other with long lances, and tried to knock each other to the ground. Each noble family had a "coat-of-arms", which was painted on their shields, so they could be recognized in armour.

A knight wore a ribbon, badge or scarf belonging to his favourite lady. This was called her "favour". If he won he brought great honour to her as well as to himself.

Village Life

In the Middle Ages, most people in Europe lived in villages. Each village was controlled by the Lord of the Manor. It usually had three fields, divided into strips, which the lord allowed the villagers to farm. They paid him by working for him and by giving him some of the food they grew.

All the peasants can use the common. They can graze their animals here and gather wood and berries.

Fisherman. The Church said people should always eat fish on Fridays.

The ford is a shallow part of the stream, where people can cross.

Ford

The villagers are holding a fair. This is their only chance to buy goods from outside the village. Jugglers, acrobats and musicians have come to perform at the fair.

Priest's house

Dancing bear

Merchants are coming to the fair to buy the villagers' wool.

Villagers harvesting wheat. Next year they will grow barley here.

Black death

In AD1348, a ship from the East arrived in an Italian port. Some sick sailors came ashore bringing with them a terrible disease, known as the Plague or Black Death.

The Plague quickly spread across Europe because people knew little about medicine or the need to be clean. About one person in every three died from it.

Everyone has their grain ground into flour at the village mill.

The Lord of the Manor lives here in the Manor House.

Lord of the Manor going hunting. The peasants are forbidden to kill any game animals because that would spoil the lord's hunting.

Stray animals are put in a "pound" and their owners have to pay a fine before they can get them out.

In this field barley is growing. Next year it will be left unplanted.

Hole for smoke to come out.

Ale house

Blacksmith

Stocks

Roof made of straw or reeds. This is called thatch.

Vegetable plot and garden.

This field has been left fallow (unplanted) this year. This will make it more fertile for wheat next year.

Spinning wool

Tinker coming to fair to mend and sell metal pots and pans.

9

Towns and Trade

This is what towns looked like in the Middle Ages. The streets were made of earth or cobbles and were narrow and dirty. There were no underground drains so people threw their rubbish into the street. Rich merchants built their houses of stone but most houses were made of wood, so fire was always a great danger. Towns were very small by modern standards and were surrounded by high stone walls.

University

Picture sign shows what the shop sells.

As trade increased and towns grew richer, townsmen wanted to organize their own affairs. Many towns obtained a charter from the king or local lord.

1 Guilds

Each trade and craft had its own guild. The guild organized its members by fixing prices and standards of workmanship.

2

A boy who wanted to learn a trade was "apprenticed" to a master. He lived in his master's house and worked in his shop.

3

After seven years he made a special piece of work called a masterpiece. If it was good enough he could join the guild.

4

The mayor and corporation, who ran the city, were chosen from the most important members of each of the guilds.

5

When the population increased men could not find places as guild members so they had to work for others for wages.

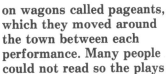

Mystery plays

On special holidays each guild acted different scenes from the Bible. These were called "mystery" plays. The guilds acted their plays on wagons called pageants, which they moved around the town between each performance. Many people could not read so the plays helped them to get to know the stories in the Bible. In many towns the guild which did the best play won a prize.

1 Trade

Banker

The first bankers were rich merchants who lent money to people wanting to organize trading expeditions.

2

Spices, jewels and silks were brought to Europe from India and China. Italian merchants controlled this trade.

3

Goods were carried overland by packhorses. Most roads were very bad and there were often bandits in lonely areas.

4

Sea travel was also difficult and dangerous. Sailors steered by the stars and tried to keep close to the land whenever they could.

The Church

The head of the Church in western Europe, the Pope, was elected by cardinals (the highest rank of priests) at a meeting called a conclave.

At one time there were three rival popes who all claimed to have been elected by a conclave. This argument was called the Great Schism.

Everyone went to church. All the services were in Latin, although only the priests and highly-educated people understood it.

Few people could read and write, except priests, so kings used priests as secretaries and advisers. Priests of high rank were summoned to parliament.

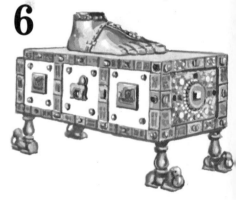

No one in Europe had discovered how to print books. All books were written by hand by monks and were often decorated with bright colours and gold leaf.

People who refused to believe everything that the Church taught were called heretics and were sometimes burnt to death. Joan of Arc was burnt as a heretic but later people decided she was a saint.

Bodies of saints or holy objects were often put into jewelled containers called reliquaries. These were treated with great respect and people worshipped in front of them.

Pilgrims

Some people went on journeys to holy places to show their devotion to God, to be forgiven for some sin or cured of an illness. These journeys were called pilgrimages.

Life in a nunnery

Some people chose to give their lives completely to God's service and to live apart from the rest of the world. Women who did this were called nuns and lived in nunneries. Men were called monks and lived in monasteries. Trainee monks and nuns were called novices.

Nuns are always ready to give food and beds to tired pilgrims and travellers.

Peasants from the village working on nunnery lands.

Abbess's house

Nun giving food to some poor people.

Stables

Visitors' houses

Cloisters where nuns take exercise.

Chapter House where meetings are held.

Dormitory

Refectory, where the nuns eat their meals. In some nunneries they eat in silence while a religious book is read to them.

Hospice where nuns look after people who are ill.

Nuns and monks promised to obey their superiors, to give up everything they owned and never to marry. Each day was divided into special times for prayer, study and work.

Like any Lord of the Manor, a nunnery had land. Rich people often left land and money to the nuns when they died, so that the nuns would pray for them. Some nunneries became extremely rich.

Key dates

AD1181/1226 Life of **St Francis of Assisi.**

AD1100s and 1200s Quarrels between popes and emperors led to wars in Germany and Italy.

AD1265/1321 The poet **Dante** lived.

AD1273 **Rudolf of Habsburg** became King of the Germans. His family ruled until 1918.

AD1307/1314 The Knights Templar were disbanded.

AD1337/1453 The "**Hundred Years**" **War** between England and France.

AD1370/1417 The Great Schism.

AD1380/1422 Quarrels between French nobles helped the English in the war.

AD1412/1431 Life of **Joan of Arc**. She led the French to victory in the war but was then burnt as a heretic.

Wars Between Religions

When invaders overran the western part of the Roman Empire, the eastern (Byzantine) half survived. The city of Constantinople was its capital.

These are priests of the Byzantine "Orthodox" Church. Over the years, eastern Christians developed slightly different beliefs from those of the west.

Between AD632 and 645 Muslims conquered part of the Byzantine Empire. Here their caliph (ruler) enters Jerusalem. Later, emperors and caliphs made peace.

Many Christian pilgrims visited the Holy Land, where Jesus had lived. Th Muslims allowed them to continue these visits.

The Crusades

In AD1095, Pope Urban II gave a sermon at Clermont in France. He inspired his listeners to go on a crusade (holy war).

The Crusaders set out on the long and difficult journey to the Holy Land to win it back from the Muslims.

The leaders of the First Crusade were French noblemen but their followers came from many different countries.

The Crusaders arrived in Constantinople and met th Emperor. At first he was friendly but really he did not trust them.

The Muslims, under a great leader called Saladin, won back Jerusalem from the quarrelling Christians. Several new crusades set out from Europe to try to win it back.

The feeling between the Byzantines and the European Crusaders became so bad that one group of Crusaders attacked Constantinople itself and set up their own emperor.

Richard the Lionheart of England, Frederick II of Germany and St Louis of France tried to save Outremer but by AD1291 the Muslims had recaptured the Holy Land.

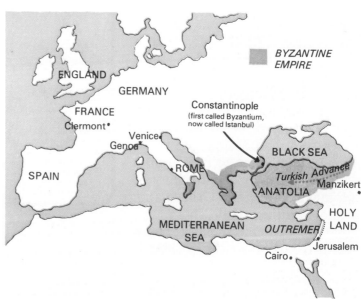

BYZANTINE EMPIRE

ENGLAND
GERMANY
FRANCE
Clermont •
Venice •
Genoa •
SPAIN
ROME
MEDITERRANEAN SEA
Constantinople (first called Byzantium, now called Istanbul)
BLACK SEA
Turkish Advance
Manzikert •
ANATOLIA
HOLY LAND
OUTREMER
Jerusalem
Cairo •

5 In the 11th century*, Seljuk Turks, who were also Muslims, arrived in the area from the east. They were very unfriendly to the Christians.

6 When the Turks defeated the Byzantines at the Battle of Manzikert, the western Christians felt they must go and fight to protect the Holy Land.

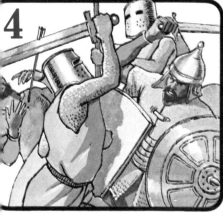

4 The Crusaders left Constantinople and went to fight the Muslims. They were very successful. The Holy Land became a Christian kingdom, called Outremer.

Knight Templar

Knight Hospitaller

Teutonic Knight

5 Special groups of soldier-monks were formed to care for pilgrims and to fight the Muslims. One knight from each of the three most important groups is shown here.

6 Some Crusaders settled in Outremer. When new Crusaders came out they were shocked to find the settlers quarrelling with each other but making friends with Muslim rulers.

10 The Byzantines won back Constantinople but the days of their wealth and power were over. In AD1453, with the help of cannons, the Turks finally captured the city.

How to spot a Crusader's tomb

Here is the tomb of a knight. His crossed legs show that he was a Crusader. Look out for a tomb like this if you go inside a church.

Key dates

AD632/645	Muslims seized parts of Byzantine Empire.
AD638	Caliph Omar took Jerusalem.
AD1000/1100	Turks invaded Byzantine Empire.
AD1071	Battle of Manzikert.
AD1095	Sermon at Clermont.
AD1096	First Crusade. Jerusalem taken. Outremer founded.
AD1187	**Saladin** took Jerusalem.
AD1191	Crusade of **Richard the Lionheart**.
AD1204	Sack of Constantinople.
AD1228/1244	**Emperor Frederick II** won back Jerusalem for a while.
AD1249/1270	Crusades of **St Louis**
AD1261	Byzantine Emperor recaptured Constantinople.
AD1291	The end of Outremer.
AD1453	Turks captured Constantinople. (End of Byzantine Empire.)

This means the 100 years between AD1000 and AD1100.

How Muslim People Lived

The Arabs were the first Muslims and they conquered a huge empire. At first the whole Muslim empire was ruled by one caliph, but later it split into several kingdoms. Life for the Muslims was often more advanced than life in Europe. After they had conquered the eastern provinces of the Roman Empire, they absorbed many of the ideas of ancient Greece and Rome. Trading made them wealthy, and this brought more comfort and luxury into their lives.

Many Arabs were nomads, who moved with their animals in search of water and pasture. They did not change their way of life even after they conquered their huge empire.

Peasants in Muslim lands went on working their fields. Much of the land was hot and dry and they had to work hard to keep it watered.

Muslim cities

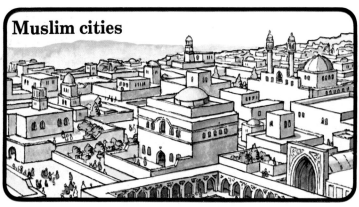

Houses in Muslim cities were often covered with white plaster, which helped to keep them cool. They faced inwards on to open courtyards, which provided shade. The streets were usually narrow and there were few open spaces except around the mosques.

Market

Towns usually had a souq (market). The streets where it was held were often roofed over. Shops in one street usually sold the same kind of goods.

Baths

Palaces and many private houses had baths and there were also public baths. They were copied from the designs of Roman baths.

1 Learning

Arabic writing

Arabic numbers

0 1 2 3 4 5 6 7 8 9
Our numbers

The Muslims developed a way of writing which read from right to left. Their system of numbers was simpler than the Roman figures used in Europe.

Muslim scholars studied Greek and Roman learning. They were especially interested in mathematics, the stars, geography, law, religion and medicine.

The Arabs made complicated instruments, like this one, which measured the position of ships at sea, by looking at the stars. This instrument is called an astrolabe.

Muslim doctors followed ancient Greek methods of treating the sick. Hospitals were built to care for people who needed special treatment.

Harem windows

Muslim rulers built themselves huge palaces, like this one. These were beautifully decorated by skilled craftsmen, and were very comfortable, compared with European castles built at this time. They usually had gardens set out in patterns around fountains. Life in these palaces was very formal, with lots of ceremonies.

Part of a house was set aside for women only. This was called the harem. No man from outside the family could enter it. In the street, Muslim women wore veils.

Arab traders

Arab dhow

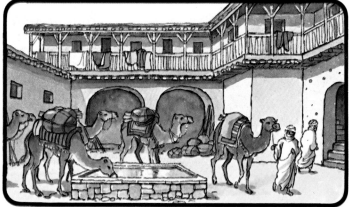

Trading played an important part in Muslim life. Arabs travelled to many different countries to find new customers. By sea they travelled in fast ships, called dhows. Some Arabs still use dhows today.

On land, merchants travelled by camel in groups called caravans. On main routes, caravansarays (shelters) were built at a day's journey from each other. Travellers could spend the night there.

Muslim art

Close-up of tiles

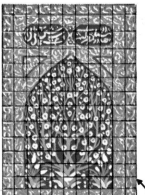

Tiles

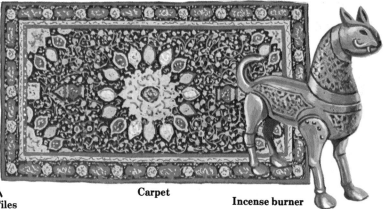

Carpet

Incense burner

Their religion did not allow Muslim artists to make sculptures of the human figure. They used patterns, flowers, animals and birds as decoration. Tiles were often used for decorating buildings.

Muslim craftsmen were famous for the manufacture of beautiful carpets and for their metal work. The bronze lion, shown above, was used for holding burning incense. Crusaders who returned to the west took treasures like these back with them. The work of Muslim craftsmen became popular in Europe.

17

Genghis Khan and his Empire

The Mongols were nomads who wandered across the plains of Asia with their herds of horses. From AD1206, a chief called Temujin overpowered all the Mongol tribes and conquered a huge empire. He became known as Ghengis Khan, the Great Prince. His sons raided Europe and his grandson, Kubilai Khan, conquered China. The Mongols were then weakened by family quarrels and fierce resistance. Later, a chief called Tamerlane* conquered an empire of his own and invaded India.

Muslim city being destroyed by Mongol raiders.

Mongols fought on horseback, using lances or bows and arrows.

Mongol commander. The Mongol army was very well-disciplined and could travel vast distances very quickly.

Here the Mongols are moving off after destroying an enemy city. The Mongols were very cruel to their enemies. Millions of people were killed or made slaves.

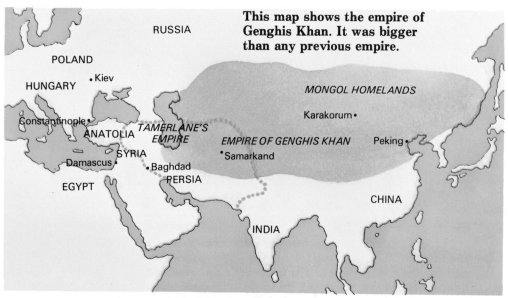

This map shows the empire of Genghis Khan. It was bigger than any previous empire.

RUSSIA

POLAND

HUNGARY

Kiev

Constantinople

ANATOLIA

TAMERLANE'S EMPIRE

SYRIA

Damascus

Baghdad

PERSIA

EGYPT

MONGOL HOMELANDS

Karakorum

EMPIRE OF GENGHIS KHAN

Samarkand

Peking

CHINA

INDIA

A friar visits the Mongols

A Christian friar, called William of Rubruck, was sent by St Louis of France to visit the Mongols. The Mongols had their own gods, but several of their

Tamerlane is sometimes known as Tamburlaine.

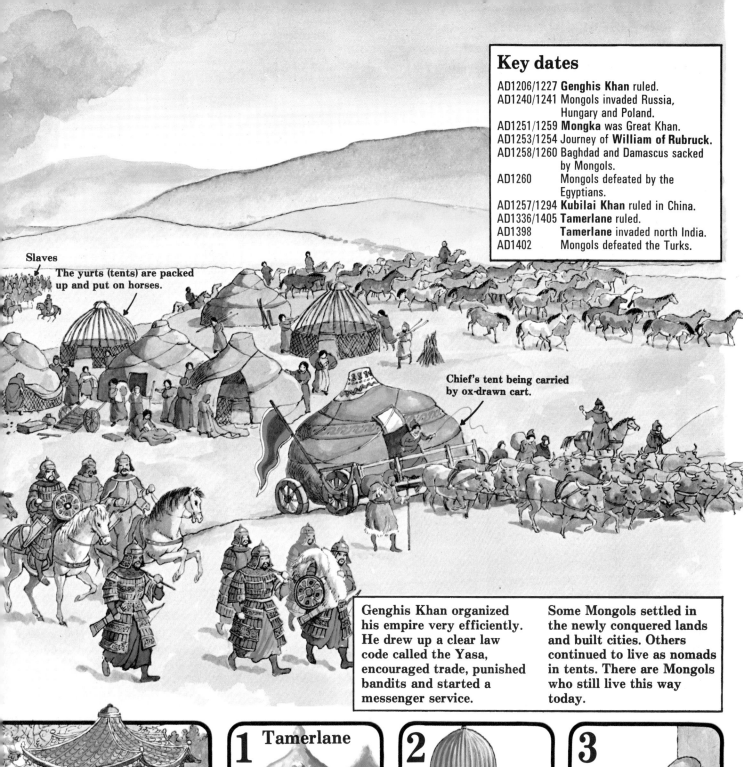

Slaves

The yurts (tents) are packed up and put on horses.

Chief's tent being carried by ox-drawn cart.

Genghis Khan organized his empire very efficiently. He drew up a clear law code called the Yasa, encouraged trade, punished bandits and started a messenger service.

Some Mongols settled in the newly conquered lands and built cities. Others continued to live as nomads in tents. There are Mongols who still live this way today.

princes had married Christian princesses. The Christians thought the Mongols would help them fight the Muslims, but this never happened.

1 Tamerlane

This is the Mongol chief Timur the Lame, known in Europe as Tamerlane. He ruled his empire from the city of Samarkand.

2

This is the building in Samarkand where Tamerlane was buried. Russian archaeologists have opened his tomb.

3

By using modern methods scientists built up a face on his skull, so that we now know what he looked like.

Princes and Temples

India was divided into kingdoms ruled by wealthy princes. They built themselves luxurious palaces and kept musicians and dancers to entertain them.

Indian villagers worked hard to keep their fields watered for growing rice. Each village was run by a headman who carried out the orders of the local ruler.

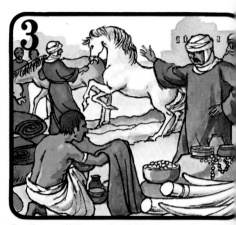

Indians did most of their trade with Arabs. They sold silks, ivory, pearls, spices and perfumes and bought Arab horses, which were especially beautiful and could run fast.

Many people, both inside and outside India, had accepted the teachings of the Buddha. Pilgrims, like this Chinese monk, travelled a long way to visit sacred Buddhist shrines.

The ancient Hindu faith became popular again. There were many gods and goddesses but the god Shiva, shown above, was one of the most important ones.

Hindus believe that all rivers come from the gods. The river Ganges, shown above, is especially holy. For thousands of years they have bathed in it to wash away their sins.

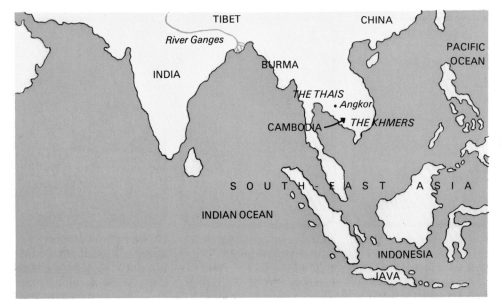

Indian ideas in other countries

Indian religions, ideas and ways of life spread to other countries, especially in South-East Asia. This is a Buddhist temple at Borobudur on the island of Java in Indonesia.

Angkor

One of the countries that was influenced by Indian ideas was Cambodia. In the ninth century a people called the Khmers rose to power there. They worshipped their own kings as gods on earth, but they also worshipped Hindu gods and built huge temples, like this one at Angkor. In AD1431 a people called the Thais invaded Cambodia. The great cities and temples of the Khmers were abandoned and the jungle grew up and covered them.

In AD1296 a Chinese visitor to Cambodia saw a procession like this and wrote an account of it.

How we know

Pictures, like this, were cut into the stone of Angkor. They tell us about the battles, on land and rivers, fought by the Khmers against their enemies the Chams and Thais.

The stone carvings at Angkor also tell us about the everyday life of the Khmers. This picture shows two men and their friends getting ready to watch a fight between two cockerels.

Silk and Spice Traders

In AD589 a new dynasty (family line) of emperors, called the Sui, began to rule China. They brought peace to the country after a time of long and difficult wars between rival Chinese groups.

Civil servants helped the Emperor to rule. They had to take exams before they were given jobs in government. In the countryside, the nobles, who owned most of the land, gradually became more powerful.

Buddhism had spread from India in the first century AD and was very popular. But many people still believed in the teachings of Confucius and the Taoist religion. At times Buddhists were persecuted.

A trading city in China

Some merchants travelled by sea to Africa and the Middle East.

Chinese inventions

The Chinese were the inventors of several things that were unknown to the rest of the world at this time.

They discovered how to make porcelain, a very hard, fine type of china.

At this time, the Chinese were using compasses to find their way across land and sea. This one is made of lacquered wood.

By the 10th century they were using wooden blocks to print books. This is probably the oldest printed page in the world.

Gunpowder was first used for fireworks. By the 13th century the Chinese were also using it for bombs and other weapons.

22

2

Chinese craftsmen were very skilful. At the time when the T'ang family were emperors (AD618/906) they made especially fine pottery figures of animals and servants. These were placed in tombs.

3

In AD1279 the Mongols, led by the great Kubilai Khan, overran China, which they then ruled for nearly 100 years.

Key dates

AD589/618	Sui Dynasty ruled.
AD618/906	T'ang Dynasty ruled. Buddhism very popular.
AD960/1279	Sung Dynasty ruled. Growth of trade. Mongols started attacking northern frontier.
AD1279/1368	Mongols ruled China.
AD1276/1292	**Marco Polo's** trip to China.
AD1368	Mongol rulers overthrown.
AD1368/1644	Ming Dynasty ruled.

Silk, porcelain (fine china) and carved jade were taken to the west and traded for silver and gold. Many cities grew rich because of this trade.

This caravan of camels is setting out with goods destined for the Middle East and Europe.

1 Marco Polo

Many foreign merchants, especially Arabs, came to China to trade. Later, a few adventurous Europeans arrived. Two of the European merchants who visited China were the brothers,

Niccolo and Maffeo Polo, from Venice. On their second visit they took Maffeo's young son, Marco. Here they are meeting Kubilai Khan, the Mongol emperor of China.

2

Marco Polo travelled around Kubilai Khan's empire for nearly 17 years. When he returned home, he wrote a book about his travels. This is the first page of his book.

Land of the Samurai

Japan is a group of islands off the coast of China. We know little about its early history because the Japanese had no writing until it was introduced from China in the fifth century AD. The Buddhist religion also came from China and won many followers, although Japan's ancient religion, Shinto, was still popular. Japanese arts, crafts, laws, taxes and the organization of government were also based on Chinese ideas.

SEA OF JAPAN

JAPAN

• Heian (now Kyoto)

PACIFIC OCEAN

This is part of the Imperial city, Heian, later called Kyoto. The emperor was at the centre of power, but noble clans (families) gradually took over and ruled for him. Many emperors retired to Buddhist monasteries. As "Cloistered Ex-Emperors", some re-established their power for a time.

Legally all the land in Japan was owned by the emperor. He allowed farmers, like these, to use it in return for taxes and services. Later, the nobles began to acquire their own private lands because the Emperor was not strong enough to stop them. Many battles were fought about the possession of land and nobles gave it to their supporters as rewards.

This is Yoritomo, military leader and the chief of the Minamoto clan. In AD1192 he began to use the title "Shogun". This became the name for the head of government and was passed from father to son.

Poetry

Poetry was popular, especially among the people at court. People made trips to look at the cherry blossom and see the maple leaves turning red. This inspired them to recite and write poems. There were several famous women poets.

Novels

The Japanese liked novels. This is Murasaki Shikibu, a court lady, who wrote a famous novel called *The Tale of Genji*.

Armour making

Japanese warriors wore suits of armour made of tough leather strips. This is an armourer's shop where the suits were made.

Helmets were made to look like the face of the wearer.

Armour made from tough leather strips.

Curved swords made by highly-skilled swordsmiths.

The Mongol Invasion Scroll

The Mongol ruler of China, Kubilai Khan, twice tried to invade Japan, but his men were driven back by the Samurai and by storms called Kamikaze. This scroll tells the story.

Japanese warriors were called Samurai. They fought for the nobles and had to be absolutely loyal to them. They were rewarded with land and wealth, but were expected to die for their lords if necessary.

The Samurai fought hand-to-hand battles, skilfully wielding deadly two-handed swords. Before attacking, each Samurai would shout his own name and tell of the bravery of his ancestors, hoping to strike fear into the heart of his enemy.

Key dates

AD538	Buddhist religion introduced to Japan.
AD794	Capital city moved from Nara to Heian (now called Kyoto).
AD794/1185	Period of Japanese history called Heian.
AD851/1115	Fujiwara clan controlled government.
AD1115/1160	Some power taken by "Cloistered Ex-Emperors".
AD1180/1185	Taira and Minamoto clans fought for control of government.
AD1192	**Minamoto Yoritomo** took the title of Shogun.
AD1185/1333	Period of Japanese history called Kamakura.
AD1274/1281	Mongol invasions.
AD1333/1336	Period of rule by the emperor
AD1392/1573	Period of Japanese history called Ashikaga.

Kingdoms, Traders and Tribes

In AD639, Arabs, inspired by their new religion, Islam, invaded Egypt and then north Africa. They traded with the local people and brought new wealth to the area.

South of the Sahara, the land was often difficult to clear and live in. There were also dangerous diseases there. As people learnt how to make strong tools from iron, tribes were able to progress further south, clearing and farming the land as they went.

1 West African kingdoms

Arab traders began to make regular journeys across the Sahara. They bought gold and salt from West Africa and sold it in busy Mediterranean ports.

MEDITERRANEAN SEA

MOROCCO

THE SAHARA

Timbuktu

KINGDOM OF MALI

AFRICA

River Niger

MUSLIM EMPIRE

ATLANTIC OCEAN

River Co

African king

KALAHARI DESERT

2

Trade made the local Africans very rich. They built magnificent cities full of palaces and mosques. The most famous city was Timbuktu shown here.

3

Arab visitors

Some of the West African rulers had large kingdoms. One of the most important was Mali. Several Arabs who travelled to these kingdoms kept records of their visits. They were very impressed by the luxury they found, especially at court. Here, some Arabs are meeting an African king.

Portuguese explorers

From AD1420 onwards, Prince Henry of Portugal, known as "the Navigator", organized expeditions to explore the West African coast and trade with the Africans.

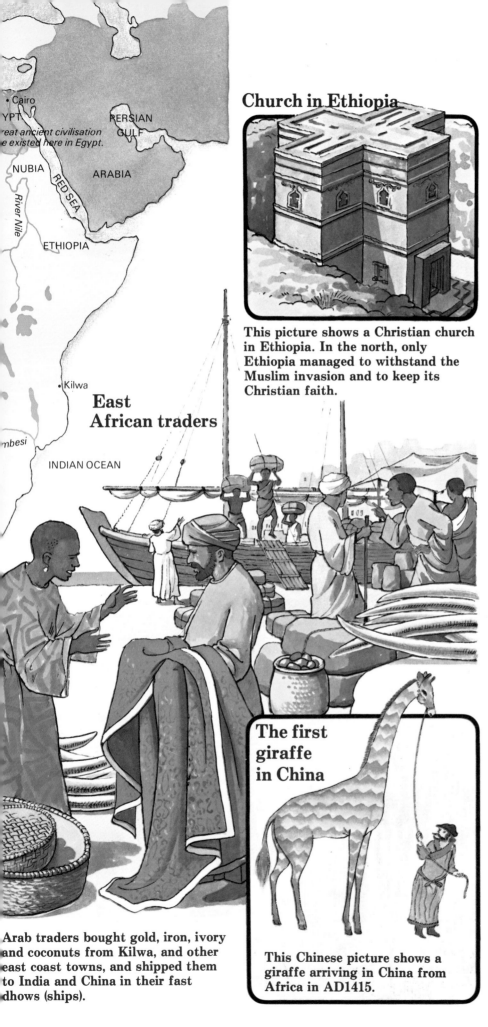

Great ancient civilisation existed here in Egypt.

Cairo
YPT
NUBIA
RED SEA
River Nile
ARABIA
PERSIAN GULF
ETHIOPIA
Kilwa
INDIAN OCEAN
mbesi

East African traders

Arab traders bought gold, iron, ivory and coconuts from Kilwa, and other east coast towns, and shipped them to India and China in their fast dhows (ships).

Church in Ethiopia

This picture shows a Christian church in Ethiopia. In the north, only Ethiopia managed to withstand the Muslim invasion and to keep its Christian faith.

The first giraffe in China

This Chinese picture shows a giraffe arriving in China from Africa in AD1415.

Life in the south

In the south different tribes adopted different ways of life.

1

In the Kalahari Desert the Bushmen hunted animals for their food.

2

Pygmies lived in tropical jungles, hunting animals and gathering berries and fruits.

3

Tribes living in the open plains of the east and south kept animals and farmed the land.

4

People who knew how to make iron tools were very useful to their tribes.

Life in North and South America

At this time there were many separate groups of people living in different parts of the huge continent of America. In the forests, mountains, plains, deserts and jungles and in the frozen north, people found ways of surviving by hunting, fishing, gathering, and later farming. The people of North America did not have a system of writing, but archaeologists have found remains of their settlements, which tell us something about their lives.

1 People in North America

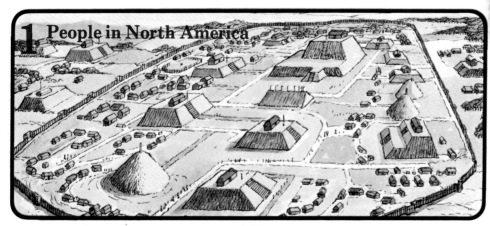

One of the most advanced groups of North American Indians were the Mississipians or "Mound Builders", who were farmers and traders. In their towns, the temples and other important buildings were built on top of great earth mounds. This picture shows part of Cahokia, one of their towns.

Underground rooms (kivas) were used for religious ceremonies.

Some Indian farmers lived in "pueblos", towns made of stone and mud. The houses were sometimes as high as five floors and were built in canyon walls.

At Huff, on the plains, traces of a village of more than 100 wooden houses, like this, have been found. The village was surrounded by a ditch and palisade (wooden fence).

Eskimos learnt how to live in the intense cold of the far north. They hunted caribou, seals and whales and also fished and trapped birds.

Mountain farmers in Peru

The first American farmers we know about lived in the area that is now Peru. They grew maize, vegetables, cotton, tobacco and a drug called coca. Later they built terraces on the mountainside, so that they could grow crops even on the steep slopes of the Andes. Alpacas and llamas provided wool and carried heavy loads.

What the Indians made

The people in Peru were skilled potters and metal-workers and expert weavers. Some of the cloth they made has lasted to the present day and is still brightly-coloured. Each of the objects shown above was made by a different people.

Towns

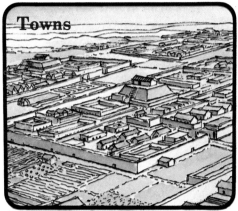

At first, the people of Peru had small settlements. Later they built great monuments and cities, such as the Chimu peoples' capital of Chanchan, shown above.

The Incas

These men are Inca warriors. The Incas were a tribe who lived in the mountains of Peru. The first Inca ruler probably lived about AD1200.

In 1438 a man called Pachacutec became their king and they spread out from the city of Cuzco, their capital, to conquer a huge empire.

Key dates

North America
AD500/1500   The Mound Builders or Mississipians lived.
AD1400/1600 People living at Huff.

South America
AD200/900   Period of Peruvian civilisation called the ''Classic Period''.
AD1100/1438 Chimu people living at Chanchan.
AD1200   **Manco Capac** ruled the Incas.
AD1438/1471 **Pachacutec** ruled the Incas.

Central America
700BC/AD900 Maya living in Yucatan.
100BC   Zapotecs living on the south coast.
AD750/990   The Toltec Empire.
AD1325   Aztecs known to be at Tenochtitlan.

The Aztecs

One of the earliest and greatest peoples of Central America were the Maya. This picture shows a procession of Mayan musicians.

Archaeologists have recently discovered, in the same area, more about a people called the Toltecs. This is a temple in Tula, their capital city.

This is an Aztec warrior. The Aztecs probably came from western Mexico before they settled at Tenochtitlan and conquered all the land around it.

Aztec numbers

The Aztecs had a system of numbers, which meant they could count and keep records of their possessions. These are some of the symbols they used.

The market place

Dogs, fattened ready to be eaten.

Avocadoes

Tomatoes

Corn

Limes

Pineapples

Trading between themselves and with people from other towns was an important part of Aztec life. They had no money so they exchanged goods for others of equal value. This is called barter. Chocolate was a favourite drink, so cocoa beans, from which it was made, were always in demand. They were often used for making small payments. Jade and turquoise were more valuable than gold and silver.

Calendar

This picture shows the "New Fire Ceremony", which marked the beginning of a 52 year cycle. There were 18 months in each year.

Schools

Children were taught by their parents. At 15 the boys went to school. Special schools trained boys and girls as priests.

The city of Tenochtitlan

This is the capital city of the Aztecs. It was built on islands in the middle of a lake. The lake no longer exists and modern Mexico City is built on top of it.

The Aztecs worshipped many gods and goddesses. They built temples where they killed human beings and ripped out their hearts, in order to please these gods.

Temple of the Rain God

Human sacrifice

Temple of the War God (Chief Aztec god)

Lake

Temple

Emperor's palace

Temple of the Feathered Serpent, one of the Aztec gods

This wall called the Serpent Wall.

Aztecs playing "tlachtli", a game using a rubber ball.

Special boats collect waste.

Mosaic and feathers

Aztec craftsmen produced beautiful mosaic work, like this mask, which is covered with small pieces of precious turquoise.

Shields, like this one, were made of feathers. The Aztecs also used feathers for making head-dresses and cloaks.

How we know

The Aztecs used a form of picture-writing. It had not developed far enough to record complicated ideas but some religious teachings and history were recorded and have survived in books like the one above. Such a book is called a codex.

31

The Slav People

Many of the people who now live in Eastern Europe and Western Russia are Slavs. They settled in these places in the 700s, after centuries of wandering across Europe. In the west, the Slav people set up several kingdoms for themselves. In the south, they were ruled by a people called Bulgars. In the east, the Slav people settled with the Vikings, who called the area "Rus" and so gave us our name "Russia".

This map show the Slav kingdoms durin the 800s.

Novgorod

BALTIC SEA

KINGDOM OF KIEV

• Moscow

THE POLES

KINGDOM OF THE FRANKS

MORAVIA

• Kiev

BLACK SEA

KINGDOM OF THE BULGARS

1

Some of the Slav kingdoms became very great and wealthy, but did not last very long. One of these was Moravia. This silver plaque is one of the few Moravian things to have survived.

2

The Southern and Eastern Slavs were converted to Christianity by Byzantine missionaries. This led them to copy the Byzantine art style, as in this picture.

3

The Western Slavs (present-day Poles and Czechs) also became Christians, but they joined the Roman Catholic instead of the Byzantine Church. This is the Polish king, Boleslav I.

4

Some Russian states became wealthy and powerful, and European kings began to take an interest in them. The mos important was Kiev. Three of its Grand Prince's daughters married European kings.

5

At the beginning of the 13th century, Russia was invaded by a group of Mongols called Tartars. They destroyed many cities and made others, including the small town of Moscow, shown here, pay them tributes.

6

One Russian prince, called Alexander Nevsky, fought a great battle against the Tartars to save his city, Novgorod. He is still remembered as a great her

Kings, Popes and Princes

This picture shows a procession in Florence, the capital city of one of the greatest states in Italy. In the fifteenth century Florence was one of the great banking centres of Europe and was also famous as a clothmaking centre. The ruling family of Florence was called the Medici.

They were very wealthy and spent a lot of money on buying paintings and sculptures and having magnificent buildings constructed, which you can still see if you visit Florence. The most brilliant of the Medici princes was Lorenzo the Magnificent.

In the 15th century Italy was a collection of separate states. The central area around Rome was ruled by the Pope. Here the Pope is receiving a messenger from a foreign prince.

The Italian states were always fighting each other. In 1494 the French joined the fighting and soon the Spaniards and the emperor of the German states joined in as well.

Venice was one of the wealthiest states in Italy. Its ruler was called the "Doge". This is a portrait of one of the Doges, wearing the special Doge's hat.

Art and Learning

At the end of the 15th century, people in Europe began to take a great interest in art and learning, and to develop new ideas about the world. They started asking questions and doing experiments, instead of just accepting existing ideas.

People began to think that civilisation had been at its best in Ancient Greece and Rome, so they revived Greek and Roman ideas. The time became known as the "Renaissance", which means revival or rebirth. It began in Italy and gradually spread across Europe.

In the Renaissance, Italians began to be interested in the remains of Ancient Rome. They dug up statues and other treasures and made collections of them.

This is the city of Florence in Italy. The new ideas of the Renaissance began here and many of the most famous men of this time lived and worked in Florence.

1 Painting

Before the Renaissance, artists painted mainly religious scenes. Everything in their pictures looked flat and the people did not look very lifelike.

2

In the late 14th and early 15th centuries, painters began to try to make the people in their paintings look as much like living people as possible.

3

Besides painting religious subjects, Renaissance painters did pictures, like this one, of everyday life, and of stories from Ancient Greece and Rome.

Sculpture

Sculptors were inspired by the statues of Ancient Greece and Rome. This marble statue was made by Michelangelo. He was also a painter, an architect and a poet.

4

For the first time artists began to use live models to help them paint life-like people. This is Simonetta Vespucci, who modelled for the artist Botticelli.

5

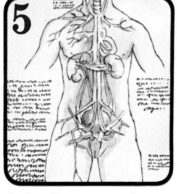

Artists began to study nature and the human body to help them draw things more accurately. This sketch is from the notebook of Leonardo da Vinci.

6

Artists learned how to show distance in their paintings, making you feel you could walk into them. This is called "perspective".

1 Learning

Many new universities and schools were founded. The main subjects were Greek and Latin grammar. In England the new schools were called "grammar" schools.

2

Scholars studied texts in Greek, Latin and Hebrew. They were excited by the thoughts and ideas of ancient times. The invention of printing helped to spread these ideas.

3

Studying ancient Christian texts made some people, like this Dutch scholar called Erasmus, criticize the Church and its priests for being corrupt.

4

People also began to study politics. This is Machiavelli, an Italian who wrote a book about politics called "The Prince", in which he said that a ruler had to be ruthless.

Architecture

Architects built wonderful palaces and churches. They used domes and copied the style of Greek and Roman temples. The towers and spires of the Middle Ages went out of fashion.

A properly educated Renaissance person was expected to be able to:

understand and collect art,

write poetry,

play a musical instrument,

read and write Latin and Greek,

speak several languages,

fight if necessary,

take part in politics,

ride and be good at sports,

show good manners to everyone.

Science and Inventions

1

The new ideas of the Renaissance made people keen to question everything about the world around them. Some people began doing experiments to test their ideas.

2

People called "alchemists", however, tried to brew potions that would cure all ills, give eternal life and turn lead into gold.

3

One of the greatest men of the Renaissance was Leonardo da Vinci. He was a painter and an inventor and he thought a lot about making a flying machine. This is a model based on one of his designs which he worked out by watching birds fly. Leonardo also studied animals and human bodies to find out how they worked and he painted the very famous picture of the Mona Lisa.

4

The printing press was probably the most important invention of this time. The first one was made by a German called Johann Gutenberg. Books could now be produced quickly and cheaply, instead of having to be handwritten as before. This meant ideas and learning spread more quickly.

5

In England, people experimented with metals and learnt how to make cheap and reliable cannons out of cast-iron. These soon replaced the expensive bronze cannons that the German and Italians had been making.

6

There were very few clocks in the Middle Ages and these were usually huge ones on public buildings. The invention of springs made it possible to make watches that could be carried around and also small clocks that people could keep at home. Pendulum clocks were also invented at this time.

7

During the 16th century, the invention and improvement of instruments like these helped sailors to steer their ships more accurately. To make the most of these instruments a captain had to know the stars and be good at mathematics. Gradually, new and better maps were produced too.

Medicine

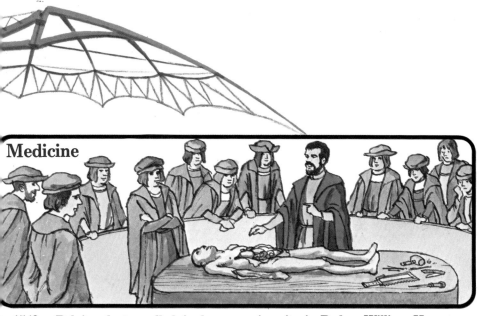

In 1543, a Belgian doctor called Andreas Vesalius published a book about how the human body worked. Here he is lecturing to his students at the university in Padua. William Harvey, another great doctor, discovered and proved that the heart pumps blood round the body.

The invention of microscopes made people realize for the first time that the world was full of minute creatures, too small to see unless they are magnified.

Ideas about the universe

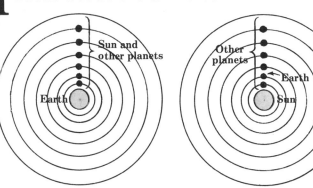

Sun and other planets

Earth

Other planets

Earth

Sun

From the time of the Ancient Greeks onwards, people had believed that the Earth was the centre of the universe and that the Sun, Moon and stars moved round it. In 1543, the Polish astronomer, Copernicus, published a book showing that the Sun, not the Earth, was the centre of the universe. Many people refused to believe him.

The invention of the telescope in the early 17th century meant that people could get a better view of the stars and planets. The Italian scientist, Galileo, made a telescope strong enough to show the separate stars of the Milky Way. He supported Copernicus, but the Catholic Church forbade him to teach his theories.

The new interest in science led to the founding of scientific societies. Special places were built, like the Royal Observatory near London, for the study of stars.

This wall has been cut away.

The discoveries of the English scientist, Sir Isaac Newton, changed people's ideas about the universe. Here he is doing an experiment through which he discovered that white light is made up of different colours.

Key dates

AD1444/1510 Italian painter, **Botticelli**.
AD1452/1519 Italian artist/inventor **Leonardo da Vinci**.
AD1454 **Gutenberg** invented his printing press.
AD1466/1536 Dutch scholar **Erasmus**.
AD1469/1527 Italian writer **Machiavelli**.
AD1473/1543 Polish astronomer **Copernicus**.
AD1475/1564 Italian artist **Michelangelo**.
AD1514/1564 Belgian doctor **Vesalius**.
AD1564/1642 Italian astronomer **Galileo**.
AD1578/1657 English doctor **Harvey**.
AD1600 (approx.) Invention of telescope and microscope.
AD1642/1727 English scientist **Newton**.

New Ideas About Religion

The people of Western Europe were all Roman Catholics, but by AD1500, many were unhappy with the way the Church was being run. The Popes and many of the priests seemed interested only in wealth and power and set a bad example in the way they lived their lives. This led to a movement, which became known as the "Reformation", to change and reform the Christian Church. People who joined the movement were called "Protestants" because they were protesting about things that they thought were wrong.

In 1517 a German monk called Martin Luther nailed a list of 95 complaints about the Church and the way priests behaved, to the door of Wittenberg church in Germany.

Luther believed that everyone should be able to study God's message for themselves. So he translated the Bible from Latin into German. Versions in other languages quickly followed.

The Catholics fight back

The Pope called a meeting of churchmen at Trent in Italy. They laid down exactly what the beliefs and rules of the Catholic Church were and ordered complete obedience to them.

This is St Ignatius Loyola who founded the Society of Jesus. The members, who were known as Jesuits, tried to win Protestants back to the Catholic Church.

Many Protestants disapproved of decorated churches and destroyed those they took over. But the Catholics introduced an even more elaborate style, shown here, called Baroque.

Murders and executions

Holland was ruled by the Kings of Spain at this time. William of Orange led a revolt of the Dutch Protestants against the Spanish. He was murdered by a Catholic.

So many people in France became Protestants that the Catholics laid a plot. On 24 August 1572, the eve of St Bartholomew's Day, they murdered all the Protestants they could find in Paris.

Mary, Queen of Scots, was a Catholic. She plotted against Elizabeth I, the Protestant Queen of England, and was taken prisoner by the English. She was executed at Fotheringay Castle.

Luther was condemned by a Church court, but several German princes supported him. He also won followers across Europe.

King Henry VIII of England wanted to divorce his wife and marry Anne Boleyn. The Pope would not let him, so Henry made himself head of the Church in England.

Soon there were other religious leaders and the Protestants split into different groups. This is John Calvin, who set up a new Church in Geneva.

Priests on both sides were tortured and even hanged. Both Protestants and Catholics believed they were saving their opponents from hell by doing this.

In Spain, the most fiercely Catholic country in Europe, there was an organization called the Inquisition, which hunted out anyone who was not a good Catholic. The officers of the Inquisition used torture to make people confess their beliefs. Protestants who refused to become Catholics were burnt to death at special ceremonies called "Auto-da-fe" (Spanish for "acts of faith"), which were watched by huge crowds.

This is a map of Europe in about AD1600. It shows which areas were still Catholic and which had become Protestant.

Protestant

Catholic

ENGLAND
GERMAN STATES
FRANCE
Mixture of Catholic and Protestant
PORTUGAL
SPAIN
ITALIAN STATES

Key dates

AD1483/1546	Life of **Martin Luther**.
AD1517	Luther nailed 95 theses to Wittenburg church door.
AD1534	**Henry VIII** became head of the Church of England.
	Ignatius Loyola founded the Jesuits (Society of Jesus).
AD1536	**John Calvin** began work in Geneva.
AD1545/1563	The Council of Trent.
AD1555	Fighting between Catholics and Protestants in Germany ended by treaty called Peace of Augsburg.
AD1572	The Massacre of St. Bartholomew's Eve.
AD1584	**William of Orange** was assassinated.
AD1587	**Mary, Queen of Scots**, was executed.

War and Weapons

Guns were invented at the beginning of the 14th century. It was many years before they came into general use, but over the next few centuries they completely changed the way wars were fought. The knights and castles of the Middle Ages gradually disappeared. Their armour was no protection against bullets, so they could not get close enough to the enemy to use their swords and lances. Castle walls could not stand up to an attack of cannon balls.

From about 1300 onwards, archers started using longbows which were very effective against knights. They had a long range and were quite accurate.

Castles and walled towns had been very difficult to capture, but when cannons began to be used in the 15th century, even the thickest walls could be quickly battered down.

Armour and weapons were expensive. When peasants rebelled, as they often did in the 15th and 16th centuries, they had little chance against well-armed knights and nobles. This is a German knight charging a peasant.

When hand-guns were first invented they took a long time to load and were not very accurate. Pikemen were positioned next to the gunmen to protect them against charging cavalry while they reloaded.

Then guns called muskets were invented. They fired more accurately but at first they were too heavy to hold. The musketeers had to use forked sticks to support their guns.

Pistols were less accurate than muskets and fired a shorter distance. They were usually used by cavalry who rode at the enemy, fired at them and rode away to reload.

Towards the end of the 17th century soldiers started to use bayonets (blades which attach to the end of a gun). Gunmen could now defend themselves at close-quarters.

8 Instead of relying on their nobles to raise armies, or hiring mercenary soldiers, kings began to set up permanent armies of their own. These armies were much more highly-trained than before and could obey orders at speed. Commanders had to study hard to learn how to plan their battles and campaigns.

9 War at sea changed too. The Dutch and English developed lighter ships which could turn much more quickly. This helped the English fleet to defeat the Spanish Armada.

10 On ships, cannons were placed along each side. Enemies tried to fire "broadside" at each other so they would have more chance of hitting their target.

11 Disease, bad food and harsh punishments made life at sea very hard. Governments often used "press-gangs" to kidnap men for the navy and take them to sea by force.

Key dates

AD1455/1485 **Wars of the Roses**: civil war in England.

AD1494/1559 **Italian Wars**: Italian states fighting each other. France and the Holy Empire joined in.

AD1524/1525 **Peasants' War** in Germany: the German peasants rebelled.

AD1562/1598 **Wars of Religion in France**: fighting between French Catholics and Protestants.

AD1568/1609 **Dutch Revolt**: the Dutch rebelled against their Spanish rulers.

AD1588 The **Spanish Armada** was defeated by the English fleet.

AD1618/1648 **Thirty Years War**: fought mainly in Germany. Involved most of the countries of Europe.

AD1642/1649 **Civil War** in England.

AD1648/1653 **Wars of the "Fronde"**: two rebellions against the French government.

AD1652/1654, **Wars between the Dutch and**
1665/1667 & **the English.** Fought at sea.
1672/1674 Caused by rivalry over trade.

AD1701/1714 **War of the Spanish Succession**: France and Spain against England, Austria and Holland.

AD1733/1735 **War of the Polish Succession**: Austria and Russia against France and Spain about who should rule Poland.

AD1740/1748 **War of the Austrian Succession**: Austria, Britain and Russia against France and Prussia.

The Incas

The Incas lived in the mountains of Peru in South America. Their capital was a city called Cuzco. From about 1440 onwards they began to conquer neighbouring lands and build up a huge empire. The empire lasted about a hundred years before Spanish soldiers arrived in search of gold and conquered them.

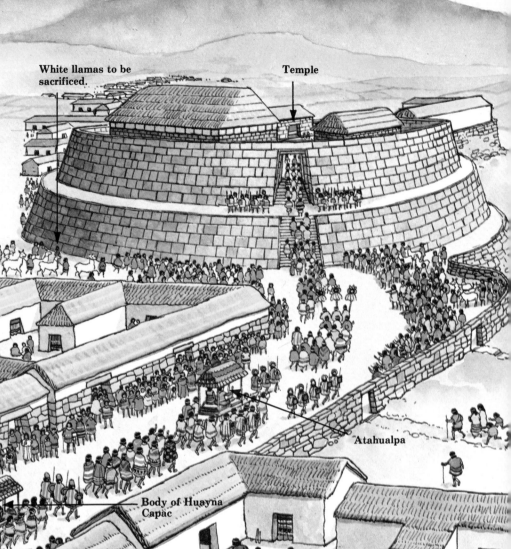

White llamas to be sacrificed.

Temple

Atahualpa

Body of Huayna Capac

Musicians with drums, rattles and flutes.

The emperor of the Incas was called the Inca. His people thought he was descended from the Sun and when he died his body was preserved and treated with great honour.

This is the funeral procession of an emperor called Huayna Capac. His son, Atahualpa, became the new emperor by fighting his half-brother, Huascar.

Unfortunately this war, was just before the Spaniards arrived and it greatly weakened the Incas in their fight against the European invaders.

Inca priests were very important people. They held services, heard confessions and foretold the future by looking into the fire. The Sun was their chief god.

Women were taught how to weave and spin wool. Some women, who were specially chosen for their beauty, became priestesses called the Virgins of the Sun.

The Incas were very skilled at making things out of gold. This gold glove was found in a tomb. Beside it is a model of a god, set with precious stones.

A farming village

Land has been terraced so that crops can be grown on the steep mountainside.

Peasants dig fields with pointed sticks.

Buildings made with heavy blocks of stone have been put together without the help of machinery or iron tools.

Villagers eat mainly maize and vegetables.

Women weaving

Guinea pigs are kept for food.

Men drinking "chicha" beer

All the land belonged to the Inca. One third of the crops was kept by peasants, who lived in mountain villages, like this one, and worked on the land. Another third went to the priests and the last third went to the Inca. With his share he paid his officials, soldiers and craftsmen.

Keeping records

The Incas had no system of writing but their officials used "quipus" to help them record things. Coloured strings stood for objects. Knots tied in the strings stood for numbers.

Roads and messengers

A well-maintained network of roads linked all parts of the huge Inca empire. There were hanging bridges, made of twisted straw and vines, across the mountain chasms. These roads and bridges were built and repaired by peasants sent from their villages to serve the emperor. There were no wheeled vehicles so goods were carried by llamas and relays of fast runners carried messages and quipus across the empire. There were rest houses, a day's journey apart, for people on official business to stay in.

The Discovery of America

Until the end of the 15th century, Europeans did not know that the huge continent of America existed. Explorers and traders had made long and difficult journeys eastwards to China and India, bringing back spices, silks and jewels. These were in such demand in Europe that people thought there might be a quicker way to the Far East by sea. The Portuguese sailed to the east round Africa, but others thought it might be quicker to go westwards. When they did, they found America in the way.

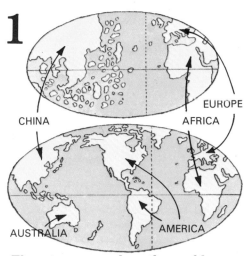

These two maps show the world as people in Europe thought it looked in about 1490 (top) and as it really looked (bottom).

An Italian, called Christopher Columbus, persuaded King Ferdinand and Queen Isabella of Spain to pay for an expedition to find China by sailing west instead of east. He set off in 1492 with three ships.

1 The Spanish conquerors

Spanish adventurers ("conquistadors") started to explore the mainland, hoping to find treasure. They discovered the Aztecs in Mexico and the Incas in Peru.

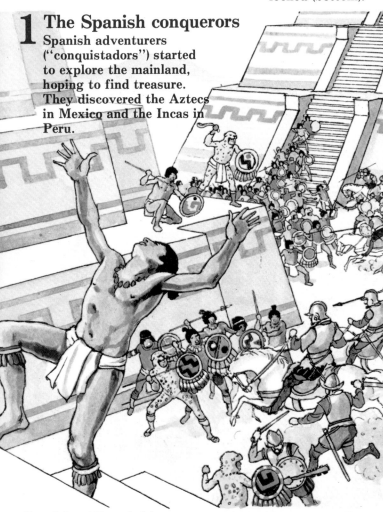

Spanish soldiers, led by Hernando Cortes, attacked the Aztecs in their capital city, Tenochtitlan. Although there were fewer of them, the Spaniards had much better weapons than the Indians, who had never seen horses before. The Spaniards soon conquered the whole of Mexico and called it New Spain.

With the help of his Indian interpreter, Dona Marina, Cortes won the support of several Indian tribes, who helped him to defeat the Aztecs.

In Peru, the Spanish, led by Pizarro, captured the Inca emperor. To buy his freedom he filled a room with gold. But he was killed and Peru conquered.

The Spanish tried to make all the Indians become Christians. Indians who went on worshipping their own gods were burnt to death.

The Spaniards treated the Indians very cruelly. Many were put to work in silver mines. Thousands died of illnesses brought over from Europe.

3 After five weeks, Columbus reached what he thought were islands off China but were, in fact, the West Indies. Later, he made three more voyages and reached the mainland of America.

4 To stop Spain and Portugal fighting about who owned the newly discovered lands, the Pope drew a line on the map. All new lands east of the line went to Portugal, those to the west went to Spain.

5 There were many expeditions to explore the new lands. The first to sail round South America was led by Magellan. He was killed on the way, but his ship returned and was the first to sail right round the world.

Slave trade

The Spanish and Portuguese brought ships full of Africans over to work as slaves. They tried to stop other countries joining in this trade, but some captains, like the Englishman John Hawkins, ignored their ban.

Pirates

Spanish treasure ships were often attacked by pirates on their way back to Spain. The French and English governments even encouraged their sea-captains to be pirates, rewarding them for bringing back treasure.

AZTEC EMPIRE

INCA EMPIRE

Columbus's route

WEST INDIES

Pope's line

Magellan's route

Key dates

AD1492	First voyage of **Christopher Columbus.**
AD1494	The Pope divided the new lands between Spain and Portugal.
AD1498	**Vasco da Gama** sailed round Africa and reached India.
AD1500	**Pedro Cabral** claimed Brazil for the Portuguese government.
AD1519/1522	**Magellan's** voyage round the world.
AD1519	**Hernando Cortes** landed in Mexico.
AD1521	Fall of Aztec capital, Tenochtitlan.
AD1533	Murder of the Inca, **Atahualpa.**
AD1562/1568	**John Hawkins** shipping African slaves to Spanish America.

Muslim Empires

From about 1300, a Muslim people called the Ottoman Turks began to build up an empire. In 1453 they captured Constantinople, the centre of the Orthodox Christian Church, and renamed the city Istanbul. Its great cathedral, St Sophia, shown here, became a mosque.

The Ottomans wanted to conquer Europe. Led by Sultan Suleiman the Magnificent, they defeated the Hungarian army at the Battle of Mohács, and took control of Hungary. They continued to threaten Europe until 1683, when they besieged Vienna and were heavily defeated.

The Sultan's palace

The Ottoman Sultans spent much of their time in the Topkapi Saray, their splendid palace in Istanbul. Here the Sultan is receiving an envoy from Europe. European princes were eager to buy Turkish goods and make alliances with the Turks.

Slaves

This is a slave. The Ottomans chose boys from the Christian areas of their empire, took them away from their families and brought them up as Muslims.

Most of the boys were trained to be soldiers called Janissaries. They were the best troops in the Ottomans' army.

The cleverest of these boys were given a good education, and later they were made government officials.

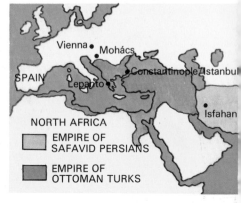

Vienna • Mohács

SPAIN · Lepanto · Constantinople/Istanbul

Isfahan

NORTH AFRICA

EMPIRE OF SAFAVID PERSIANS

EMPIRE OF OTTOMAN TURKS

Muslims in Persia

1

The Persians, like the Ottomans, were Muslims, but they belonged to a different group of Muslims, called the Shi'ites. This mosque is in Isfahan, their capital city.

2

The Persians and Ottomans often fought each other over religion and land. Their wars lasted on and off for over 200 years.

3

The royal family of Persia was called the Safavids. During the reign of their greatest shah (king), Abbas I, the luxuries of Persia became famous throughout the world.

1 Spain and the Muslims

Muslims had overrun Spain in the 8th century. They were finally driven out when King Ferdinand and Queen Isabella conquered Granada, the last Muslim kingdom in Spain.

2

Some Muslims stayed on in Spain and became Christians. But the Spaniards never trusted them and years later their descendants were banished.

3

The Spanish wanted to keep the Ottomans out of the Mediterranean Sea. In 1571, they defeated them in the great Battle of Lepanto.

4

Fierce pirates from North Africa raided the coasts of Spain and other European countries and carried off people to sell as slaves in Muslim lands.

The Habsburgs

SPANISH HABSBURG LANDS

AUSTRIAN HABSBURG LANDS

The Habsburgs were the most powerful ruling family in Europe in the 16th century. They were the rulers of Austria and most of Central Europe and in 1516 the Habsburg Archduke, Charles V, inherited Spain and the newly won Spanish territories in America too. When Charles died, his empire was divided between his son, Philip II of Spain, and his brother Ferdinand, Archduke of Austria, and from then on Spain and Austria were ruled by separate branches of the Habsburg family.

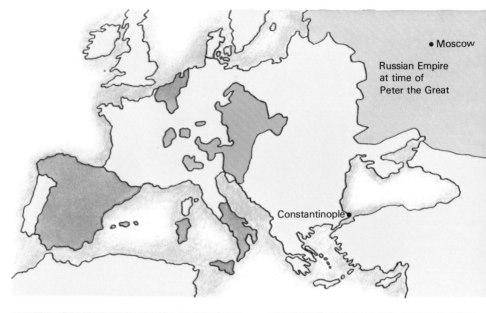

• Moscow

Russian Empire at time of Peter the Great

Constantinople •

1 Fabulous riches were sent to Spain from South America, but wars against the French, the Protestants and the Turks cost so much that the kings of Spain were always in debt.

2 You can see some of the magnificent clothes worn at the Spanish court in the paintings of Velasquez, King Philip IV's court artist. This is Philip's daughter, Margarita Teresa.

3 The Spanish kings were strong supporters of the Catholic Church. They encouraged the Inquisition to find and punish heretics and declared war on Protestant countries.

4 At this time there were many famous writers and artists in Spain. This is Don Quixote with his servant Sancho Panza, from the book *Don Quixote* written by Miguel de Cervantes.

Holy Roman Emperors

This is the Holy Roman Emperor, who was elected by a group of seven German princes. They always elected the Habsburg Archduke of Austria because the Habsburgs were so powerful. This meant that the

Archduke ruled over the hundreds of different German states. This was a difficult task as many of the German princes had become Protestant and resented having a Catholic ruler.

The Tsars

Before 1450, Russia was divided into several different states, each with its own ruler. During the 15th century, the Grand Prince of Moscow gradually gained control of all the states. The Russians belonged to the Orthodox Christian Church, which had its centre at Constantinople. But when the Turks, who were Muslims, conquered Constantinople in 1453, Moscow saw itself as the centre of the Orthodox Church.

Grand Prince Ivan III of Moscow was the first to use the title "Tsar" and have this double-headed eagle as his emblem.

Ivan III ordered that Moscow's fortress, the Kremlin, should be rebuilt. He brought in Italian architects who built the cathedral, shown here, inside its walls.

Ivan IV (1533/1584), often known as Ivan the Terrible because of his cruelty, won great victories over the Tartars and also gained control of all the Russian nobles.

He encouraged trade with Europe and is here receiving envoys from Elizabeth I of England.

When Ivan the Terrible died, the nobles fought for power until a national assembly chose Michael Romanov, shown here, to be the Tsar.

Peter the Great

Tsar Peter the Great (1689-1725) wanted Russia to become a powerful modern state. He forced his nobles to become more European by making them cut their beards off.

Peter went to Holland and England to learn about ship-building. He brought European craftsmen back with him to build him a strong, new navy.

In 1709, Peter led the Russians to a great victory over Sweden, their main rival, at the Battle of Poltava.

Peter wanted Russia to have the grandest capital city in Europe, so he built St Petersburg (now Leningrad) on the edge of the Baltic Sea.

The Elizabethans

From 1485 to 1603, England was ruled by a family called the Tudors. The best-known of the Tudor rulers are Henry VIII, who separated the English Church from the Roman Catholic, and his daughter, Elizabeth I. When Elizabeth was only three, her mother, Anne Boleyn, was executed. During the reigns of her half-brother Edward VI and half-sister Mary, Elizabeth's life was often in danger, but she survived to become one of England's most brilliant rulers.

This is a painting of Elizabeth. She reigned for 45 years, keeping a magnificent court where she inspired writers, artists and explorers. She never married.

This is a Protestant preacher. Elizabeth declared that the Church of England was Protestant, but she did not persecute people who had other beliefs unless they plotted against her.

Explorers

This is Sir Walter Raleigh. He introduced tobacco and potatoes to England from America. He also tried to start a colony in America, but it was unsuccessful.

Some explorers tried to find a way to the Far East by sailing north-west or north-east. They all failed because their ships could not break through the ice.

Once the explorers had discovered new lands and sea-routes, merchants banded together to form companies to trade overseas, licensed by the government.

The Globe theatre

The more expensive seats are in the galleries.

Pit where poorer people and apprentices stand.

The theatre is built of wood with a thatched roof so there is always a danger of fire. (It did, in fact, burn down in 1613.)

Francis Drake

Francis Drake was a great sailor who led daring attacks on Spanish ships and colonies in South America and captured a lot of treasure from them. The Spaniards hated him, but after he had sailed round the world the queen had him knighted on his ship, the Golden Hind. Later, when the Spaniards sent an Armada (fleet) to invade England, Drake played a leading part in their defeat.

By avoiding expensive wars, Elizabeth helped England become very wealthy. The nobles and middle classes spent their money on splendid houses, furniture and clothes.

Beggars and thieves were a terrible problem. A new law was made which said that all districts must provide work for the poor and shelter those who could not work.

Portraits

We know what many famous Elizabethans looked like from the miniature portraits by an artist called Nicholas Hilliard. This is a picture he painted of himself.

Musicians

Several great musicians lived at this time. Two of the most famous were Thomas Tallis and William Byrd. They composed music to be played at home as well as a great deal of church music.

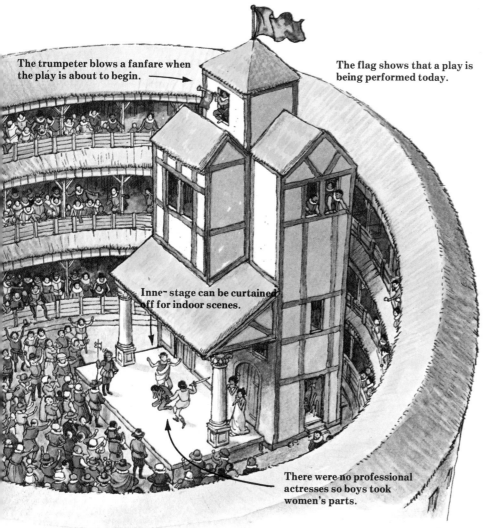

The trumpeter blows a fanfare when the play is about to begin.

The flag shows that a play is being performed today.

Inner stage can be curtained off for indoor scenes.

There were no professional actresses so boys took women's parts.

The Globe in London was the most famous of the theatres built at this time. The first one was opened in 1576. Before this, plays were performed in inn courtyards and town squares.

Shakespeare was an actor and writer with one of the London companies. He wrote at least 36 plays and many of them were first performed at the Globe theatre.

51

European Settlers

An Indian village

Boys fishing

Land cleared by burning.

Chief

Long houses made of bark.

Party of hunters bringing a deer home.

Palisade made of tree trunks.

Ritual dance

When the first Europeans arrived in North America, there were hundreds of different tribes of native people there. Each had their own customs, language and way of life. Those on the east coast, where the settlers first landed, were farmers, hunters and food gatherers. They lived in small villages and grew corn and some vegetables. This picture is based on drawings made by some of the early European settlers. The arrival of Europeans in the early 17th century was a disaster for these Indians. Many of them died of diseases brought from Europe and many others were killed or driven from their lands.

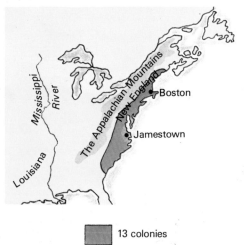

Mississippi River

Louisiana

The Appalachian Mountains

New England

Boston

Jamestown

13 colonies

In 1607 a group of English settlers set up a colony at Jamestown in Virginia. Here, their leader, Captain John Smith, is being rescued from death by Pocahontas, the daughter of the local Indian chief.

Another group of English people, who became known as the Pilgrim Fathers, sailed to America in 1620 in the ship, "Mayflower". They were Puritans, who wanted freedom to worship God in their own way.

3 The Puritans called the area where they settled New England. During their first winter they had a terrible struggle getting enough food.

4 Local Indians helped the English to survive. After their first harvest they held a feast to thank God. "Thanksgiving Day" is still celebrated in America.

5

Many other Europeans sailed with their families and belongings to live in America. Here is a ship full of settlers unloading. Some of them went because they wanted religious freedom, some were escaping from troubles at home and others came in the hope of finding adventure, or a better life and land of their own. The settlers on the east coast soon formed 13 colonies, each with their own laws and system of government. Gradually they were all brought under the control of the British government.

6 Most colonists settled down as farmers, at first. It was hard work clearing the land, growing crops and defending themselves against hostile Indians.

7 In the south the colonists started growing tobacco. There was a craze for it in Europe so they grew rich by making African slaves work for them.

8 Trade with Europe became profitable and some of the money was used to build towns. This is part of 18th century Boston.

9 A few people, mainly Frenchmen, chose to live as trappers and hunters. They explored along the Mississippi River, claiming land for France.

Plantations and Trading Forts

1 West Indies

Sugar cane

Plantation owner

Overseer

From the 1620s onwards, most of the islands known as the West Indies were taken over by the French and English. They set up sugar plantations and imported African slaves to work on them.

2

Fierce pirates infested the Caribbean Sea at this time. One English pirate called Henry Morgan was eventually knighted by King Charles II.

Key dates

AD1497	**John Cabot** discovered Newfoundland.
AD1523	French begin to explore Canada.
AD1607	English colony set up in Virginia.
AD1608	French founded the settlement of Quebec.
AD1612	First English colony in West Indies set up on Bermuda.
AD1620	The Pilgrim Fathers sailed to America in the Mayflower.
AD1655	English captured Jamaica from Spaniards.
AD1682	The French set up settlements in Louisiana.
AD1759	**General James Wolfe** captured Quebec from the French.
AD1763	Treaty of Paris. England took over Canada from French.

Canadian trading fort

Many French and English people settled in Canada. Some of them were farmers but many of them made a living by trapping animals for fur and catching and salting fish, especially cod. The trappers sold their catch and bought supplies at forts set up by trading companies. The fish and furs were then sent to Europe where they were in great demand.

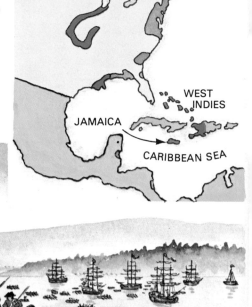

BRITISH

SPANISH

FRENCH

Hudson's Bay Company

Quebec

CANADA

JAMAICA

WEST INDIES

CARIBBEAN SEA

The capture of Quebec

The lands belonging to England's Hudson Bay Company in Canada and the 13 colonies in America were separated by the French colonies in Canada. From the 1680s onwards, rivalry between the French and British grew and fighting broke out. Here British troops, led by general Wolfe, are reaching the top of the very steep cliffs above the St Lawrence River before making a surprise attack on the French city of Quebec. After the capture of Quebec, the English went on to gain control of the whole of Canada.

The Kingdom of Benin

Today Benin is a small town in Nigeria, but between AD1450 and AD1850 it was the capital city of a great kingdom. European explorers brought back reports that Benin's warriors were highly disciplined and very brave, and were constantly fighting to win more land and slaves.

The people of Benin had no system of writing, but they made bronze plaques to record important events. This plaque shows their king, who was called the Oba, sacrificing a cow. The Obas spent most of their time in religious ceremonies and let their counsellors govern.

The Portuguese were the first Europeans to explore the coast of Africa. Soon others came, eager to buy ivory, gold and especially slaves sold by the local chiefs.

The most promising boys were trained as hunters. If they were very good they could become elephant hunters, armed with blow-guns and poisonous darts.

Benin lost its power in the 19th century, but the people still survive. This present-day chief is dressed for a festival in honour of the Oba's father.

Music

This carving shows a drummer playing at a ceremony at the Oba's court. The musicians of Benin also played bells and elephant-tusk trumpets.

Carvings

The people of Benin made beautiful portrait heads, like this one of a queen mother. It was the queen mother's duty to bring up the Oba's heir.

There were many skilled craftsmen in Benin. Besides bronze plaques and portrait heads, they made lovely things from ivory, like the bracelets, shown above.

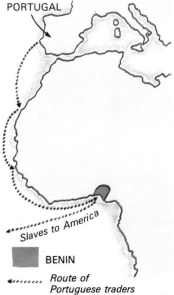

PORTUGAL

Slaves to America

BENIN

Route of Portuguese traders

55

The Mogul Empire

Muslim warriors had been invading and setting up kingdoms in India since before the 10th century. The most famous Muslim invaders were the Moguls, who were descended from the Mongols. In 1526, they founded the great Mogul Empire in north-west India which lasted until 1858. During their rule, great progress was made in the arts and sciences. Most Indians continued to work on the land, however, as their ancestors had done for centuries before them.

This is the first Mogul emperor, Babur (1526-1530). He was a descendent of the Mongol chiefs, Tamerlane and Genghis Khan.

This is the court of Babur's grandson, Akbar (1556-1605), greatest of the Mogul emperors. He was a good soldier and a wise ruler. He encouraged artists and brought scholars of all religions together to try to find one religion.

The Moguls were strongly influenced by Persian art and learning. This is Akbar's son, whose wife was Persian. Her name, Nurjahan, meant "Light of the World".

Many wonderful buildings were put up by the Moguls. The most famous is the Taj Mahal. It was built by Emperor Shah Jahan, as a tomb for his wife Mumtaz Mahal.

The Mogul emperors and nobles enjoyed hunting. Sometimes they used cheetahs for hunting gazelle. They also hunted tigers while riding on the backs of elephants.

European merchants came to India to buy silks, cotton, ivory, dyes and spices. Gradually they set up trading posts throughout India.

As the power of the Mogul rulers grew weaker, the British and French used the rivalry of lesser princes to increase their own power. Here, one of the princes is preparing for battle.

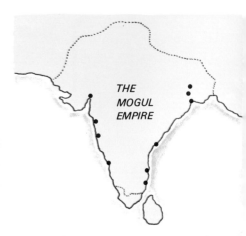

THE MOGUL EMPIRE

• BRITISH AND FRENCH TRADING POSTS

Ming and Ch'ing Emperors

The emperors of China lived in Peking, in a fantastic palace called the 'Forbidden City''. Here they were surrounded by richly decorated buildings and lovely gardens. The Ming dynasty (family line) of emperors (AD1368/1644) cut themselves off from the government and let their officials rule for them. In AD1644 the last Ming emperor committed suicide and the Ch'ing dynasty won power. They ruled until AD1911. Many of the Ch'ing emperors were clever rulers and brought peace and prosperity to China.

1 This figure, carved in ivory, represents a public official. To obtain this job he had to take a series of very difficult exams.

2 Chinese doctors knew how to prepare medicines by boiling up herbs. They also treated patients by sticking needles in them (acupuncture).

3 Here is a scene from *The Water Margin*. This was one of China's few novels. It tells a story about bandits who protected the poor against wicked officials.

4 European missionaries, like these Jesuit priests were, at first, welcomed by the emperors, but later they were driven out.

5 Porcelain Silk Lacquer Jade Tea

Many people in Europe wanted to buy beautifully-made Chinese goods, like these. But Europeans had to pay in gold and silver because China did not want European goods.

Farming

In the countryside life continued with few changes. New crops, such as maize, were introduced from America by Spanish and Portuguese traders. During the period of peace under the Ch'ing emperors the population began to increase. At first this did not matter, but later, it became difficult to grow enough grain to feed everyone.

57

Life in Japan

The emperors of Japan were greatly honoured, but had no real power. The country was ruled by an official called the Shogun. The first Europeans reached Japan in the 1540s and for nearly a century they traded with the Japanese. But then the Shogun expelled all foreign merchants, except the Chinese and the Dutch, and the Japanese people remained totally cut off from the rest of the world until 1854.

In 1467, civil war broke out. For over 100 years, the local barons, called daimyos, fought each other. They built huge castles like this one, half-fortress, half-palace, where they lived with their warriors, the samurai. The samurai believed that the only honourable way of life was to fight for and give loyal service to their daimyo. Eventually, a powerful daimyo called Tokugawa Ieyasu, succeeded in uniting Japan. He became Shogun and ruled from his capital in Edo (now Tokyo). The Tokugawa family held power until 180

1

The ancient Japanese Shinto faith became popular again in the 18th century. Here a new baby is being brought to a Shinto shrine.

2

Tea drinking developed into an elaborate ceremony, which still plays an important part in Japanese life. Both the ceremony and the tea were originally brought from China by Buddhist monks. The way in which the tea is prepared, served and drunk follows strict rules.

3

Christianity was brought to Japan by Jesuits. They converted many people but later the Shoguns banned Christianity and had many Christians executed.

4

Arranging flowers was a special art, called Ikebana, which at first only men were allowed to do. The type of flowers and the way they are arranged have special meanings.

5

Pictures made by printing from carved blocks of wood became popular at this time. Most of them illustrate the lives of ordinary people.

6

This is a street bookseller in the early 18th century. Poetry and novels were still popular but there were no longer many women writers as there had been earlier.

7

Puppet theatres and a type of musical play called "Kabuki" became very popular. These were livelier and more realistic than older Japanese dramas.

A Dutch island

From 1630 onwards, Dutch merchants had to live on this small island in Nagasaki Bay. They were not expelled completely like other foreigners because the Shoguns felt they would not try to conquer or convert the Japanese. A bridge linked the island to the land, but the Dutch were not allowed to cross it.

Key dates

AD1467/1568	Period of civil war in Japan.
AD1543	First Portuguese traders reached Japan. Other Europeans follow.
AD1549/1551	**St Francis Xavier** working in Japan.
AD1592 & 1597	Japanese invaded Korea.
AD1600/1868	Tokugawa family rule.
AD1603	**Tokugawa Ieyasu** became Shogun.
AD1606/1630	Christians persecuted.
AD1623/1639	All Europeans, except a few Dutch, left Japan.

Merchants and Trade

Once explorers had discovered new lands and sea-routes in the 16th century, there was a huge increase in trade between Europe and the rest of the world. By the 17th century the main trading countries were Holland, England and France. In these countries the merchants and middle classes who organized this trade became very wealthy and began to copy the life-style of the nobles. Even some of the ordinary working people benefited from this increase in wealth.

Groups of merchants, like these, set up trading companies in which people could buy shares. The shareholders' money was used to pay the cost of trading ventures and any profit was divided amongst the shareholders.

Many merchants bought goods from people who worked in their own homes and sold them abroad. Here a merchant's agent is buying cloth from a family workshop.

Companies hired ships to export their goods. Countries competing for overseas trade had to have good ships, sailors and ports. Dutch ships were among the best in Europe.

Rich merchants began to band together to set up banks to lend money. For this service they charged a fee called "interest". People could also bring their money to the bank

for safe-keeping. The first bankers were Italian merchants. In the 17th century London and Amsterdam became the most important banking cities.

In some of the big cities of Europe, coffee houses became the places where people met to buy and sell shares and discuss business.

It soon became more convenient to have a proper building for use as a market where people could buy and sell shares. This is the Amsterdam Stock Exchange, built in 1613. Soon there were stock exchanges like this in all the important trading centres of Europe.

Special insurance companies were set up. Merchants paid them a fee and if their trading expeditions met with disaster the insurance company stood the cost.

1 The new middle classes

As the merchant classes grew richer, they built themselves big town houses. The fashionable areas of big cities had pavements and wide streets.

2 The new middle classes wanted to live like the nobles. Many of them became rich enough to buy country estates and obtained titles. Some of the nobility looked down on them but others were happy to marry into these wealthy families.

3 Governments needed to understand business and finance so sometimes men from the merchant classes were chosen as royal ministers and advisers.

4 We know what many of the Dutch merchants of this time looked like because many of them paid artists to paint their portraits.

5 Many of the paintings of this time, especially Dutch ones, show us how merchant families lived and what their homes looked like.

6 In every country there were still many desperately poor people. Some nobles and merchants tried to help the poor. They founded hospitals, homes for old people and orphanages. Here a group of merchants' wives are inspecting an orphanage run by nuns.

Dutch merchants find Australia

On their trips to the east, Dutch sailors discovered Australia, which they called New Holland. Some people were wrecked there and tried to set up settlements but all their early attempts failed.

The Dutch controlled most of the important spice trade between Europe and the East Indies. This made Holland the greatest trading nation in Europe for much of the 17th century. This map shows the Dutch empire in the East Indies and the things they went there to buy.

- • Dutch bases
- △ Rice
- ■ Pepper
- ○ Sugar
- ▲ Cloves
- □ Nutmeg
- ◊ Ivory
- ● Diamonds
- ▲ Tin
- ♣ Precious woods

Kings and Parliaments

In the 17th and 18th centuries much of Europe was ruled by kings, queens and emperors who were extremely powerful. These rulers are known as "absolute monarchs". The court of

Louis XIV of France was the most brilliant in Europe. This is the Hall of Mirrors in his palace at Versailles. Louis encouraged the French nobles to come and live at his court, and

spend their time in a round of entertainments, so that he could keep an eye on them. Other monarchs built themselves great palaces too and tried to imitate Louis' way of life.

1 The English parliament

Parliament supporter
("roundhead")

King's supporter
("cavalier")

King Charles I of England tried to ignore parliament and rule like an absolute monarch. Many people were so unhappy with the way he ruled that in 1642 civil war broke out.

The king was defeated and executed. Oliver Cromwell, the leader of the parliamentarian army became ruler. He could not get parliament to agree with him so he too tried to rule without parliament.

Oliver Cromwell died in 1658. His son was incompetent and no one would support his government. Eventually Charles I's son was invited back and crowned King Charles II.

2 Parliaments hardly ever met. The king took all the important decisions. His ministers could only advise him and carry out his instructions. In order to keep control a successful ruler, like Louis XIV, had to spend hours every day with his ministers in meetings like this one.

3 Sometimes the king's favourites became very powerful. Louis XV let Madame du Pompadour, shown above, make important decisions.

4 The king made the laws and could put his enemies in prison if he wanted. Law-courts did what the king wanted.

5 Absolute monarchs usually kept large, permanent armies. Frederick the Great of Prussia, which is now part of Germany, was a brilliant military commander. Here he is inspecting his troops.

6 Monarchs often brought great painters, musicians and writers to their courts. As a child, Mozart played the piano at the court of Maria Teresa.

7 To add to the strength of their countries rulers set up industries. Some of these produced luxury goods such as tapestries, silk and glass. This is a glassworks.

4 Parliament's power increased, however, and the king's minister had to have the support of its members. This is Robert Walpole one of the most successful ministers of the 18th century.

5 Members of parliament formed two political parties called the Whigs and the Tories. Only people who owned property worth more than a certain value could vote.

Key dates

AD1642	English Civil War began.
AD1643/1715	**Louis XIV** ruled France.
AD1649	**Charles I** was executed.
AD1658	**Oliver Cromwell** died.
AD1660/1685	Reign of **Charles II.**
AD1682/1725	**Peter the Great** ruled Russia.
AD1715/1774	**Louis XV** ruled France.
AD1730/1741	**Robert Walpole** was Prime Minister.
AD1740/1780	**Maria Teresa** ruled Austria.
AD1740/1786	**Frederick the Great** ruled Prussia (now part of Germany).
AD1756/1791	Life of **Mozart.**
AD1762/1796	**Catherine the Great** ruled Russia.

Sports and Pastimes

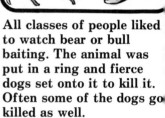

In the 16th century, nobles and kings played an early version of tennis on special courts. Bowls were also a favourite game at this time.

A cruel but popular sport was cock-fighting. Cocks were specially trained to fight, often to the death. The crowd placed bets on which bird would win.

Fox-hunting was a sport for the wealthy. Horse-racing, which was introduced later on, interested a wider audience.

All classes of people liked to watch bear or bull baiting. The animal was put in a ring and fierce dogs set onto it to kill it. Often some of the dogs go killed as well.

The English village of Hambledon had the first recognized cricket club. The game was later introduced to many of the countries in the British Empire.

Special gambling houses were set up where people could gamble on cards and dice. Huge sums of money would change hands every evening.

Fencing and shooting were sports, but gentlemen sometimes killed each other in duels with swords or pistols, fought over an insult or gambling quarrel.

Boxing grew in popularity, particularly in the early years of the 19th century. Many young noblemen learned to box, but did not fight in public contests.

In the late 18th century, sea-bathing became fashionable for people who could afford to travel to the coast.

They used "bathing machines" to stop people watching them from the beach.

Pirates, Highwaymen and Smugglers

During the 18th century traders and explorers on long sea trips were likely to be attacked by bands of pirates, who sailed the seas looking for ships to plunder. The West Indies, where many pirates hid among the islands, was an especially dangerous area.

Travel by land was slow, uncomfortable and dangerous. The roads were not made up and coaches sometimes overturned.

There were highwaymen too, who held up the coaches and demanded the passengers' money and valuables.

European countries charged taxes, called customs duties, on goods brought into the country. To avoid paying the taxes, smugglers worked secretly, often at night, bringing brandy, silks and other expensive goods from ships moored off the shore.

Towns and villages along the coast had Coast Guards and Excise Officers whose job it was to look out for smugglers. Once onshore the goods had to be hidden until they could be sold. You can still see old inns with secret cellars where smuggled goods were hidden.

When countries such as Britain and France were at war, trade between them was supposed to stop, but the smugglers went on carrying the goods and made great profits. If they were caught they were severely punished and sometimes even hung.

BRITAIN (THE AGRICULTURAL REVOLUTION): AD1700 to AD1800

A Revolution in Farming

In the 18th century farming methods in England changed completely. The experiments of a few enthusiastic landowners led to the invention of new tools, the introduction of new crops and new ways of improving the soil and breeding better animals. Landowners found it easier to introduce improvements if they gave each farmer a block of land, instead of thin strips in different fields as was usual then. These changes, known as the "Agricultural Revolution", later happened in other parts of Europe.

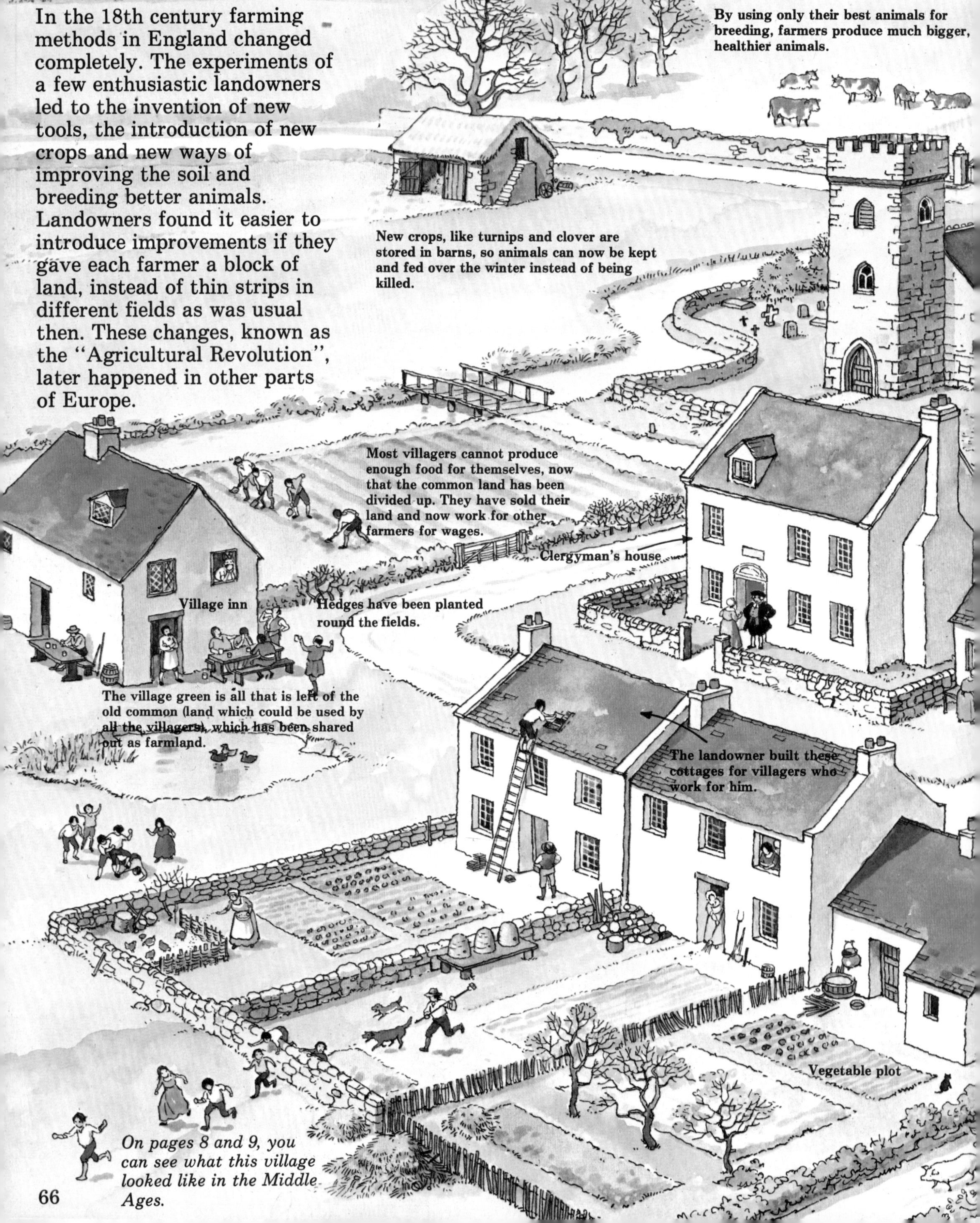

By using only their best animals for breeding, farmers produce much bigger, healthier animals.
New crops, like turnips and clover are stored in barns, so animals can now be kept and fed over the winter instead of being killed.
Most villagers cannot produce enough food for themselves, now that the common land has been divided up. They have sold their land and now work for other farmers for wages.
Clergyman's house
Village inn
Hedges have been planted round the fields.
The village green is all that is left of the old common (land which could be used by all the villagers), which has been shared out as farmland.
The landowner built these cottages for villagers who work for him.
Vegetable plot

On pages 8 and 9, you can see what this village looked like in the Middle Ages.

Village windmill for grinding corn.

House of chief landowner of the village, often called the squire. Some other villagers own their land, but he still owns the most.

This carrier has just delivered some goods to the house.

Seed drill sows seeds in straight lines.

New plough cuts deeper furrows.

Doctor's house

Ditch for draining land that used to be too wet for growing crops.

Animal manure is spread on the land to make it more fertile.

Landowner (squire)

Blacksmith

This farmer owns the land he farms.

Village shop

This family is leaving to go and work in a town.

Milkmaid

Woman spinning

Landowner's wife

Hoeing keeps the crop free of weeds so there will be a bigger harvest.

This man rents a farm from the landowner

In this field the farmer grows wheat one year, turnips the next, barley the third year and clover the fourth. This order of growing crops keeps the field fertile. Fields are no longer left unplanted every third year.

Machines and Factories

In the first half of the 18th century, most people in Britain still lived and worked in the countryside. Woollen and cotton cloth, produced in the north of England, were the chief manufactured goods. Before 1750 cloth was mainly made by hand, in people's homes. But by 1850 it was being made by machines in factories. The new factories employed lots of people and towns quickly grew up round them. These changes in working life have become known as the "Industrial Revolution".

Britain produced a great deal of woollen cloth. In the first half of the 18th century, most of it was made by villagers in their homes and sold to visiting merchants.

Then machines like this were invented. They helped spinners and weavers to work much faster. Later they were adapted to be driven by water, and later still by steam.

This is one of Watt's steam engines.

The early factories used water power to make their machines go. Various people experimented with the idea of using steam. Eventually a Scotsman called James Watt found out how to make steam engines drive the wheels of other machines and these were soon being used in factories.

This is an iron works. Iron was needed for making the new machines, but iron-smelting needed charcoal and the wood for making this was in short supply.

Coal was no good as its fumes made the iron brittle. Then, Abraham Darby discovered coal could be turned into coke which was pure enough for making iron.

People had been using coal to heat their homes for a long time, but it had been dug only from shallow mines. Deep mines were too dangerous.

Several inventions made mining safer. The safety lamp cut down the danger of explosions. Steam pumps helped prevent flooding and there was also a machine which sucked out stale air.

Underground rails made it easier to haul coal to the surface from great depths, but conditions in the mines were still very bad. Small children were used to pull the heavy trucks.

The new machines were too big to fit into people's homes and too expensive for them to buy. Clever men with money to invest built factories like this one and bought machines to put in them. People working at home could not compete with the prices of factory-made goods, so they had to go and work in the factories. They were joined by country people who thought they would make a better living in the factories than on the land.

Drive-wheel transfers power from steam engine to spinning machines.

Leather belts attach drive-wheels to machines.

Factory owner showing visitors round.

Machines for spinning cotton.

Boy climbing into machine to mend it.

Exhausted children often fall asleep at work and are punished.

Women change the bobbins (reels) and watch for breaks in the thread.

Overseer

Machine-smashing

At first, conditions in the factories were very bad. Men, women and children worked very long hours for low wages. Machines had no safety guards and there were bad accidents.

Gradually laws were passed to make the factory owners improve conditions in the factories, make working hours shorter and protect the rights of working people.

Machines were very unpopular with people who had no jobs. Some people even banded together to smash them. One group was called the Luddites after their leader, Ned Ludd.

Life in the New Towns

Where factories were built, new towns quickly grew up to house the factory workers. They were overcrowded and unhealthy places and they caused many problems.

Factory owner's house

Factories

Railway (goods lin

Chimney sweep and apprentice

Policeman

Barrel organ

Hansom cab

Gas lamp

Cheap houses, built back-to-back, were put up for the factory workers, especially in the northern towns. Often there were no toilets or running water. The streets were dirty and the air and rivers polluted by factories.

Diseases spread quickly. Until cheap ways of travelling were developed the workers had to live near the factories, which were often built near coal mines and ironworks.

Pickpocket

Fruit-seller

70

1

Key dates

AD1733/1793	Invention of several machines for spinning and weaving cloth.
AD1769	**James Watt** invented his first steam engine.
AD1812	Outbreaks of machine-smashing by the Luddites.
AD1824 & 1825	Trade Unions made legal, but with many restrictions.
AD1833	First of many laws passed to improve working conditions in factories.
AD1833, 1870, 1880, 1891, 1902	Education Acts*.
AD1845/1905	Life of **Dr Barnado.**
AD1848	First Public Health Act.
AD1875	First Housing Act.
AD1878	Salvation Army founded.
AD1900	Labour Party founded.
AD1909	Old-age pension Act.
AD1911	National Insurance Act.

An Act is a law passed by parliament.

The changes in farming and industry left some people without jobs and desperately poor. To get help they had to go and live in "workhouses". Conditions in the workhouses were very harsh to discourage lazy people from using them. Men and women lived in separate quarters so families were split up. Poor people often preferred to live on the streets.

2

Several reformers tried to help poor people. Dr Barnardo, shown here, set up children's homes and General Booth started a Christian organization called the Salvation Army.

3

Many laws were passed during the 19th century to improve people's lives by cleaning up towns, building better houses and setting up schools where all children could go without paying.

4

Old-age pensions started in 1909. These people are collecting theirs from the post office. In 1911, a law was passed which insured people against sickness and unemployment.

5

Workers began to join together to form trade unions so that they could bargain for better wages and working conditions by threatening to strike. At first the trade unions were illegal but gradually laws were passed which made them legal and gave them the right to picket (stand outside their work places and try to persuade other workers not to go in).

6

Some trade unionists and people who agreed with them formed the Labour Party. In the general election of 1906, 29 of their members were elected to parliament.

Transport and Travel

The Industrial Revolution brought about immense changes in transport and travel. Some important developments happened first in Britain, others happened first in America and other parts of Europe.

1

2

In England, companies called Turnpike Trusts were set up. They built and repaired roads and charged people tolls for using them. This is one of the tollgates. Engineers, like Telford and Macadam, found ways of building roads with hard surfaces.

New bridges were also built, many of them iron. This is the Clifton Suspension Bridge in England, designed by Brunel, a famous engineer.

3

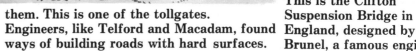

4

5

Bicycles were in general use by the 1880s. The early "penny-farthings" were ridden by men, but later models were suitable for women to ride too.

As the population increased during the 19th century, cities grew in size. People had to live further from their work and horse-drawn buses were introduced to provide them with transport. Before long, city streets became packed with traffic.

The first motor cars were made in Germany in 1885. They remained too expensive for anyone but the very wealthy until the 1920s.

1 Canals

2

In the 18th century, it was much cheaper to send heavy goods by water than by road. Where there were no suitable rivers, canals were cut to link important ports and cities. Locks, like the ones shown here, took the boats up and down slopes. The barges were pulled by horses walking along the "towpath."

In 1869 the Suez Canal, which links the Mediterranean Sea to the Red Sea, was opened. This canal cut several weeks off the journey from Europe to India. Later, in 1915, another long ship canal was opened. This was the Panama Canal in Central America which joined the Atlantic and Pacific Oceans

Railways

Early type of locomotive designed by famous railway engineer George Stephenson.

The first steam locomotive to run on rails was built in England in 1804 by Richard Trevithick. Twenty years later, the first passenger railway was opened and from then on railways became very popular. They were a quick, cheap and safe way of carrying people and goods. As train services improved, it became possible for ordinary people to go on seaside and country holidays. England's roads and canals were neglected.

London got its first long stretch of underground railway in 1863. Until 1890, when electric trains came in, the underground trains were steam-powered. The tunnels are still filled with the soot they made.

1 Sea travel

Very fast sailing ships called "clippers" were built during the 19th century and used to carry light cargoes such as tea. A completely new kind of ship was also being developed at this time. These ships were built of iron and had steam-engines. They gradually replaced sailing ships.

2

Many lighthouses were built and a life-boat service introduced, making sea travel much safer than it had been in the past.

3

Faster and safer sea travel tempted wealthy people to take holidays abroad. In 1869, Thomas Cook ran his first holiday tour to Egypt.

1 The first flights

The French Montgolfier brothers were the first people to take off into the air. This was in 1783 in a hot-air balloon. Other balloonists tried using hydrogen.

2

At the beginning of the 20th century, two Americans, the Wright brothers, built a glider like this one. Later they built an aeroplane fitted with an engine and in 1903 made the first powered flight.

Key dates

AD1663/1770	Turnpike trusts set up.
AD1783	First ascent of hot air balloon.
AD1804	First steam vehicle to run on rails.
AD1829	First railroads opened in U.S.A.
AD1839	First pedal bicycle made.
AD1863	Opening of first underground railway.
AD1869	Suez Canal opened.
AD1885	**Karl Benz** made a 3-wheeled motor car.
AD1886	**Gottlieb Daimler** made a 4-wheeled motor car.
AD1903	First powered flight.

73

French Revolution and Napoleon's Wars

The King of France, Louis XVI, and his wife, Marie Antoinette, lived in the magnificent palace of Versailles near Paris. Here they were surrounded by rich nobles who hardly paid any taxes. Louis was not a good ruler and they were all unpopular with the people.

Many nobles were very arrogant and treated everyone else with scorn. The middle classes were very annoyed by this.

The peasants had to pay taxes to the church, the government and their local lord. They also had to work for their lords.

By 1789, the government had no more money left, so the king was forced to call a meeting of the States General (parliament), which had not met for 175 years. Later the States General passed many reforms but most people were still not satisfied.

On July 14, 1789, a crowd in Paris captured a royal prison called the Bastille. This sparked off riots all over France.

The revolution became more violent. The king, queen, nobles and anyone not revolutionary enough were executed by guillotine.

European rulers were horrified by events in France and soon the French were at war with most of the rest of Europe. Here a soldier is recruiting people for the French army. Many clever young officers were found, in particular Napoleon Bonaparte.

Napoleon was so successful as a military commander that he became First Consul of France and then had himself crowned Emperor.

Napoleon gained control of much of Europe. He made his brothers and sisters rulers of the lands he conquered. This map shows the lands ruled by him and members of his family by 1810.

10 Napoleon planned to invade Britain, his most determined enemy. But after the British defeated the French at sea in the Battle of Trafalgar, he gave up the idea.

11 In 1812, Napoleon invaded Russia with an army of 600,000 men. He defeated the Tsar's army and marched to Moscow. But the Russians had set fire to Moscow and removed all the provisions. Here the French army is returning home in the middle of winter. Hundreds of thousands of them died from cold and hunger.

12 After his disastrous invasion of Russia, there was a general reaction against Napoleon in Europe. British troops helped the Spanish to drive the French out of Spain.

The Battle of Waterloo

The Battle of Waterloo was the last great battle in the wars against Napoleon. The French were completely defeated by a British army, led by Wellington, and a Prussian army, led by Blücher.

Louis XVIII was made King of France, and Napoleon was imprisoned on the small British island of St Helena in the South Atlantic Ocean, where he died in 1821.

Key dates

AD1789	First meeting of the States General.
AD1792	France went to war with Austria and Prussia.
AD1793/1794	Period called "The Reign of Terror". Hundreds of people guillotined.
AD1804	**Napoleon** became Emperor.
AD1805	Battle of Trafalgar.
AD1808/1814	War between the British and French in Spain and Portugal.
AD1812	**Napoleon's** invasion of Russia.
AD1815	Battle of Waterloo.

New Nations and Ways of Governing

The 18th and 19th centuries were times of great change in the way countries were governed.

There were many revolutions and several new, independent nations emerged.

1 Independence for America

In 1775 war broke out. The British Army were far from home and supplies. The colonists were on their own ground and their riflemen were very good shots.

In 1781 the British surrendered at Yorktown and in 1783 they signed a treaty recognizing the United States of America as an independent nation.

Most European settlers in America lived in the 13 colonies* on the east coast. In the early 18th century Britain helped them in their wars against the Indians and the French. The British then taxed them to pay for the wars. The colonists hated the taxes and sometimes attacked British tax officers.

When the new constitution (set of rules by which a country is governed) had been agreed upon, George Washington was chosen as first President of America.

Key Dates

AD1775/1783 War of American Independence.
AD1789/1797 **George Washington** President of the U.S.A.
AD1818/1883 Life of **Karl Marx**.
AD1859/1860 **General Garibaldi** drove French and Austrians out of Italy.
AD1861 Kingdom of Italy founded.
AD1871 German Empire founded. **William I** became Kaiser and **Bismarck** First Chancellor.

Germany

Early in the 19th century Germany was a group of states, the strongest of which was Prussia. In 1861 William I became King of Prussia. With his chief minister, Bismarck, he gradually brought all Germany under his control. In 1871 William was proclaimed Kaiser (emperor) of Germany.

Battleship being launched

Germany became one of the strongest countries in Europe. It quickly built a large navy, developed its industries and won colonies in Africa and the Far East.

Germans became very interested in their country's history. The operas of Wagner based on tales of German gods and heroes, became very popular.

76 *A colony is a settlement ruled by the country from which the settlers have come.*

Italy

In Italy, some states were independent, some were ruled by France and some by Austria. General Garibaldi and his soldiers, known as the "Red Shirts"(above) helped to drive the foreigners out of Italy and make it an independent nation.

ITALY IN 1866
GERMAN EMPIRE IN 1871

1 Ideas about government

In Britain, the people chose which political party should rule by voting at elections. At first few people had the right to vote but gradually it was extended to all men.

2

Some women began to demand the vote. They were called suffragettes.

They held marches and caused as much disturbance as possible to win support.

3

Rulers in many countries were afraid of democracy (people having a say in the running of the country). Soldiers were used against the people who protested.

4

People with revolutionary ideas were sometimes executed or put in prison so they could not lead the people against their ruler.

5

Some people believed any form of government was wrong. They were called anarchists and they killed many political leaders.

6

A German thinker, called Karl Marx, wrote many books with new ideas about government. He wanted people to get rid of their rulers in a revolution and then have new governments run by the working people. Communism is based on his ideas.

Slavery and Civil War

In the southern states of the United States of America there were large plantations. Since the 17th century the plantation owners had bought slaves from Africa to work for them. The northern states had small farms and industries and did not need slaves.

NORTHERN (UNION) STATES

SOUTHERN (CONFEDERATE) STATES

Washington

Richmond

The slave trade became well organized. Europeans either captured Africans or bought them from local rulers, like the King of Dahomey, shown here.

Conditions on the ships carrying the slaves to America were dreadful as the more slaves a trader could get on a ship, the greater his profit.

When they reached America, the slaves who had survived the voyage were sold at auctions. They could be sold again at any time and families were often parted.

Some slaves were lucky enough to work in their master's house but most were used as field hands on the plantation. Most estate owners grew either cotton, tobacco or sugar, all of which need constant attention. Because of the heat African slaves were thought best for this work. Some masters were very cruel but others treated their slaves quite well.

Many slaves tried to escape to the north where they would be free as there was no slavery. A black woman called Harriet Tubman, helped 19 groups of slaves escape.

AM I NOT A MAN AND A BROTHER?

Protests against slavery began to grow. In 1833 slavery was abolished in the British Empire and the Anti-Slavery Society was founded in America. This is its badge.

In the American Congress (parliament) there were bitter arguments about slavery. The northerners wanted to abolish it but the southerners were determined to keep slaves.

The outbreak of war

In 1861 the southern states elected their own president and broke away from the Union of the United States, declaring themselves a "confederacy". The north thought the states should stay united so war broke out between the Unionists (northerners) and Confederates (southerners). It lasted for four years. There were many fierce battles and nearly 635,000 people lost their lives.

Camp

Mine exploding

Southern (Confederate) flag

Northern (Unionist) flag

Barbed wire

Trench

A new style of fighting developed during the American Civil War. Soldiers made trenches protected by barbed wire. They used mines, hand-grenades and flame throwers.

At first the southerners, led by General Lee, were quite successful. But the north had more soldiers, factories to make weapons and railways to transport them. It used its navy to stop ships bringing supplies to the south. Despite terrible suffering the southerners fought bravely on, but in 1865 they were finally forced to surrender.

1 After the war

President Abraham Lincoln, who had been elected before the war broke out, hoped to make a lasting peace but he was assassinated at Ford's Theater in Washington.

2

The south had been ruined by the war and its main town, Richmond, had been burned. For years afterwards both white and black people were very poor.

3

Some southerners still regarded black people as slaves. They formed a secret society called the Ku Klux Klan. Members covered themselves in sheets and terrorized black people.

Explorers and Empire Builders

In 1750 there were still huge areas of the world where Europeans had never been. During the 19th and late 18th centuries European explorers set out to discover as much as they could about the lands and oceans of the world. Traders and settlers followed and the European countries began to set up colonies abroad which they ruled.

Captain Cook

Captain Cook led three expeditions (1768-79) to the Pacific Ocean. He visited islands such as Tahiti where he was met by war canoes.

He explored the east coast of Australia. Its strange animals fascinated the artists and scientists on the expedition.

He also sailed round the islands of New Zealand. The crew of his ship *Endeavour* landed and met the Maoris who lived there.

1 Exploring Africa

During the 19th century people began to explore and make maps of Africa. They saw wonderful sights such as the Victoria Falls, but many fell ill and died of strange diseases.

2 On a journey in search of the source of the Nile, two British explorers, Speke and Grant, stayed with Mutesa, King of Buganda, who treated them with great hospitality.

3 Some explorers, such as Dr Livingstone, were also Christian missionaries.*Missionaries set up hospitals and schools for the Africans, as well as churches.

4 The Frenchman, René Caillé, was one of the earliest European explorers in the Sahara Desert. He was also one of the first Europeans to see the ancient African city of Timbuktu.

5 There were also several women explorers in the 19th century. This is Alexandrine Tinné, a wealthy Dutch heiress, who travelled through much of North Africa and the Sudan.

*People who went to foreign lands to teach the people about Christianity.

ther expeditions

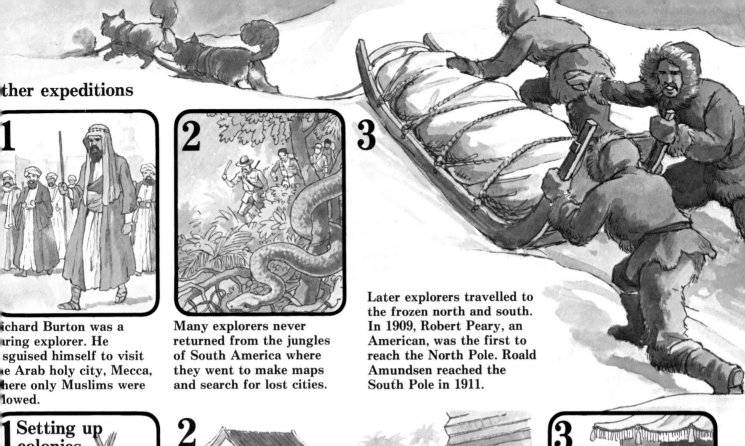

1 ichard Burton was a aring explorer. He sguised himself to visit e Arab holy city, Mecca, here only Muslims were lowed.

2 Many explorers never returned from the jungles of South America where they went to make maps and search for lost cities.

3 Later explorers travelled to the frozen north and south. In 1909, Robert Peary, an American, was the first to reach the North Pole. Roald Amundsen reached the South Pole in 1911.

Setting up colonies

1 uropeans wanted new laces to sell their factory-ade goods. They also anted to buy raw aterials such as cotton nd tea.

2 If quarrels between local rulers threatened trade, the Europeans sent armies. These often stayed after the fighting was over.

3 They also sent officials to organize and govern the territory for them, thus setting up a colony there.

4 More and more Europeans went to he colonies and settled there with heir families. They organized vast states where the local people worked nd grew tea, rubber, cotton and foodstuffs or reared sheep and cattle. Later, when minerals were discovered, factories and railways were built and still more people went to live in the colonies.

5 In Europe, politicians were worried by the increase in population and they encouraged people to go and settle in the colonies where there was land and work for them.

Europeans in Africa

1 North Africa

In the early 19th century most of the countries of North Africa were part of the Ottoman Empire*. But the Ottoman Empire was breaking up and European powers began to move in.

The French gained control of Algeria and later Tunisia and Morocco. Here, desert tribesmen are attacking one of the French forts, which is defended by the famous French Foreign Legion.

2

The ruler of Egypt needed money, so he sold his shares in the Suez Canal to Britain. Britain became involved in Egyptian affairs and later took over the government.

3

Egypt also ruled the Sudan. In 1883 a religious leader, the Mahdi, led a revolt. Britain sent an army led by General Gordon, but it was defeated at Khartoum.

Trading in the West

These gold objects were made by the Ashanti, a people who live in west Africa. They grew rich by trading in gold and slaves. They fought the British in several wars and were defeated in 1901.

Zimbabwe

Zimbabwe was the capital city of a rich kingdom in south-east Africa. It was destroyed probably in the early 19th century by rival tribes. The people were clever builders and this is the remains of a temple in the city.

Empire of Muslim people from Middle East called the Ottoman Turks.

South Africa

Cecil Rhodes

Cecil Rhodes made a fortune from diamond and gold mines, then formed a company to build a railway from the British colony to the mining area north of the Boer states. In 1895 this area became known as Rhodesia.

Dutch settlers had first arrived in South Africa in 1652. They set up Cape Colony on the Cape of Good Hope. Most of them were farmers and they became known as "Boers" (Dutch word for farmers). In 1814 an international treaty gave Cape Colony to the British. The Boers hated being ruled by the British and between 1835 and 1837 many of them set off northwards, with all their possessions in wagons, to find new lands free from British rule. This movement is called the "Great Trek".

The Grab for Africa

☐	FRENCH
☐	BRITISH
☐	GERMAN
☐	PORTUGUESE
☐	BELGIAN
☐	SPANISH
☐	ITALIAN

In 1880 much of Africa was still independent of any European country. Between 1880 and the outbreak of World War I in 1914, the European powers carved up nearly the whole of Africa between them. This map shows Africa in 1914.

The Boers came into conflict with the Zulus, the fiercest of the neighbouring African tribes. The British helped the Boers and eventually, in 1879, the Zulus were completely defeated.

The British gradually increased their control over the Boer states. In 1886, gold was discovered in one of them and many more British people came out to work in them.

In 1899 war broke out between the Boers and the British. The Boers did very well at first. They rode fast horses, were good at stalking the enemy and knew the countryside.

The British destroyed the Boers' farms and animals and put all the Boers they could find, including women and children, into special prison camps. In 1902 the Boers surrendered.

Key dates

AD1814	Britain gained control of Cape Colony.
c. AD1830	Collapse of Kingdom of Zimbabwe.
AD1830	French began to take over North Africa.
AD1835/1837	The Great Trek.
AD1875	Britain bought Egypt's shares in the Suez Canal.
AD1878/9	Zulu War.
AD1885	Fall of Khartoum.
AD1896	Britain took over Matabeleland which became Rhodesia.
AD1899/1902	Boer War.
AD1901	Ashanti kingdom became British.
AD1910	Union of South Africa set up.

The British in India

This is a court of the British East India Company which started as a trading company. By the 19th century it governed most of India.

The British built railways and schools and tried to modernize India. They also tried to stop some of the Indians' religious customs. The Indians resented this interference. In 1857 some *sepoys* (Indian soldiers in the British Army) mutinied and the revolt quickly spread. The British eventually regained control but in future changes were made more carefully.

After the Mutiny the East India Company lost its right to rule and the British Government appointed its own officials. Indian princes also lost their power but were very wealthy and still lived in great luxury.

Queen Victoria became Empress of India in 1876. Many Indians felt this created a special tie with Britain and the royal family often went to India.

The British brought their own customs and entertainments to India. They introduced cricket which became one of the national sports of India.

Most Indians were very poor. The cities were crowded and outbreaks of disease and famines were common. Improvements could be made only slowly.

The two main religious groups in India were the Hindus and the Muslims. They were rivals and sometimes there were riots and people were killed.

The Indians had little say in how their country was ruled so a group of them formed the National Congress. At first they just wanted reforms but later they began to demand independence from Britain.

Convicts and Settlers

In 1788 the British Government began to send criminals to Australia as a punishment. Many stayed on there after they had served their sentence.

Soon many other settlers arrived. Most of them wanted land where they could raise sheep and cattle. Some went in search of gold and minerals.

Life in Australia in the 19th century was hard and often dangerous. There were "bushrangers" (outlaws). The most famous was Ned Kelly.

As more settlers arrived they took land from the Aborigines (native Australians), many of whom were killed, or died of diseases brought by settlers.

INDIA

Key dates

AD1788 First convicts sent to Australia.
AD1840 Britain claimed New Zealand.
AD1857 Indian Mutiny.
AD1876 **Queen Victoria** became Empress of India.
AD1885 Indian National Congress party founded.

BRITISH TERRITORY IN 1914

AUSTRALIA

NEW ZEALAND

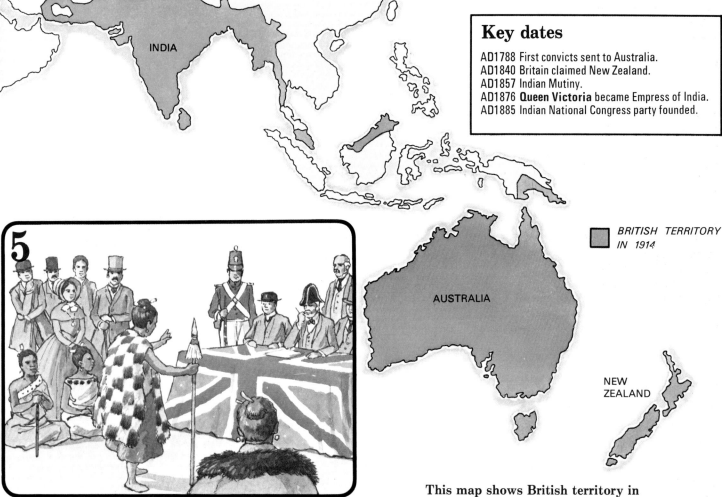

European settlers first arrived in New Zealand in the 1790s. In 1840 the British Government took over the country. The Governor and the Maori chiefs made a treaty agreeing how much land the settlers could have, but this did not prevent fierce wars between the Maoris and the settlers.

This map shows British territory in India, South-East Asia, and Australia in 1914. By this time Australia and New Zealand had gained the right to rule themselves but they were still part of the British Empire.

Indians and Settlers

Many tribes of Indians lived in North America, each with its own way of life and language. The Indians of the Great Plains lived by farming until they captured horses from the Spaniards in the 16th century. Then most of them became nomads, hunting buffalo across the Plains and rearing horses. They lived like this for about 200 years until European settlers moved west and took the Indians' hunting grounds for their farms.

Tepee (tent made of buffalo hide)

Buffalo hunt. The buffalo provided Indians with food, clothing and shelter.

Chiefs

Traders

Meat drying

Travois (sledge)

We have removed part of this tepee wall so you can see inside.

Preparing buffalo hide

Medicine man

The Plains Indians lived in tepees which could be packed up when the buffalo moved on. The first white men to meet the Indians were traders who sold metal goods, blankets and guns and bought buffalo hides and horses.

1 Settlers move west

As more settlers from Europe moved into the original 13 States of the United States of America, more land was needed. In 1803 the Americans bought Louisiana from the French.

Settlers began to cross the Appalachian Mountains and the Great Plains, looking for land to farm. They travelled with wagons packed with everything they needed for their new homes, so most people, except for guards and cattle herders had to walk. It usually took many months to reach a suitable area.

The settlers made treaties with the Indians promising not to take all their land. But the treaties were soon broken when settlers wanted more land.

In 1848 gold was discovered in California. Thousands of people flocked there in the "goldrush" hoping to make fortunes.

Railways were built to link the east and west coasts. These brought more settlers to the Great Plains, leaving less and less land for the Indians.

The men who built the tracks had to be fed. They employed hunters armed with rifles who killed most of the buffalo on which the Indians had depended.

The Indians fought the settlers. The wars were bitter and both sides were cruel. The Indians won victories such as at Little Big Horn when they killed General Custer and his men. But the settlers had more soldiers and better weapons and many Indian tribes were almost wiped out.

The Indians were left with only small areas of land called reservations. They were controlled by government agents and most were very unhappy.

The Wild West

In the United States of America, many of the people who moved westwards to the vast plains and prairies started raising cattle or growing corn. Towns, like this one, grew up to supply their needs. At first they were wild, lawless places, especially when cowboys from the ranches came into town. They brought great herds of cattle to the railway depots from which they were taken to feed the people in the cities.

Large industries and cities like New York and Chicago grew up. The first skyscrapers were built. By 1890 the United States was one of the world's most powerful industrial nations.

At first life was hard for the farmers on the plains, but soon they started using tougher crops and steel ploughs and later bought machines for harvesting and threshing. Before long they were producing vast quantities of grain which were sold all over the world.

From all over Europe poor people and people persecuted for their ideas came to the United States to start a new life. Some were lucky, but many of them ended up working in factories and living in hard conditions in the big cities.

New Countries in South America

1 Between 1810 and 1825 a series of revolutions ended the rule of Spain and Portugal in South America and set up 11 new states. This is Simon Bolivar, one of the revolutionary leaders who helped to achieve this.

2 Coffee was brought from Arabia to South America and grown on large estates. By 1860 it was the main export of many states.

3 Another important export was rubber. It was made from the juice of trees growing in the Amazon jungle.

4 Many of the Indian tribes in the Amazon jungle attacked the white men who came to take over their lands.

5 On the vast pampas (grasslands) of the southeast, there were huge ranches where great herds of cattle were reared by cowboys called "gauchos".

The cattle were used for making canned meat which was sold abroad.

Mexico

1 Mexicans and Americans were always quarrelling about who should control Texas. It belonged to Mexico but many Americans had settled there and wanted to be part of the United States. Here Davy Crockett and a group of other Americans are defending the Alamo Fort against a Mexican attack.

2 In 1863 the European powers, led by France, tried to get control of Mexico by making Archduke Maximilian of Austria, Emperor of Mexico. In 1867 the Mexicans shot him.

3 From 1867 onwards the Mexicans ruled themselves. In the early 20th century civil war broke out. One of the revolutionary leaders was Pancho Villa, shown here.

89

Life Under the Tsars

1

The Tsars (emperors) of Russia governed their huge country from St Petersburg. There was no parliament and the Tsars and nobles, from whom they chose their ministers and officials, were very cut off from the rest of the country. Much of their time was spent at balls and receptions.

2

Most Russians were members of the Orthodox Christian Church, which supported the idea that the Tsar was chosen by God and that he alone had the right to rule.

3

Talking or writing about government reforms was forbidden. Secret police tracked down anyone suspected of wanting to change the government.

4

Many people who criticized the government for its inefficiency and cruelty, were executed or sent into exile in a part of Russia called Siberia.

5

During the 19th century there were several great novelists, playwrights and composers at work in Russia. The Russian ballet became world-famous.

6

Many Russians were serfs—peasants who lived on nobles' estates and were treated as slaves. Serfs could be bought and sold. They had to do any work their estate owner demanded and they were often given cruel punishments for small mistakes. There were frequent uprisings and riots. Eventually, in 1861, Tsar Alexander II freed the serfs. The government lent them money to buy land, but they were too poor to buy farming equipment and pay back the loans. Their lives were not much improved and some were even worse off than before.

The Crimean War

The Russians wanted to expand their empire. In the late 18th and early 19th centuries they expanded eastwards. They also won land around the Black Sea, by helping the people of these territories free themselves from the Turkish Empire. The countries of Europe were suspicious of Russia's ambitions. In 1853 Britain and France tried to capture the area called the Crimea, to stop Russian expansion. One incident in this war was the Charge of the Light Brigade (shown here). A British force misunderstood an order and charged the Russian guns.

1 Discontent grows

This is Nicholas II, who became Tsar in 1894. He was a well-meaning and kind man but he was not strong enough to be a good ruler.

2

Nicholas's wife, Alexandra, was under the spell of a monk called Rasputin. She believed he could cure her son of a blood disease, but others thought him evil.

3

Factories and industrial towns were growing up in Russia. Living conditions in the towns were very bad and many people started demanding changes.

4

In 1905 a crowd of workers went on strike and marched to the Tsar's palace to tell him their problems. Soldiers, fearing a revolution, fired on them.

5

The Tsar allowed a *Duma* (parliament) to meet for a while but then dismissed it. Meanwhile, a group of people in exile, led by Lenin, were planning a revolution.

Key dates

AD1762/1796	Reign of **Catherine the Great**.
AD1812	Invasion of Russia by Napoleon.
AD1853/1856	Crimean War.
AD1855/1881	Reign of **Alexander II**.
AD1861	Serfs freed.
AD1894/1917	Reign of **Nicholas II**.
AD1904/1905	Russia defeated in war with Japan.
AD1905	Massacre of strikers outside Tsar's palace.
AD1906	Meeting of Duma (parliament).

Western Ideas in the East

Japan

It was hundreds of years since any emperor of Japan had had any real power. An official called the Shogun ruled the country for the emperor. This is the last Shogun of Japan.

From about 1640 onwards Japan had no contact with the countries of the west, except for a few Dutch traders. Then, in 1853, Commodore Perry, the commander of a squadron of American warships, sailed to Japan and got permission for America to trade with Japan. Soon European powers followed and Japan made trade agreements with many European countries.

In 1868 the 15-year-old Emperor left the old capital, Kyoto, and set up a new one in Edo (Tokyo). Here he is arriving in Edo, where he took back power from the Shogun and set up a western-style parliament.

The small picture above shows the opening of the first parliament.

The Samurai (warriors) were replaced by a new army, trained in modern methods of fighting by advisers from France and Germany.

The Japanese learnt many other things from the west. They built railways and factories and started producing large numbers of goods quickly and cheaply.

The Japanese wanted to win power overseas. They started to interfere in China and Korea. This made them rivals with the Russians and in 1904 Japan and Russia went to war. The new, efficient Japanese army and navy quickly defeated the Russians.

1 China

Between 1644 and 1912, China was ruled by the Ch'ing (also called the Manchu) Emperors. One of the greatest was Ch'ien Lung (1736-95), shown here.

The Ch'ing emperors fought many wars to protect their frontiers, win more territory and put down rebellions. At first they were successful but the wars were very expensive and later emperors found it more and more difficult to pay for them. The country slowly became weaker.

The Chinese population was growing quickly but farming methods were still very old-fashioned. It was difficult to grow enough food for everyone.

The Chinese Government did not like foreigners and allowed them to trade only in certain areas. The British were keen to extend these areas and in 1839 they went to war.

The British won the war in 1842. They forced the Chinese to sign a treaty which gave them Hong Kong and allowed them to trade in certain other ports.

Some Chinese decided to strengthen China by adopting certain Western ideas and inventions, such as railways, and steamships. But many still hated foreign ideas.

People who hated foreigners formed a secret society called the "Boxers". In 1900 they started attacking all the foreigners they could find in China. Here they are storming a foreign embassy.

This is the Empress Tzu Hsi. From 1862 to 1908 she ruled China, first for her son, then for her nephew. She often plotted with those who hated foreigners.

In 1911 there was a revolution and the last Ch'ing Emperor was expelled from China. This is Sun Yat-sen the first President of China.

Time Chart

	North America	Central and South America	Europe	Africa
	Mound Builders living on the plains.		Gradual conversion of barbarian kingdoms to Christianity.	North Africa and Egypt part of the Byzantine Empire. North Africa and Egypt overrun by Muslim Arabs.
AD800			Invasion of Spain by Muslims. Battle of Poitiers. Muslim advance into Western Europe halted. Viking raids begin. **Charlemagne** crowned Holy Roman Emperor.	Various tribes start living south of the Sahara Desert.
AD900		Decline of Maya civilization in Mexico.		
AD1000	Vikings may have reached America.		Normans invade England. Normans invade Italy.	First Iron Age settlement at Zimbabwe.
AD1100		Chimu people living in Peru.	First Crusade.	Zimbabwe becomes a powerful kingdom.
AD1200			The Mongols invade Eastern Europe. Eighth Crusade.	Arab merchants known to be trading in West and East Africa. Rise of Empire of Mali in West Africa.
AD1300		Rise of Aztec Empire in Mexico.	Beginning of Hundred Years War. Black Death from Asia spreads through Europe.	
AD1400	People living at Huff.	Spread of Inca Empire in Peru.	First firearms developed. Invention of printing. Ideas of the Renaissance spreading from Italy .	Chinese merchants trading in East Africa. Kingdom of Benin set up.
AD1500	Voyage of Christopher Columbus.	Arrival of Spaniards. End of Aztec and Inca Empires. Arrival of Portuguese.	European explorers discover America. Beginning of Reformation. Wars of Religion between Catholic and Protestants.	Portuguese expeditions explore west coast and start trading with Africans. Turks conquered Egypt. Mali Empire destroyed. Beginning of slave trade.
AD1600	Spaniards brought horses to America. First European settlements. Pilgrim Fathers arrive in New England.		Development of trade between Europe and other parts of the world. English Civil War.	Dutch settlers arrive in South Africa.
AD1700	England wins Canada from the French. War of American Independence.		Beginning of Agricultural Revolution in Britain. Beginning of Industrial Revolution in Britain.	Rise of Ashanti power on west coast.
AD1800	United States buys Louisiana from the French. California goldrush. American Civil War.	Spaniards and Portuguese driven out of Central and South America. War between Mexico and United States of America.	French Revolution. Wars of **Napoleon** Unification of Italy. Unification of Germany.	Slave trade abolished within British Empire. The Great Trek. Opening of Suez Canal. European powers build up empires in Africa. Boer war begins.
AD1900		Mexican Revolution begins.	World War I.	Union of South Africa established.

94

Russia and Asia	Middle East	India	China and Japan	Far East and Pacific
Slavs in Russia.	Byzantine Empire controls much of Middle East.	India ruled by many princes.	T'ang Dynasty in China.	
Muslims conquer Persia.	Death of **Muhammad.** Spread of Muslim Empire. Muslims conquer much of Byzantine Empire.			
			Japanese capital moved to Kyoto.	
Vikings settle in Russia.				Rise of the Khmers in Cambodia.
Kiev becomes most important city in Russia.				First settlers reach Easter Island and New Zealand from Polynesia.
Russia becomes offically Christian.	Seljuk Turks invade Byzantine Empire.		Sung Dynasty in China.	
	Invasion of Seljuk Turks.			
	The First Crusade.			
	Kingdom of Outremer founded.		Appearance of Samurai in Japan.	Large statues erected on Easter Island.
	Life of **Saladin.**		Military rulers in Japan take the title "Shogun".	
Mongols invade and conquer Russia.	Sack of Constantinople by Crusaders.		**Marco Polo** visits China. The Mongol ruler, **Kubilai Khan,** conquers China.	
	End of Kingdom of Outremer.			
			Ming Dynasty in China.	
		Mongols invade northern India.		
Rise of Moscow. Russia gradually united.	Sack of Constantinople by Ottoman Turks.	First European sea voyage to India and back, led by **Vasco da Gama** (Portuguese).	Long period of war in Japan.	Europeans first see Pacific Ocean.
Ivan III becomes first Tsar and throws off Mongol power.	End of Byzantine Empire.			
Rise of Safavid Dynasty in Persia.	**Suleiman the Magnificent.** Turks threaten Europe.	Mogul Empire set up.	Arrival in Japan and China of European traders and missonaries.	First Europeans cross Pacific Ocean on their way round the world.
Tsar Ivan the Terrible. Development of trade between Russia and England.	Turkish advance into Europe halted.			
	Europeans try to extend their trade with Turkey and Persia.	British start regular trade with India.	All Europeans, except Dutch traders, expelled from Japan. The Manchu family start the Ch'ing Dynasty in China.	Expansion of Dutch trade in East Indies.
Tsar Peter the Great.				
		British destroy French power in India.		Dutch land in Australia. **Captain Cook** reaches Australia and New Zealand. British colony of Australia founded.
Napoleon's expedition to Moscow.	Ottoman Empire falling apart. Russia tries to help parts of Empire break free.	Britain gradually gains control of the whole of India. Indian Mutiny.	War between the British and Chinese. **Commodore Perry** arrives in Japan.	Britain takes possession of New Zealand.
Crimean War.		**Queen Victoria** proclaimed Empress of India.		French build up empire in Indo-China.
Nicholas II becomes Tsar.			Boxer uprising in China. War between Japan and Russia.	
Meeting of the First Duma (parliament).	World War I.		Revolution in China. Last Ch'ing Emperor expelled.	

95

Index

Going Further

Books to read

These are just some of the books available on these periods of history. If you look in your local library or book shop, you will probably find many others.

AD600 to AD1450

The Time Traveller Book of Viking Raiders by Anne Civardi and James Graham-Campbell (Usborne).
The Time Traveller Book of Knights and Castles by Judy Hindley (Usborne).
Castle by David Macaulay (Collins).
Living in a Medieval Village, *Living in a Medieval City* and *Living in a Crusader Land*—3 books by R. J. Unstead (Black).
Knight Crusader by Ronald Welch (Puffin).
The Children's Crusade by Henry Treece (Puffin).
Vinland the Good by Henry Treece (Puffin).
The Buildings of Early Islam by Helen and Richard Leacroft (Hodder and Stoughton).
The Samurai of Japan and *Genghis Khan and the Mongols*—2 books by Michael Gibson (Wayland).
Peoples of the Past, The Aztecs by Judith Crosher (Macdonald).

AD1450 to AD1750

Everyday Life in Renaissance Times by E. R. Chamberlin (Carousel).
The Story of Britain in Tudor and Stuart Times by R. J. Unstead (Carousel).

Europe Finds the World, *The Birth of Modern Europe*, *Martin Luther* and *Benin*—4 books in the Cambridge Introduction to the History of Mankind (Cambridge University Press).
Cue for Treason by Geoffrey Trease (Puffin).
Popinjay Stairs by Geoffrey Trease (Puffin).
The Strangers by Anne Schlee (Puffin).
Jack Holborn by Leon Garfield (Puffin).

AD1750 to AD1914

The Old Regime and the Revolution, *Power for the People*, *The War of American Independence* and *Transported to Van Diemen's Land*—4 books in the Cambridge Introduction to the History of Mankind (Cambridge University Press).
Honest Rogues: The Inside Story of Smuggling by Harry T. Sutton (Batsford-Heritage).
Freedom and Revolution and *Age of Machines* by R. J. Unstead (Macdonald).
Ishi: Last of his Tribe by Theodore Kroeber (Puffin).
Underground to Canada by Barbara C. Smucker (Puffin).
Children on the Oregon Trail by A. Rutgers Van Der Loeff (Puffin).
Escape from France by Ronald Welch (Puffin).
Castors Away! by Hester Burton (Puffin).
*These books are novels.

Places to visit

Look out for great houses and houses once lived in by famous people. Look out too for factories and farms built after 1750. *History Around Us* by Nathaniel Harris (Hamlyn) and *History Hunter* by Victor E. Neuburg (Beaver Books) will help you to recognize them.

In London the British Museum, The Victoria and Albert Museum and the London Museum all have collections of things from these periods of history.

In Australia the National Gallery of Victoria in Melbourne has a good collection of objects from Cambodia, China and Japan. It is also worth visiting the museums in Perth and Sydney.

In Canada the best museums to visit are the Royal Ontario Museum in Toronto and the McCord Museum in Montreal.

There are lots of places where you can see things from these periods of history. Most museums have furniture, costumes, weapons and everyday objects in their collections. If you live in Britain, two books that will help you find out about places to visit in your area are *Museums and Galleries* (British Leisure Publications) and *Historic Houses, Castles and Gardens in Great Britain and Ireland* (British Leisure Publications), which you can buy in newsagents and book shops. Both these books are published every year.

Paintings can tell you a lot too, They often show the clothes and houses of the people who had them painted. Look in art galleries and at art books in libraries. Photographs can tell you a lot about the latter part of the period.

ENGLISH HERITAGE

ENGLISH HERITAGE HISTORICAL REVIEW

VOLUME 1, 2006

Front cover: The Reverend Edward Williams, *The south and east ranges of Moreton Corbet Castle from the south-east*, 16 September 1790 (see page 43)
Title page: Edward Haytley, *Juliana, dowager countess of Burlington, in the garden of Chiswick House*, late 1740s (see page 82)

Contents

Editorial

English Heritage owns or manages some 420 properties dedicated to public presentation. Probably no other governmental body in the world has so many. And the range of English Heritage's properties is arguably the widest anywhere, from prehistoric sites to nuclear bunkers. It includes Stonehenge and much of Hadrian's Wall, ruins of the greatest medieval religious houses, seats of the greatest medieval and early modern magnates, Renaissance fortifications, landscapes from the age of sensibility, a deserted Bronze Age village and a deserted medieval village, the world's first iron bridge and the world's first iron-framed mill, the greatest of London's aristocratic houses, a coal mine, Queen Victoria's island retreat, the Boscobel oak, the Albert Memorial, the most famous of Rembrandt's self-portraits, Darwin's diary and the duke of Wellington's boots. *English Heritage Historical Review* is dedicated to this.

English Heritage is an executive agency, not an academic institution. It determines practical and topical issues which arise in the course of managing the material evidence of the nation's past. Yet it would not be fulfilling its managerial responsibility in the necessary depth if it did not think about the nature of the properties which it manages. Whether executive or contemplative, many of these issues require fundamental investigation. On occasion this investigation is scientific, technological, financial, commercial, legal, educational or aesthetic. But, as English Heritage is the *Historic* Buildings and Monuments Commission for England, all its properties require at least periodic audits of the available historical information, and often a more penetrating scrutiny.

English Heritage employs professional historians and also engages historians as consultants for specific tasks. Although we do other things as well, we undertake historical research as part of our job. We make historical discoveries like those which are presented on these pages. Some of these discoveries are made by archaeologists and by archaeological means, but their consequences are historical.

Not all of our discoveries are suitable for the publication series which English Heritage has always produced. English Heritage guidebooks may summarise them. English Heritage archaeological reports may present the material data which underpins them. They may well be peripheral to the scope of our published architectural investigations, or be relatively inconspicuous within them. *English Heritage Historical Review* has therefore been conceived to present new historical discoveries about our own properties, as discrete items. This volume is the first of what is intended to be an annual publication.

The articles in it and its successor volumes provide information which might be distracting or overwhelming in guidebooks, and which require more interpretation and contextualisation than even the more generous length of archaeological reports allows. They cover all periods from prehistory to the present; they cover all aspects of material culture – landscapes, structures and smaller artefacts; they do not just record, but contextualise and interpret. The information in them is previously unpublished; it may be generated by documentation, survey, excavation, scientific examination or by interpretation; it is supported by the *apparatus scholasticus* necessary for verification, endorsement and further investigation. In short, *English Heritage Historical Review* presents discoveries about the past in a manner recognised as historical.

The Roman Amphitheatre at Chester: An Interim Account

Tony Wilmott, Dan Garner and Stewart Ainsworth

This article summarises the important discoveries made by English Heritage and Chester City Council by excavation and landscape study of the remains of Chester's Roman amphitheatre in 2004–5. These included the bases of applied stone columns, of which there were probably two superimposed orders, seldom found north of the Alps, and familiar from the Colosseum and the amphitheatre of El Djem, Tunisia. The excavation revealed the existence of two amphitheatres, both stone built, and external features which gave some idea of their associated activities. In contrast to the excavation of 1965–9, it recorded all the developments from the Roman period to the present, and this interim analysis is thus able to assess the effect of the amphitheatre on the growth of Chester over 2,000 years.

Fig. 15: John McGahey, detail from a view of Chester made from a tethered balloon, 1852. The oval plan of the amphitheatre, seen behind the church, is still discernible after nearly 1,800 years

Chester amphitheatre lies on high ground on the banks of the River Dee, just outside the south-east corner of the legionary fortress of Deva. This siting, visible to anyone approaching from the south and east, and from the river, would have been deliberate, as the amphitheatre, one of the most imposing and original building types invented by the Romans, expressed Roman identity and power in a way few other structures could.

The amphitheatre was discovered by W J Williams in 1929 during the installation of heating to the Dee House convent school.[1] Before this, the only evidence for such a structure was the discovery in nearby Fleshmongers Lane of a slate relief depicting a gladiator (a *retiarius* armed with trident and net, apparently left-handed, and possibly a representation of a specific individual) in 1737.[2] Williams's identification of the scant remains as an amphitheatre was an interpretative *tour de force*, and was confirmed in the following years by excavations carried out by R Newstead and J P Droop.[3] In 1965–9 extensive excavations of the northern half of the amphitheatre by F H Thompson culminated in the consolidation of this part of the site, and its opening as a public monument in 1972.[4]

In Thompson's highly influential excavation report he was forthcoming about the flaws in his methodology. In particular he acknowledged that his wholesale clearance of the arena by machine down to what were believed to be Roman levels had destroyed evidence for the post-Roman periods on the site. Thompson's conclusions have been widely accepted and influential in the interpretation of amphitheatre excavations in Britain.[5] The discovery of timber slots beneath the seating bank running concentrically and radially to the arena wall led to the conclusion that the first amphitheatre was entirely of timber construction. Thompson's second amphitheatre was stone built, and he believed that all of the stone elements were contemporary. These were the arena wall, the main outer wall, the stone-built gates and entrances, and a wall 5ft 11in inside the outer wall which Thompson termed the 'concentric wall'. Archaeological dating evidence for the timber phase was not forthcoming, so this phase was dated theoretically to the mid-70s AD, as it was assumed that the amphitheatre was contemporary with the earliest timber phase of the legionary fortress. The stone phase was dated by archaeological means to AD *c.*100, a date derived from finds from the arena wall. In the centre of the arena itself a complex of post-holes was interpreted as the foundation for a platform associated with arena activities such as military parades.

1 W J Williams, 'Roman Amphitheatre in Ursuline Convent School Grounds', *Journal of the Chester Archaeological Society*, new ser, XXVIII (2), 1929, 218–19.
2 R Jackson, 'The Chester Gladiator Rediscovered', *Britannia*, XIV, 1983, 87–96.
3 R Newstead and J P Droop, 'The Roman Amphitheatre at Chester', *Journal of the Chester Archaeological Society*, new ser, XXIX, 1932, 5–40.
4 F H Thompson, 'Excavation of the Roman Amphitheatre at Chester', *Archaeologia*, CV, 1976, 127–239.
5 N C W Bateman, 'The London Amphitheatre, Excavations 1987–96', *Britannia*, XXVIII, 1997, 51–85.

The southern half of the amphitheatre remains overbuilt, and until 2004 was separated from the displayed portion by an unlovely concrete retaining wall. The western quadrant of the amphitheatre lies beneath the 18th-century Dee House, listed grade II, but with later additions of varying architectural merit. To the east of Dee House lies a garden area. South of Dee House is the recently completed Civil Justice Centre building and its car park. Part of the latter building and of the car park overlies the southern arc of the amphitheatre. The eastern edge of the structure is under the minor thoroughfare leading from Little St John Street, on the eastern side of which is the church of St John the Baptist (Fig. 1).

The foundation of St John's is traditionally dated to 689.[6] It is likely that the church was founded adjacent to the amphitheatre, either to reflect a tradition of Christian martyrdom in the arena, or because of a post-Roman reuse of the amphitheatre

6 K J Matthews and E M Willshaw, *Heritage Assessment of Dee House and Environs, Chester*, Chester: Chester City Council, 1995, 12.

Fig. 1 (above): The study area, photographed from the air on 23 July 2004

Fig. 2 (right): The study area, showing the extent of the amphitheatre and the area of non-invasive survey

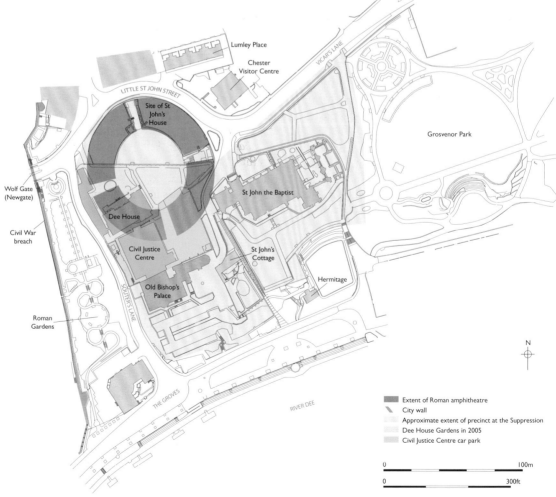

as a fortification or as the centre of a local power structure. The church was used as a cathedral from 1075 to 1102, when the see of Lichfield was moved to Chester, and was an important collegiate church throughout the medieval period, until its suppression in 1547.[7] Despite much rebuilding, parts of the original Norman cathedral structure survive inside the current church and in a ruinous state outside.

The future of the amphitheatre and of Dee House has frequently been discussed within the last 20 years, and different proposals have been drawn up for the monument, resulting in a number of archaeological evaluations on the unexcavated portion of the monument.[8] A small-scale excavation and subsequent archaeological watching brief were also undertaken between 1999 and 2001 on the southern edge of the amphitheatre, during the construction of the Civil Justice Centre.[9] In addition, from 2000, Keith Matthews directed three seasons of small-scale, targeted excavation on the amphitheatre, demonstrating that more *in situ* archaeology existed in the displayed area than had been thought. During Spring 2002, discussions between English Heritage and Chester City Council were held during which the future of the amphitheatre was considered. This resulted in the development of a joint English Heritage and Chester City Council project to investigate it. Three strands of work were undertaken: an archaeological research framework, non-invasive survey of the amphitheatre and its environs, and excavation within the amphitheatre area (Fig. 2). The interim results of the latter two are presented in this paper. Three areas of the amphitheatre were excavated: Area A comprised a quadrant which had previously been partially excavated by Thompson, Area B was the nearest practicable area to St John's, and Area C was in the centre of the arena (Fig. 3).

PREHISTORY
A small number of prehistoric flints from the site hints at early occupation. During the last few days of excavation two intercutting post-holes were found beneath the pre-amphitheatre buried soil horizon. Radiocarbon determinations will establish the dates of these features. Palynological analysis

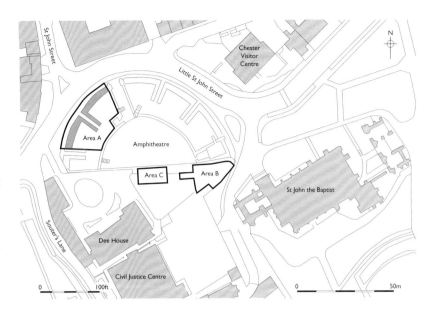

Fig. 3: The location of the three excavation areas

of the immediate pre-Roman ground surface shows that the late Iron Age landscape was cleared of large timber, and used for both pastoral and arable agriculture.[10]

THE FIRST AMPHITHEATRE
The legionary fortress at Chester appears to have been established AD *c.*74–5. It is possible that this was the culmination of earlier military activity, and that earlier camps and forts remain to be found on the site. The amphitheatre site produced a small assemblage of early material which might have derived from such occupation. Once the fortress was established, a civilian settlement or *canabae* began to develop. By the end of the first century AD this settlement extended eastwards of the fortress for some 330yds beyond the defences.[11]

Despite Thompson's interpretation, the earliest amphitheatre (Phase 1) was a stone building, and Thompson's 'concentric wall' may now be understood as its outer wall. This wall was built first, and the arena was then excavated, though to what depth we do not know. The spoil from the arena was dumped against the outer wall to form a seating bank. The date of this construction has not yet been determined, but the presence of dumps of rubbish incorporating Roman finds in the primary bank suggests that settlement was well established before its construction. An arena wall would also

7 A T Thacker and C P Lewis (eds), *The Victoria History of the Counties of England, A History of the County of Chester, Vol V, Part 1 The City of Chester, General History and Topography,* London, 2003, 88.
8 K Buxton, *Dee House, Chester, Cheshire – Archaeological Evaluation*, Lancaster, 1993; R Cleary, J Edwards and K Matthews, *Dee House, Chester: Evaluation March 1994*, Chester Archaeology Service Evaluation Report 30, 1994.

9 D Garner, *Dee House, Chester: An Archaeological Excavation and Watching Brief*, Gifford Report no. B2159C/D.01, 2005.
10 We are indebted to the preliminary analysis by Dr David E Robinson for this opinion.
11 D J P Mason, 'The town and port of Roman Chester', in P Carrington (ed), *Deva Victrix: Roman Chester Reassessed*, Chester, 2002, 53–74.

Fig. 4: A mineralised timber truss, showing post and brace in section

have been necessary, and it is probable that in this incarnation the amphitheatre comprised a stone-built outer wall and arena wall, with an earthen seating bank on which bleacher-style seating would have been positioned. Apart from the stone outer wall, this would be consistent with most other amphitheatres in Britain.[12] Metalled surfaces developed outside the outer wall, and access to the seating was probably via one of four entrances, the positions of which dictated the location of entrances in succeeding phases.

It was probably not long before the amphitheatre was radically altered (Phase 1a). Though the outer wall remained, the seating bank was cut away, forming a flat terrace. On this terrace was built a system of timber-framed seating. Slots were cut into the terrace, radiating from the arena wall, and these were linked by a pair of concentric beam-slots which were also concentric with the line of the outer wall and the arena wall. Thompson had interpreted this beam-slot pattern as the footings for a timber amphitheatre. The data recovered has the potential to tell us a great deal about the way in which it was constructed. The timbers survived

Fig. 5: Samian ware bowl depicting fighting gladiators

in semi-mineralised form, and it will be possible to recover their dimensions. Ground-fast beams, upright and diagonal members were recorded (Fig. 4). In each joint there was an iron nail. Some of these nails retained the imprint of wood grain, from which it is possible to say that the timber used was not oak. It may have been beech. The upright and diagonal members were not jointed, as might be expected, but simply nailed together. Once the timber framework to support the seating was erected it seems that the arena was deepened, and it was probably at this stage that it was excavated to bedrock. This would have necessitated a new arena wall. Upcast from the excavation of the arena was again deposited in the *cavea* (seating bank), this time to hold in position the base-plates of the timber framework. In the area south-east of the unexcavated part of the amphitheatre (Area B) the relationship was established between the *cavea* deposits and the arena wall, and it is clear that the arena wall belongs to this phase. Fortunately a coin was found in the foundation slot of one of the radial timbers. It was a *sestertius* of Domitian dated to the last year of his reign, AD 96. This provides an important *terminus post quem* for the construction of Phase 1a, and is so far the only positive dating we have for any amphitheatre phase.

Simultaneously with the internal alterations new access arrangements were provided to the upper seats in the form of a stone stairway engaged against the outer wall. The foundation for this stair cut the metalled surface of Phase 1. The dimensions of the stair, and a preliminary calculation of practicable gradients, suggest that the outer wall stood to a height of some 15ft 9in. Such an external stairway is rare in amphitheatres, the only currently known parallel being the amphitheatre of Pompeii, though external staircases can also be seen at the *Ludus* in Rome, a training arena for gladiators situated next to the Colosseum.[13] At about the same time as the external staircase was erected, the service road running around the circumference of the amphitheatre was moved away from the outer wall creating a concentric zone about 5ft 7in wide and its new edge was defined by a formal kerb. This may have been done to prevent the new staircase from causing an obstruction to the regular flow of traffic outside the amphitheatre.

The deposits which built up around the outside

---

12 J Wacher, *Towns of Roman Britain*, 2nd edn, London, 1995, 49.
13 J-C Golvin, *L'amphithéâtre Romain: essai sur la theorisation de sa forme et ses fonctions*, Paris, 1988, 33–7.

of the amphitheatre during Phase 1a are a unique survival, protected as they have been by being enclosed within the shell of the second amphitheatre. These deposits give unrivalled evidence for the activities that took place outside amphitheatres during their use. Post-holes and surfaces suggest the existence of short-lived timber buildings. These existed within a pattern of deposition leading to the accumulation of almost a metre-depth of material. The predominant element of these deposits was fine yellow sand, quite different from the coarse red sand native to the site, and clearly imported, probably from the area of Boughton, 1¼ miles upstream on the River Dee. It seems likely that this represented sand imported to the amphitheatre for use in the arena (the Latin for sand is *arena*). A number of factors, not least the presence in this material of a human tooth, suggest that this was deposited during the clearing of the arena after spectacles had taken place. Close to the north entrance of the amphitheatre was a small, three-sided, stone-built structure with a plastered and painted interior. This was probably a small shrine. Shrines in analogous positions occur at Carleon, Wales and Carnuntum, Austria,[14] while a furnished burial was found in a comparable position at the amphitheatre of Merida, Spain.[15] It seems likely that this specific location, adjacent to a main entrance on the long axis of the amphitheatre, possessed some ritual importance in amphitheatre ceremonial. Other finds from these external deposits included animal bones such as chicken and beef ribs, possibly relating to the sale and consumption of snack food, a fragment of a *gladius* hilt, and a miniature Samian ware bowl (Fig. 5) depicting gladiatorial combat, which was conceivably sold to a spectator as a souvenir of an event.

THE SECOND AMPHITHEATRE

At some time, probably in the second century, though the dating evidence is yet to be analysed, the amphitheatre was extended and enlarged (Phase 2). A new outer wall, almost 6ft 7in thick, was constructed 5ft 11in outside the outer wall of the first structure (Fig. 6). This wall had foundations over 3ft 3in deep, and was founded on bedrock. A small part of the superstructure survived, and even the bottom two courses of the inner face of the wall were more carefully dressed and laid than the masonry of the outer wall of the

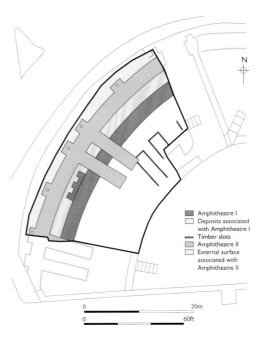

Fig. 6: Simplified plan of Area A showing the phasing of the amphitheatres

Amphitheatre I
Deposits associated with Amphitheatre I
Timber slots
Amphitheatre II
External surface associated with Amphitheatre II

first amphitheatre.[16] Although the original four entrances into the arena were retained, the upper part of the auditorium was now accessed by *vomitoria*, vaulted stairways within the structure of the building which led directly into the face of the *cavea*. This suggests that the outer wall was now very much higher, and that it was no longer possible to use external stairways. Two *vomitoria* were provided in each quadrant of the amphitheatre, giving eight *vomitoria* in all. Marking-out lines for the bottom step found in the one threshold excavated demonstrate that the stairs opened direct from the street. Flanking each entrance and *vomitorium* were pairs of projections from the wall face. Thompson interpreted these as buttresses. However, they were only one stone thick and did not penetrate to the base of the foundations. In two cases semicircular mortar pads on the upper face of these blocks betray their true identity: they were foundation stones for substantial engaged half-columns. This suggests an exterior decorative treatment extraordinary for the northern provinces, and seldom found north of the Alps. If there were one storey of such pilasters, laws of proportion would demand that there should be two with an entablature in between. The most obvious and grandest parallels to this form of ornament are the Colosseum itself and the amphitheatre of El Djem, Tunisia.[17] It is hoped that analysis of the architectural scheme according to

---

14 R E M and T V Wheeler, 'The Roman Amphitheatre at Caerleon, Monmouthshire', *Archaeologia*, LXXVIII, 1929, 111–218.
15 R-M D Cabello, *El teatro y el anfiteatro de Augusta Emerita*, British Archaeological Reports International Series, 1207, Oxford, 2005, 214.

16 We are indebted to Dr Peter Hill for this information.
17 D Bomgardner, *The Story of the Roman Amphitheatre*, London, 2000, 147.

Fig. 7: Stone block in the centre of the arena, Area C

classical proportions, and the angle and rise of the *vomitorium* stairs, will enable us to reconstruct the height and grandeur of the second amphitheatre.

Re-examination of the upstanding masonry by Matthews in 2001–3 revealed a complex sequence of modifications to the east entrance, which probably continued into the post-Roman period: the outer end of the entrance was completely sealed by a blocking wall; the arena end was narrowed on at least two occasions; two rows of decorative columns were added to the narrowed entrance; and part of a series of steps on the southern side of the entrance leading to an upper level were heavily worn through use. Cartographic assessment indicates that there was a continuity of structures over this entrance, possibly as late as the 16th century. A plan which shows St John's allegedly in 1589 shows a building located over or very close to this entrance.[18] Matthews also identified still *in situ* archaeological features and deposits relating to the early history of the amphitheatre, which survive beneath the modern gravel surface of the entrance; these remain unexcavated.[19] Thompson also identified a wall foundation running parallel to and to the north of the east entrance; a second was identified in the 2004–5 excavations in Area B. These walls extended from the arena wall to the outer wall and as such must belong to the second amphitheatre. Thompson's original suggestion that an officers' box sat above the east entrance seems to be strengthened by the presence of these walls.[20] Both walls have been extensively removed by stone-robbing and in the case of the wall in

Area B no intact masonry was identified despite excavating the robber trench to a depth of 2m.

In the centre of the previously unexcavated part of the arena (Area C) excavation revealed a large stone block placed virtually in the centre. This had an iron fitting fastened into its upper surface with lead, and was certainly a piece of arena furniture (Fig. 7). A very similar block is depicted twice on the gladiator mosaic from the villa at Bignor, West Sussex, where a pair of gladiators fight across a block with an iron ring in the top.[21] It can only be interpreted as a point to which arena victims, whether animal or human, could be chained during spectacles. Thompson found two similar stones in the northern half of the arena.[22] The discovery of the third, and that in the centre of the arena, allows the conclusion that these were evenly spaced. It is possible that two similar blocks continued the line across the centre of the arena to the south. This would provide a number of anchor points across the centre of the long axis of the arena, allowing at least five victims to be chained, affording spectators a clear view of whatever was happening, and preventing victims from sheltering against the arena wall, where they could be seen by only half of the audience.[23] We can only speculate whether humans or animals were chained, whether the chains were long or short, or whether chains passed through the ring on the stone allowing a degree of free movement. The latter interpretation derives from the depictions of a bull and a bear chained together in order to enrage each other in the arena at Pompeii[24] and El Djem,[25] suggesting that such a spectacle was widespread and popular. Research into depictions and descriptions of arena events in the Roman world may shed further light on the use of the blocks.

The scale of the amphitheatre – the most elaborate in Roman Britain – begs a number of questions on the status of Roman Chester. It was to all intents and purposes a legionary fortress with associated civilian settlement (*canabae*), throughout the Roman period. Although Chester never reached the status of *colonia* like the city of York (similarly a legionary garrison), it has been suggested by analogy with *canabae* in the Danubian provinces and Mainz (Upper Germany)

18 London, British Library, Harleian MS 2,073, fol 98 (hereafter BL, Harleian 2,073); copy at the Cheshire and Chester Records Office, P51/7/176. There is uncertainty about the date of the plans as there are a number of versions, but 'The survey was taken Ano 1589' appears on fol 99.
19 K J Matthews *et al*, *Chester Amphitheatre: Investigations Summer 2000*, Chester City Council, 2001.

20 Thompson, *op. cit.*, 174.
21 T Wilmott, 'Chester Roman Amphitheatre', English Heritage *Research News*, II, 2006, 37.
22 Thompson, *op. cit.*, 154.
23 Bomgardner, *op. cit.*, 8.
24 L Jacobelli, *Gladiators at Pompeii*, Oxford, 2004, 60.
25 D G Kyle, *Spectacles of Death in Ancient Rome*, New York, 1998, Fig. 1.

that Chester's civilian settlement may have achieved the status of *municipium* during the third century.[26] However, Chester contained within the legionary fortress some extraordinary structures – a very elaborate bath suite,[27] for example, as well as the so-called elliptical building.[28] These structures together with the amphitheatre all suggest that there was at least an aspiration towards high status for Chester, whether or not this was ultimately realised.

THE SUB-ROMAN AND ANGLO-SAXON PERIODS

In Area C it became clear that the area around the stone block in the arena was the site of intensive activity after the arena had ceased to be used. A long and complex stratigraphic sequence of pits and post-holes, culminating in the construction of a small post-hole building, spanned the period (broadly) from the end of the Roman use of the arena to the 11th century. The dating of this sequence is as yet unknown, but the possibility that it represents occupation, possibly of high status, within the sheltering walls of the amphitheatre is clear. To add substance to this theory, Thompson discovered that the main east entrance was walled-up at some point, and in the half of the seating bank area which he examined (Area A) one of the *vomitoria* entrances was similarly treated.[29] The essence of an amphitheatre was to allow a large number of people to enter. Walled-up entrances suggest that its function had altered, and it is possible that this might indicate that the amphitheatre was made defensible, as a free-standing fort for occupation or refuge. The amphitheatre at Cirencester was reused in exactly this way,[30] as were many continental amphitheatres, like Trier, Germany.[31]

The royal church of St John's was established in the 7th century by the Mercian king Æthelred.[32] It is possible that the siting of the church immediately outside the eastern main entrance of the amphitheatre was linked with memories and traditions of Christian martyrs, the existence of a high status settlement within a fortified amphitheatre, or both. It is as yet not possible to assess the status of the occupation within the arena, but this almost certainly provides the context for the foundation of St John's. The 6th-century monk Gildas mentions the martyrs Aaron and Julius, at a place called *Legionum Urbs* (the City of the Legions).[33] Though traditionally thought to have been Caerleon in South Wales, the name might equally apply to Chester, whose Old Welsh name, *Cair Legion*, is a direct translation of *Legionum Urbs*.[34] It is further possible that the east entrance of the amphitheatre may have been reused as the crypt of the early church. This entrance was certainly altered in the post-Roman period.

It is possible that royal patronage in this landscape may have encouraged settlement and trade activities during the 7th to 9th centuries, particularly along the riverside between the Groves and Lower Bridge Street, where settlement evidence including a sunken-floored building and imported pottery has been found.[35] Following the Viking raid of 893, however, this development halted, and in 907 Æthelflæd, Alfred the Great's daughter and queen of Mercia, strengthened the decayed Roman fortress walls and extended them down the river to create a *burh* or fortified town.[36] Whatever the status of the amphitheatre as a fortification, it is likely that it was eclipsed by the creation of the *burh*, and this period may, therefore, have seen the beginning of its slighting through the robbing of stone to build the new city walls.

St John's may well have lain at the centre of an episcopal enclave that survived the refortification of the *burh* in 907. If so, it seems likely that by the end of the late Saxon period there would have been a definable boundary around the church, which would have separated it from any settlement outside. By the time of the Norman Conquest, St John's was held by the Bishop of Lichfield and is described as being *in burgo episcopi* (in the bishop's borough) and the manor of Redcliffe. Redcliffe was the focus of the ecclesiastical enclave known as the bishop's borough and was surrounded by its own ditch probably from early

26 D J P Mason, 'The Status of Roman Chester: A Reply', *Journal of the Chester Archaeological Society*, LXVIII, 1986, 53–8.
27 D J P Mason, *Excavations at Chester: The Elliptical Building: An Image of the Roman World*, Grosvenor Museum Archaeological Excavation Survey Reports, XII, Chester, 2000.
28 D J P Mason, *Excavations at Chester: The Roman Fortress Baths: Excavation and Recording, 1732–1998*, Grosvenor Museum Archaeological Excavation Survey Reports, XIII, Chester, 2005.
29 Thompson, *op. cit*., 176.
30 N Holbrook, 'The amphitheatre: excavations directed by J S Wacher 1962–3 and A D McWhirr 1966', in N Holbrook (ed), *Cirencester: The Roman Town Defences, Public Buildings and Shops*, Cirencester Excavations, V, 1998, 145–71.
31 H Cüppers, *Trier Amphitheatre*, Mainz, 1979, 26.
32 Thacker and Lewis, *op. cit*., 16–21.
33 K J Matthews, 'Chester's Amphitheatre after Rome: a Centre of Christian Worship', *Cheshire History*, XLIII, 2003, 12–27.
34 *Idem*.
35 P Carrington, *Chester*, London, 1994, 53; Thacker and Lewis, *op. cit*., 16–21.
36 *Ibid*., 16–17.

Fig. 8: John Speed, map of Chester, 1610. The extract below shows the area of the amphitheatre and St John's church at a larger scale

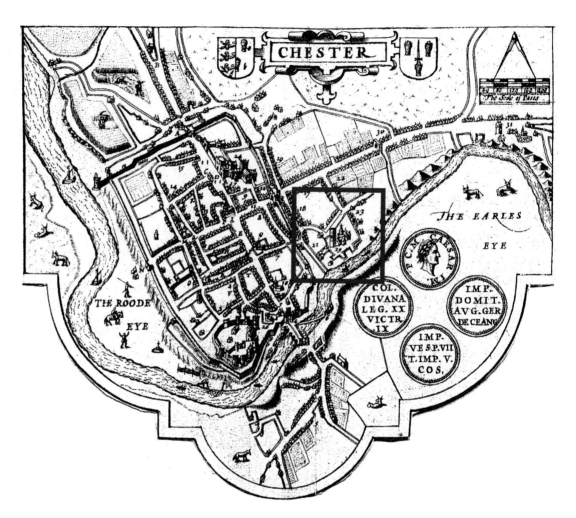

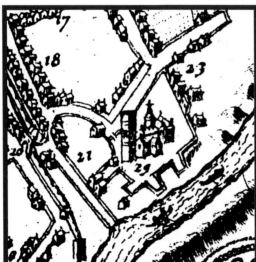

times.[37] The recent non-invasive survey work has shed some new light on this enclave, with the possibility emerging that the deeply cut Souter's Lane and the western curve of the amphitheatre may have formed part of the surrounding ditch of a pre-Æthelflædian enclave, possibly reusing the line of an earlier route down to quarries and the river. The retention of some of the boundaries of this enclave and the continuing presence of St John's College and its precinct in the developing townscape of this part of Chester in the medieval period are likely to have played an important part in the retention of the open green spaces and lack of suburban development that characterise this area today.

In the late 10th century St John's was still an important religious establishment with a monopoly of burial rights outside the defences, and it retained royal and aristocratic patronage. It was used by King Edgar in 973 for an important political gathering at which British and Viking princes demonstrated their submission by rowing Edgar up the river to the church.[38] Archaeological finds also indicate activity around St John's in the

---

37 *Ibid.*, 17, 24–5; Matthews, 'Chester's Amphitheatre after Rome ... ', *cit.*, 12–27.

38 Thacker and Lewis, *op. cit.*, 23.

10th century; fragments of several sandstone crosses have been recovered from the churchyard, demonstrating the presence of an important stone-carving workshop.[39] Some 40 coins from the reign of Edward the Elder (899–944) were found just west of the present church in the 19th century,[40] and during evaluation prior to the erection of the Civil Justice Centre in 1999–2000, two 10th-century burials were found in what is now the car park.[41] Some late Saxon pottery was also recovered from amphitheatre excavations between the 1960s and 2004.[42]

THE MEDIEVAL PERIOD

Following the Norman Conquest the walls of the *burh* were extended, and the castle was built within the circuit, dominating the harbour and town.[43] Despite its position outside the walls, St John's was also maintained, undoubtedly because of its earlier historical and ecclesiastical importance. The church was elevated to the status of a cathedral from 1075 when the see of Lichfield was moved to Chester, and by 1086 a college of canons had been established. In 1102 the see was transferred to Coventry. St John's remained an important collegiate church throughout the medieval period and retained bishop's and archdeacon's residences in its precincts until the 19th century. In the 12th century the area around St John's, the bishop's borough, formed a distinct quarter,[44] some of the boundaries of which can still be identified in the layout of the study area and its penumbra. Further development within the bishop's borough has been tentatively identified through examination of cartographic sources. The college was suppressed in 1547.[45] Despite much rebuilding, parts of the original Norman cathedral structure survive inside the current church and in a ruinous state outside. The fine Norman nave, some of the finest Norman architecture in Cheshire, belongs to the rebuilding which took place during the 11th and 12th centuries.[46] Excavation in Area B showed that the amphitheatre walls on the eastern side were almost totally robbed. A 10th-century Hiberno-Norse pin found in the bottom of one of the robber trenches gives a *terminus post quem* for

the robbing, which was probably thus undertaken in order to provide stone for the construction of the cathedral church.

By the end of the 11th century there was a precinct around the church, which included other churches and chapels as well as the bishop's residences.[47] The recent study has shown that some divisions within the precinct can be identified through historic cartography and matched with surviving structures and standing walls. The boundaries are still legible in the modern landscape. This is illustrated by the retention of the northern curve of the amphitheatre, which has remained as a boundary to this day. Even the open space occupied by Grosvenor Park probably owes its origins to the protective bounds of the bishop's borough mentioned at Domesday. The modern pattern of roads and paths around St John's and the amphitheatre had been established in the landscape by the 15th century, some skirting their way round the precinct boundaries and others leading into St John's.[48] The presence of ecclesiastical boundaries prevented the intensive building of domestic and commercial properties along the sides of roads, which is seen elsewhere in Chester in the medieval period, although a

Fig. 9: Shards of enamelled glass from the 16th-century pit, Area C

39 *Ibid.*, 125.
40 *Idem.*
41 We are indebted to Mr Dan Garner for this information.
42 R Cleary, J Edwards and K Matthews, *Dee House, Chester, Evaluation March 1994*, Chester Archaeological Service Evaluation Report 30, 1994, 25; K J Matthews, 'Chester Amphitheatre: Research Agenda', Chester Archaeological Service unpublished draft report, 2000, 3.
43 S Ainsworth and T Wilmott, *Chester Amphitheatre: From Gladiators to Gardens*, Chester, 2005, 11.
44 Thacker and Lewis, *op. cit.*, 208.
45 *Ibid.*, 88.
46 A Menuge, L Monckton, S Taylor and N Wray, *The Environs of Chester Amphitheatre: Preliminary Building Assessments*, English Heritage Historic Buildings and Areas Research Department Report Series B/016/2004, 2004, 5.
47 Thacker and Lewis, *op. cit.*, 126.
48 *Ibid.*, 214–16.

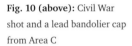

small amount occurred opposite the Wolf Gate and along the north side of the amphitheatre site where excavation has revealed cess pits from about 1200 onwards. These pits occupy the back land of medieval tenements, and it seems that Area A comprised at least three such properties. The medieval layout of the immediate amphitheatre area is hard to define, but the cartographic evidence points towards a perimeter area of collegiate land around the northern fringe of the amphitheatre having been released for commercial development and roadside properties opposite the Newgate, possibly as early as the 14th century.[49] These properties were probably associated with the pits excavated in Area A. Medieval pits in all three excavation areas produced finds and environmental material with huge potential to enhance knowledge of domestic life in medieval Chester. In Areas C and B it was clear that the early medieval occupation in the arena was followed by the gradual accumulation of apparent agricultural cultivation soils. The arena wall finally disappeared from view beneath these soils in the 14th century. In Area B the walls

of a number of successive medieval buildings were found overlying both the *cavea* and the arena of the amphitheatre, with the corner of one building founded on the arena wall itself. The rest of the former amphitheatre area may well have been relatively open ground within the precincts, as indicated on a map by Speed of 1610 (Fig. 8).

THE SUPPRESSION

At the suppression of St John's in 1547 the college of canons was surrounded by a large precinct, which contained other college buildings, chapels and bishop's and dean's residences. One of the buildings attested in Area B is likely to be a structure represented immediately north of a building annotated as the Dean's House on the 16th-century plan referred to earlier.[50] Evidence for elaborate decoration was found, including panels of fine plaster moulding and ceramic floor and wall tiles. A pit in Area C belonging to the mid-16th century produced evidence for feasting, including the bones of many types of wild and domestic birds, fish including large salmon and rays, and a great deal of beef bone.

---

49 We are indebted to Ms Jane Laughton for this information.

50 BL, Harleian 2,073.

Fig. 10 (above): Civil War shot and a lead bandolier cap from Area C

Fig. 11 (right): Edward Wright, *City of Chester*, 1690, detail showing the riverside and St John's church

Fig. 12 (facing page top): Alexander de Lavaux, map of 1745, detail

Fig. 13 (facing page bottom): Murray and Stuart, map of 1791, detail showing the area of St John's church and the amphitheatre

Finds included a tin-glazed earthenware jug in the shape of an owl, and even some imported enamelled glass (Fig. 9), probably made in France, but in the style of Venetian glass.[51] An area of curved bedding trenches appears to be a garden feature relating to this pre-suppression high-status phase.

Following the suppression, the former collegiate buildings around the precinct became residences for the local gentry, and a bishop's and archdeacon's residence were retained.[52] In 1581 the choir, chapels at the east and transepts were largely demolished as St John's church was too large for the parishioners to maintain, and it was relegated to the status of a parish church.[53]

The first detailed map of Chester, produced by John Speed in 1610 (Fig. 8), shows how the amphitheatre, together with St John's and its precincts, remained a distinct unit outside the walls, free from the development of medieval properties which characterise the areas to the north along what are now St John Street, Foregate Street and Love Street.[54] There was also extensive open ground to the east. The curve of Little St John Street around the amphitheatre site is very striking, and demonstrates how later boundaries associated with defining the precincts of St John's had preserved the imprint of this monument. However, ongoing analysis indicates that Speed's map contains a number of inaccuracies, particularly the positioning of the eastern boundary of St John's. The eastern boundary is still more or less marked by the wall which separates the churchyard from Grosvenor Park, rather than further east as suggested by Speed's map. The modern Souter's Lane formed the western side of the ecclesiastical zone, and the walled inner precinct to the south is clearly defined as it follows the ins and outs of the old quarries along which it ran. Parts of this survive today. Individually drawn buildings on Speed's map are shown around the precinct, and include former college buildings and chapels. Following the suppression, they had mostly become private residences for the wealthy, and this part of Chester was becoming the preserve of the gentry.[55] In contrast, St John's became a simple parish church. Within 32 years, however, the growing secular

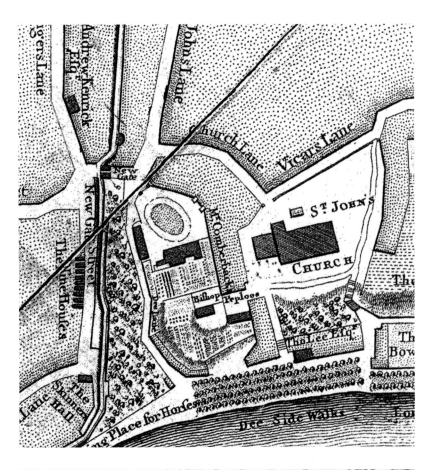

51 I Smith and J Edwards, 'Feasting in Tudor Times', *Past Uncovered*, Chester, 2005.
52 Thacker and Lewis, *op. cit.*, 131.
53 *Idem*.
54 Chester, Cheshire and Chester Record Office (hereafter CCRO), PM 14/7, J Speed, *Plan of Chester*, 1610.
55 We are indebted to Ms Jane Laughton for this information.

Fig. 14: Moses Griffith, view from the south, late 18th century, showing the Groves and St John's church

Fig. 16 (facing page top): A compilation of 1:500 scale Ordnance Survey sheets Chester XXXVIII.15.12 and XXXVIII.11.18, surveyed 1874

Fig. 17 (facing page bottom): Interpretation of features as mapped by the Ordnance Survey in 1874, showing the position of the amphitheatre and the modern road system

exclusiveness and tranquillity would be shattered by the savagery of the Civil War.

THE CIVIL WAR

The area of the amphitheatre and St John's church played an important role during the Civil War siege of Chester.[56] As the principal port for Ireland, and with extensive road connections to the North, Midlands and North Wales, Chester was a place of great strategic importance. Though the city walls had been neglected, when the political situation deteriorated and civil war threatened, they were strengthened by earthen ramparts piled up behind. An extensive network of outworks was also hastily constructed to protect the suburbs and provide a first line of defence. To deny cover to the attackers, many properties close to the walls were demolished, and it is likely that some of the prestigious residences formed by the former college buildings of St John's suffered this fate. This probably included the buildings partially excavated in Area B. Finds of building material, including fine moulded ceiling plaster and ceramic tiles, certainly indicate the demolition of the high-status buildings prior to the deposition of Civil War ammunition on the site (Fig. 10).

The city was garrisoned for the king in 1645. On 19 September the outworks were breached by the parliamentarian army, and the suburbs fell. Two days later the defending commander, Lord Byron,

was surprised when two or more cannon were brought up and installed in St John's churchyard under cover of buildings which had not been demolished, as Byron had asked; he had also asked that the tower of St John's be demolished. After 32 shots had been fired, a breach was made in the city wall. The delayed assault which followed was beaten back by fierce resistance. The rebuilt breach can still be seen today from Roman Gardens. The city was bombarded from numerous points and the combination of the weakness of the king's position, destruction, starvation and disease caused the royalists to surrender on 3 February 1646.[57] Within Area B over 100 pieces of spent lead shot were found. These varied in calibre, including both pistol and musket balls. The cap of a bandolier cartridge and a lead powder-flask spout were also found. These were identical to similar finds from Beeston Castle, from where some of the troops in the besieging army came, and it is possible that this equipment from both sites belonged to the same unit.[58]

THE CIVIL WAR AFTERMATH

Chester suffered greatly during the Civil War, and the scars of that conflict lasted for many years. Gradually, the city's trade, almost wiped out by the siege, recovered. After the restoration of the monarchy in 1660 many properties were rebuilt, and by the end of the 17th century many wealthy citizens had started to build elegant mansions,

56 J Barratt, *The Great Siege of Chester*, Stroud, 2003; S Ward, *Excavations at Chester: The Civil War Siegeworks 1642–5*, Grosvenor Museum Archaeological Excavation Survey Reports, IV, Chester, 1987. **57** Barratt, *op. cit.*, 35.

58 P Ellis, *Beeston Castle, Cheshire: Excavations by Laurence Keen and Peter Hough, 1968–85*, English Heritage Archaeological Reports, XXIII, London, 1993.

often in brick.[59] During the amphitheatre excavations of the 1960s, a stone inscribed with the date 1664 was recovered from under St John's House which was situated to the east of the northern entrance of the amphitheatre. This may indicate that new building was going on within the area of the old amphitheatre, though no structural evidence was found.

Edward Wright's 1690 topographical drawing provides a vivid picture of the area around the amphitheatre and St John's during this period of revitalisation (Fig. 11). The three-storey building by the riverside appears to be a house with shaped gables. This building also appears on a drawing of 1760 by Joseph Winder, as well as de Lavaux's map of 1745 (Fig. 12) and Murray and Stuart's of 1791, which also shows extensive gardens in the area behind and to the east (Fig. 13). The introduction of these ornamental features outside the walls by the river may have been the first stage in the re-birth of the area, which again became one of Chester's most fashionable locations.

THE 18TH CENTURY

The early 18th century marked a rise in the commercial and social importance of the city. Much rebuilding took place, including fashionable houses and large formal gardens. The city walls were repaired and converted into a promenade connecting the city with the river, and a new, fashionable riverside walk called the Groves was created.[60] The area of the former amphitheatre and gentry houses around St John's assumed a new importance in this phase. With few surviving buildings it offered suitable open space and had long traditions of ecclesiastical and gentry ownership. By the mid-18th century some eight mansions and their gardens had been established in the area between the amphitheatre site, St John's and the Groves; two others were located up river to the east. The character of the landscape and architecture towards the end of the 18th century is well represented on a watercolour by Moses Griffith (Fig. 14). Only three buildings of this period now survive in the amphitheatre environs: Dee House, the Old Bishop's Palace, and St John's Rectory. Two of these houses, Dee House and St John's House, occupied the site where the amphitheatre had been.

Dee House and its gardens were built over the

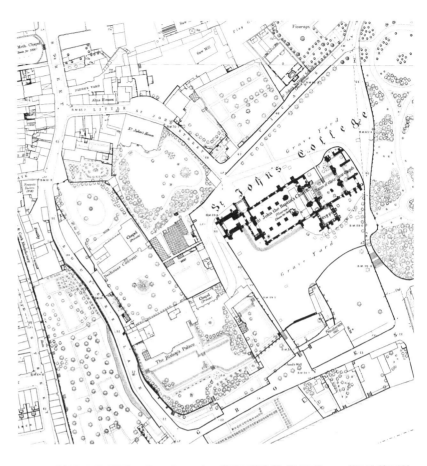

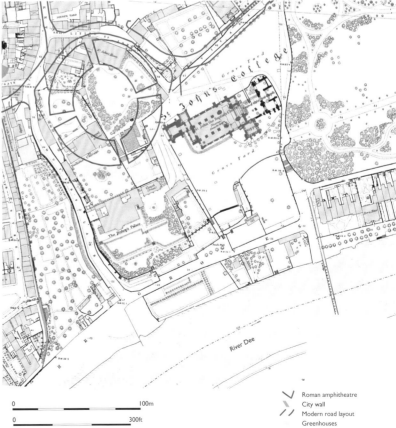

59 P Carrington, *Chester*, London, 1994, 91–5.
60 Thacker and Lewis, *op. cit.*, 217, 301.

Roman amphitheatre
City wall
Modern road layout
Greenhouses

Fig. 18: Dee House viewed from the north in May 2006

south and western parts of the amphitheatre about 1730,[61] and St John's House and its gardens were built over the north-eastern and south-eastern sides slightly later. Dee House is likely to have been built for James Comberbach (d.1735), a former mayor and alderman of Chester.[62] Its plot was originally within the former precincts of the medieval collegiate church of St John and its boundaries were influenced by the layout of the college. At least part of one of the collegiate buildings shown on the 17th-century plan of St John's falls within the eastern end of the present Dee House gardens.[63] The plot is shown on the map of 1745 by Alexander de Lavaux.[64] It was rectilinear, with its long axis north-west to south-east. The western boundary of the plot along the east side of Souter's Lane perpetuated that of the outer precinct of St John's, whilst the eastern boundary was laid parallel with the general line. The southern boundary followed a subdivision of the precinct boundary shown on an earlier map of 1610.[65] To the east, south and west were gardens, of which the southern one was the largest, laid out in a formal pattern of four rectangular beds separated by paths. Bedding trenches for the gardens associated with Dee House were found during excavation in Areas B and C. The house was

set back from the public road rather than fronting onto the street. Between the house and gates was a carriage-turning circle, and to the west were a stable block and coach-house, creating a large forecourt facing the junction and the city walls. At the rear were formal gardens overlooking the river.

The original plan of Dee House is intact. It consists of a double-pile main block with a five-bay north front and a service range projecting westwards from the rear half. It has three storeys, with cellars under the northern half of the main block. The principal reception rooms are on the ground floor in the eastern half of the main block, with smaller rooms in the western half on either side of the large stair hall. The latter was the only space to be lit only from one of the end walls, where opportunities for windows were restricted by the presence of chimney stacks. The construction is of brick with red sandstone details, and the internal walls are executed in studwork with brick nogging. Cellars for this building have been dug into the area of the amphitheatre.

Changes to the footprint of Dee House can be seen between de Lavaux's map of 1745 and the later one by Murray and Stuart of 1791. These maps show that by the later date, the Bishop's Palace, to the south, had been extended west and

61 Menuge *et al*, *op. cit*., 21.
62 *Idem*.
63 This is the building discovered in Area B. See note 50.

64 CCRO, PM 18/3, Alexander de Lavaux, *Plan of the City and Castle of Chester*, 1745.
65 CCRO, PM 14/7.

Fig. 19: View looking east from Wolf Gate (Newgate) in 1957. St John's House is on the left and the entrance gate to Dee House is at bottom right

north, so that it bordered the southern garden boundary of Dee House, and to the south-eastern boundary had been added a long range of what appear to be outbuildings.[66] These form one side of an enclosed garden lying between the Dee House gardens and the churchyard. Deeds suggest that the owner of Dee House may have had a detached garden to the south of St John's Cottage, although this has not yet been formally identified.[67] To the east of Dee House gardens, the 1791 map shows more formal gardens within a similar-sized plot to that of Dee House, between its eastern boundary and the former inner precinct boundary, then the western boundary of the churchyard. However, to the north, the plot has a triangular-shaped boundary separating it from the gardens of St John's House. The remains of the eastern side of this boundary and the cellared building adjoining it were discovered in Area B of the recent excavations within the present Dee House gardens, confirming the accuracy of the map. The irregular nature of the boundaries to the north and north-east of Dee House, combined with evidence from the excavations, suggests a network of divisions and property boundaries which pre-date the establishment of the building.

It is clear that the amphitheatre environs had retained a broadly coherent character since at least the medieval period, and that this character survived despite the replacement of medieval buildings and closes by Georgian town houses and gardens. At the end of this period the former area of the amphitheatre can be divided into four discrete blocks, their boundaries a mix of old and new. About 80 per cent of the amphitheatre area was enclosed within the gardens of Dee House and St John's House; about 15 per cent was occupied by roadside properties; and about 5 per cent was within the former inner precinct of St John's Church, by then the churchyard, which overlapped the south-east quadrant of the former amphitheatre. The wealth of the inhabitants of Dee House is reflected in some of the finds material from the excavation, notably fine Chinese porcelain.

THE 19TH AND 20TH CENTURIES
During the 19th century the character of the area continued to retain its historical identity, a cross between a villa suburb and a cathedral close (Fig. 15, see page 6). Extensive gardens covered much of the former amphitheatre area (Figs 16 and 17). Towards the end of the century, the area suffered a significant loss of Georgian buildings, with the demolition of five large houses.[68] The

---

66 Chester, Grosvenor Museum collection 1960.148.101, Murray and Stuart, *Plan of the City of Chester*, 1791.
67 Menuge *et al, op. cit.*, 21.

68 This is indicated on mapping between that of John Wood's *A Plan of the City of Chester*, 1833 [CCRO, PM 18/5] and the Ordnance Survey 1:500 scale map of 1874.

tower of St John's, which had dominated the area, collapsed in 1881.[69] The open character of the wider area was retained with the formalisation of the earlier garden and park landscape of Cholmondeley House into the Grosvenor Park in 1867.[70] This period also saw regeneration of the ecclesiastical character of the area, with major restorations of St John's church by Christopher Hussey and John Douglas, and major extensions to the Old Bishop's Palace.[71] Continuity of clerical occupancy in the landscape was also maintained by the presence of the archdeacon's house, whilst Dee House had a number of clerical tenants throughout its life. The 19th century also witnessed the architectural reassertion of the Roman Catholic presence in town and city centres, not only through church-building, but also through the establishment of convents and other institutions. Dee House (Fig. 18) became part of this resurgence in 1854, when it was acquired by the Faithful Companions of Jesus as a convent and girls' boarding school. It became an important institution in the education of the poor in Chester. In 1867 a purpose-built three-storey chapel block and schoolrooms were added by the architect Edmund Kirby in the Middle Pointed style.[72] The northern section of the range along Souter's Lane, consisting of five bays and two storeys, appears to be contemporary and is probably also by Kirby.[73] In the last quarter of the 19th century a three-storey infill block, roughly matching the original house in its details, was built in the angle formed by the main block and service wing.

In 1925 continuity of a religious and educational focus to the area was maintained when Dee House was acquired by the Ursuline Order and new school buildings were subsequently erected to the south.[74] It was this building activity which resulted in the discovery of the amphitheatre in 1929. Shortly before, controversial proposals had been submitted by the City Corporation to straighten Newgate and Little St John Street between the city wall and St John's church.[75] The discovery of the amphitheatre increased hostility to the proposals when it was realised that the new road would run across its centre. The scheme was finally blocked

in 1933 against a background of extensive national and local protest, and the curved road pattern around the amphitheatre, embedded in the landscape for generations, was retained. A final glimpse of the amphitheatre area before the major excavations in the 1960s is provided by a photograph taken from the city walls (Fig. 19), which shows the gardens in the foreground, the wall marking the boundary of the proposed road, and St John's church in the distance.

CONCLUSIONS

There is little doubt that, despite changes in the landscape and buildings immediately around the amphitheatre over a period of some 2,000 years, there has been a strong physical identity maintained between the amphitheatre and St John's, illustrated by the probable preservation of its boundaries within those of St John's precincts. Although the construction of the church and possibly also the *burh* walls no doubt contributed to the demise of the amphitheatre fabric in the late Anglo-Saxon and early medieval periods, the retention of its extent within the layout of the later ecclesiastical landscape is striking. The foundations of its current character of exclusivity, tranquillity and open space were thus cemented into the landscape at an early date.

The archives of the excavation and non-invasive projects are currently in assessment, and their potential for analysis is being established. Following this process full analysis will be undertaken. This article can only be a first statement of the more obvious results. These will be expanded and enhanced as the research results, records, artefacts and ecofacts from the excavation are studied. It has, however become clear that there is a very different story to be told than that accepted since 1975, both in the understanding of the amphitheatre itself and the evolution of Chester's landscape.

69 Matthews and Willshaw, *op.cit.*, 14.
70 Ainsworth and Wilmott, *op. cit.*, 42.
71 Menuge *et al*, *op. cit.*, 10, 32.
72 *The Builder*, 14 December 1867, 914 [*ex inf*. Dr R McD O'Donnell]; Menuge *et al*, *op. cit.*, 24; Matthews, *op. cit.*, 59.
73 Kirby (1838–1920) has not been the subject of detailed research and his work is only beginning to gain appropriate recognition. He was educated at St Mary's College, Oscott, where his drawing skills were supposed to have been noticed by A W N Pugin, and at the Royal Academy Schools. He was a pupil of Edward Welby Pugin (A W N Pugin's son) before 1864, and later of John Douglas, Chester's most

celebrated architect, before establishing his own practice in Liverpool in 1867. He worked extensively in Cheshire and Liverpool and the Catholic Church was one of his most important clients. His principal work in Chester is St Werburgh's Roman Catholic church, located nearby on Grosvenor Park Road (1873–5). Kirby's additions to Dee House were undertaken comparatively early in his career and perhaps helped him to win the church commission. [We are indebted to Mr Adam Menuge and Dr R McD O'Donnell for this information.]
74 Matthews and Willshaw, *op. cit.*, 6.
75 Matthews, *op. cit.*, 7.

APPENDIX
THE CHESTER AMPHITHEATRE PROJECT 2003–05

The results of the project are intended to provide baseline data to inform the development of proposals for the future of the site, its presentation and interpretation. The research framework was produced by Oxford Archaeology[76] and funded by the English Heritage Archaeology Commissions Programme, building on the work already carried out by Keith Matthews and Chester Archaeology.[77] Non-invasive survey began in 2004. This work, designed and co-ordinated by Stewart Ainsworth, has included topographic and analytical landscape survey, geophysics, terrestrial photogrammetry, aerial photography, architectural survey, documentary work and laser scanning.[78] The survey takes as its geographical limits the area between the city walls to the west, Grosvenor Park to the east, the River Dee to the south, and the amphitheatre itself to the north.

Excavation has been a key element in the project, and in December 2003 Tony Wilmott was appointed project director for English Heritage, charged with developing a project design for a large-scale excavation programme to be carried out in the summer months of 2004 and 2005. This was resourced and run jointly by English Heritage and Chester City Council, and in May 2004, Dan Garner was appointed as the excavation co-director for Chester Archaeology.

The excavation strategy was enshrined in a project design drawn up for the work. It had become clear that the limits of the usefulness of small-scale evaluative work had been reached, and that the questions to be asked of the site could only be answered by relatively large-scale area excavation. Area A was designed to establish the extent of Thompson's work on the *cavea* and to re-examine his phasing of the structure and its dating. It was further intended to examine the post-Roman archaeology of this area. In Area B, the brief was to excavate thoroughly and examine all aspects of the post-Roman archaeology of the site down to the top of Roman levels in order to establish the post-Roman sequence lost by Thompson. The site chosen for this excavation was the closest possible to St John's church, and it was hoped that evidence might be forthcoming to demonstrate a connection between the amphitheatre and the siting of the early church. Area C was excavated in order to examine the history of the infilling of the arena, and the consequent disappearance from sight of the amphitheatre in the townscape. It was further hoped that the true context of post-holes discovered by Thompson in the centre of the arena would be established.

The excavation was designed from the beginning to be highly accessible. To this end a public walkway was installed along the centre of the amphitheatre, and information boards were constantly updated. A newsletter was produced, and went through a total of eight editions, which were dispensed on the walkway and at the nearby Chester Visitor Centre, which also hosted a display presenting the project and its ongoing results. A dedicated website was set up to provide details of the project and up-to-date information (www.chesteramphitheatre.co.uk). This included a webcam through which the excavation could be followed in real time. In addition, a booklet was produced explaining the results of the project to date.[79] Although the excavation was fully staffed by professional archaeologists, including the permanent staff of Chester Archaeology and contract staff, volunteers played an important role, as did students who participated in the training programme developed on site for undergraduates of the Universities of Liverpool and Chester.

Excavation ended in September 2005, and work immediately began on post-excavation assessment. The assessment will generate a project design for the analysis and publication of the results in accordance with MAP2 (English Heritage, 1992). This means that the broad conclusions contained in this interim report will be subject to alteration, expansion and confirmation in the final publications. In particular, very little of the dating evidence has been examined. This article can only be a first statement of the more immediate results.

76 I Wain, 'Chester Amphitheatre Resource Assessment and Research Agenda', Oxford Archaeology, 2003.
77 Matthews *et al*, *op. cit*.

78 S Ainsworth, 'Chester Amphitheatre: The Role of Non-invasive Survey', *English Heritage project design*, 2003.
79 Ainsworth and Wilmott, *op. cit*.

The Dating of the Pyx Door

Warwick Rodwell, Daniel Miles, Derek Hamilton and Martin Bridge

The former door of the Pyx Chamber of Westminster Abbey has recently been identified as reused from the earlier abbey built by Edward the Confessor c.1042–65. The dendrochronological investigation concluded that the door is the oldest scientifically dated door in Britain, and immediately sparked a controversial counter-claim that an early medieval door in Essex is in fact older. This short piece reviews the evidence and disposes of the Essex claim.

Fig. 1: The north face of the former Pyx door, seen from the chapter house vestibule. This was originally the back, the door having been reversed when it was rehung here in the mid-13th century

In 2005 dendrochronology was undertaken on six medieval doors in Westminster Abbey. One of these, the Pyx door, which hangs today in the chapter house vestibule (Fig. 1), has been identified as the oldest scientifically dated door in Britain for which a felling date range rather than a *terminus post quem* date can be ascribed. This door most likely originated from the Saxon abbey of Edward the Confessor and was constructed between 1032 and 1064. This claim has sparked interest among the broader public, and generated a counter-claim that an early medieval door in the church of St Botolph, Hadstock, Essex, is older.

THE DOOR CALLED PYX

The Pyx door is an almost inconspicuous door in the south wall of the chapter house vestibule (Fig. 2). It does not now open into the Pyx chamber, the chamber that held records and samples of coinage to test for purity, although it did so in the 13th century. It opens into a cupboard separated from the Pyx chamber in the early 14th century. Its simple appearance is misleading, for although it has no ornament, its carpentry is expert.

The door is constructed of five oak boards of varying widths. Close inspection of the boards during sampling indicated that they were all converted tangentially by sawing through-and-through. This observation contrasts with Cecil Hewett's statement that they were 'cut on the quarter' and radially converted to 'avoid warp or winding'.[1] However, the boards had been fully seasoned prior to joining, and so the deformation that might be expected from through-and-through conversion was not evident.[2]

The board edges are rebated and edge-pegged,

and the entire piece is held together by three flush inset ledges, one each at the top and bottom of the back and one in the centre of the front, thus maintaining a smooth surface on both sides. The original front of the door, now the back, was once covered with skin, the remains of which were still plainly visible in the 19th century.[3] Although legend held that this was human skin, recent analysis shows that it is from some other animal; skins of cow and pig were commonly used as coverings for doors and chests.[4] Wrought-iron hinges, straps and other decorative details were then fixed to the door, trapping the layer of skin between the timber and the metalwork. Most of the original fittings have been lost from the Pyx door, but their tell-tale scars remain (Figs 3a and 3b). The central decorative strap with curled ends still survives, and the outlines of two elaborate hinges are delimited by surface scars and their fixing holes.

The door has been altered and reduced in width by at least 4 inches on both vertical edges; the hinges were removed when this was done, and the scars indicating the outline of their scrolled ends now run off the edges of the boards (Fig. 4). The top, which has also been truncated, may have been arched. The pattern of nailing for fixing the skin covering suggests that the door was significantly taller than it is now: that being so, the placement of the hinges only makes sense if the door was arched, not square-topped. The door was inserted into its present position when the vestibule was constructed, together with the chapter house, c.1250.[5] The original location of the door is unknown, but it may have come from a Saxon chapel here, or from the Saxon chapter house.[6]

---

1 Cecil A Hewett, *English Cathedral and Monastic Carpentry*, Chichester, 1985, 155.
2 Daniel Miles, 'The Interpretation, Presentation and Use of Tree-ring Dates', *Vernacular Architecture*, XXVIII, 1997, 40–56.
3 It is mentioned in numerous accounts: see, for example, G G Scott, *Gleanings from Westminster Abbey,* 2nd edn, 1863, 283. There is still a

fragment, trapped behind an iron strap.
4 Jane Geddes, *Medieval Decorative Ironwork in England*, Society of Antiquaries of London Research Report, LIX, 1999, chapter 1.3.
5 Paul Binski, *Westminster Abbey and the Plantagenets*, London, 1995, 13–17.
6 Hewett, *op. cit.*, 155.

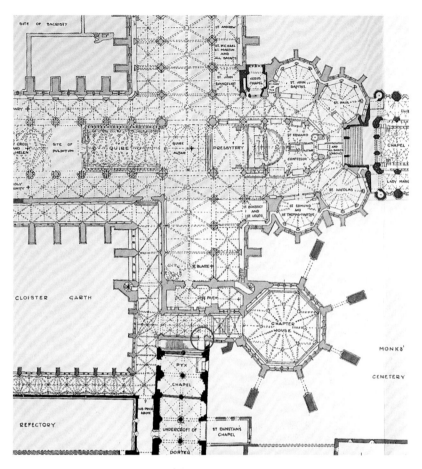

Fig. 2: A plan of Westminster Abbey. The red circle shows the location of the door in the chapter house vestibule

Fig. 4: The south face of the Pyx door, showing its current setting

THE DATE OF THE DOOR

The first attempt to date the Pyx door scientifically took place about 30 years ago. The Department of the Environment then commissioned Dr John Fletcher of the Archaeology Research Laboratory at Oxford University, to carry out dendrochronological analysis on the door. He made two visits to the abbey and measured two of the boards *in situ* simply using a graticule. The growth-ring patterns on the boards were found to cross-match one another, but did not cross-match well enough with any reference chronologies at that time to be considered publishable.

As part of the 2005 programme of tree-ring dating at Westminster Abbey, dendrochronologists from the Oxford Dendrochronology Laboratory re-evaluated the 1970s data from Fletcher's archive that had been stored in punch-card format. With the benefit of 30 more years of tree-ring dating, the old data cross-matched quite well, but it was realised that more material would be needed to bolster the statistical values to acceptable limits.

Four out of the five boards were therefore sampled using a specially designed micro-borer, which produces a 5mm diameter core, instead of the larger 12mm core sample normally produced. This allowed samples to be taken from boards where the ends were too damaged to allow adequate measurements to be taken without destructive re-surfacing of the historic surface patination. The new samples taken from the same boards as the original Fletcher measurements were found to cross-match one another and the original data, confirming the precision of Fletcher's earlier work. Both the Fletcher data and the 2005 core samples were combined to produce a 107-ring site master sequence.

After initial statistical, and subsequent visual, comparison with over 1,300 British reference chronologies, the site master was dated as spanning the years 924–1030. The matching also illustrated that the timber originated from a source near to London, as exceptionally good matches were made with more localised chronologies, but it also suggested that the timber source was subject to unusual climatic or management trends.[7]

Remarkably for doors, the two planks that were dated also retained either the heartwood/sapwood boundary or some of the sapwood (the outer portion of the tree that grows while the tree is alive). Because of this, it is possible to ascribe a

7 D W H Miles and M Bridge, *The Tree-ring Dating of the Early Medieval Doors at Westminster Abbey, London*, English Heritage, Centre for Archaeology Report XXXVIII, 2005, 8.

felling date range to the timbers. It contrasts with many dated doors and furnishings, where the final surviving ring is within the heartwood and can only provide a *terminus post quem*, or 'felled after' date. In the case of the Pyx door, using an average heartwood/sapwood boundary date of 1023, the felling date range of 1032–64 was produced and reported.[8]

This makes the Pyx door the oldest scientifically dated door in Britain, and one which has a definite *terminus ante quem* or end-of-range date due to the fortuitous presence of sapwood. It also makes the Pyx door the earliest-known example of square-rebated boards by about a half-century,[9] and the earliest-known example of post-Roman sawn timber boards. Until now, the use of sawn, rather than riven or split boards, was thought to have been re-introduced by the Normans in the latter part of the 12th century, over 100 years later.[10]

THE COUNTER-CLAIM OF ST BOTOLPH, HADSTOCK

The release of the date of the Pyx door opened up a debate. Its precedence was challenged by Robin Stummer, claiming that the church of St Botolph at Hadstock, Essex, had an older door than Westminster Abbey.[11] The Hadstock claim is based partly on scientific and partly on historical grounds. In 2003 the Oxford Dendrochronology Laboratory dated the door at Hadstock. It found that the timber was not felled earlier than 1034, and was most probably felled in the 1060s. But Stummer proposed that the Hadstock door 'predates the 1040s because there is no documentary evidence' suggesting that it could be later.[12] We find this process of thought flawed.

It is true that there is no documentation that can be applied to any part of the 11th-century church: we simply do not know when it was built, or by whom. Possible associations with King Cnut in 1020 (following the battle of Assandun in 1016), although locally championed, remain unproven.[13] Moreover, the door and the ornate stone arch in which it hangs are secondary insertions into the north wall of the nave.[14] Art historians have paid much attention to the doorway and there has long

been a consensus that it dates from the 1060s or 1070s.[15] To claim it as any older would require the invention at Hadstock of early Romanesque moulding detail about two decades before it appeared in France (whence it spread to England), which is not credible. The published date range for the Hadstock door of 1050–75 is in complete accord with the arch in which it hangs.[16]

We must remember that dendrochronology is a precise discipline, and every tree-ring present in these doors represents a specific calendar year.[17] Carpenters usually trimmed off the bark and most, or all, of the sapwood from the edges of the planks. Consequently, in nearly all cases, the exact years in which the trees were felled cannot be established. However, a critical point in the life of a tree is the boundary between the heartwood and sapwood. At Westminster Abbey that boundary is present on two planks, one dating to 1020, the other to 1026. At Hadstock, the boundary is not preserved, having been cut away by the carpenter, who trimmed all growth back to the 1025 ring. We cannot tell how many heartwood rings he removed, but the more that have been lost, the later the felling date of the tree.

When the allowance for sapwood is made, the earliest possible felling date for the Westminster trees is 1032, and for the Hadstock tree, 1034. Taking all factors into consideration, a difference of about 10 to 20 years between the two doors is most likely. Admittedly, they are not very far apart in age, but the Westminster Abbey door is probably the older of the two. Hadstock can, however, take consolation from the fact that the tree from which its door was made was of great antiquity, having been growing before *c*.600.

ACKNOWLEDGEMENTS

We would like to thank the Dean and Chapter of Westminster for collaborating with English Heritage over the dating of all six medieval doors in Westminster Abbey, and the Parochial Church Council of Hadstock for collaboration over the dating of its door. Dr Jane Geddes was instrumental in obtaining a grant through the Society of Antiquaries of London for the dating of the Hadstock door, and assisted Dr J M Fletcher with the Westminster door in the 1970s.

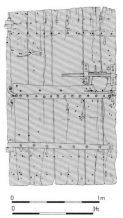

Fig. 3a (top): Reconstruction of the probable appearance of the south face of the door before it was cut down and rehung. This was originally the exterior and was covered with animal hide

Fig. 3b (bottom): Drawing of the south face of the door, showing scars and fixing holes for the original ironwork: the only surviving piece is the central strap

8 *Idem*.
9 Geddes, *op. cit*., 26–9.
10 We are indebted to Mr Damian Goodburn for this opinion.
11 Robin Stummer, 'Oldest Door: Hadstock Fights Back', *Cornerstone*, XXVI (3), 2005, 7.
12 *Idem*.
13 Warwick Rodwell, 'The Battle of Assandun and its memorial church: a reappraisal', in J Cooper (ed), *The Battle of Maldon: Fiction and Fact*, London and Rio Grande, 1993, 127–58.
14 Warwick Rodwell, 'The Archaeological Investigation of Hadstock Church, Essex: An Interim Report', *Antiquaries Journal*, LVI, 1976, 64.

15 Eric Fernie, *The Architecture of the Anglo-Saxons*, London, 1983, 169–71; Eric Fernie, 'The Responds and the Dating of St Botolph's, Hadstock', *Journal of the British Archaeological Association*, CXXXVI, 1983, 62–73.
16 D H Miles, M J Worthington and M C Bridge, 'Tree-ring Dates', *Vernacular Architecture*, XXXV, 2004, 95–113.
17 M G L Baillie, *Tree-ring Dating and Archaeology*, London, 1982; M G L Baillie, *A Slice Through Time: Dendrochronology and Precision Dating*, London, 1995; English Heritage, *Dendrochronology: Guidelines on Producing and Interpreting Dendrochronological Dates*, London, 1998.

Thomas, Earl of Lancaster, and the Great Gatehouse of Dunstanburgh Castle

Jeremy Ashbee

Is Dunstanburgh Castle on the Northumberland coastline the whitest of white elephants? This article looks at the architecture of the gatehouse built by Edward II's cousin and rival, Thomas, earl of Lancaster, in particular the upward extension of the front walls, to give the false illusion that the building was five storeys high. It notes that the gatehouse does not face either of the possible approach routes, but out to sea, above what has recently been identified as a man-made harbour. With royal castles within sight along the coast, the author concludes that Earl Thomas's gatehouse was simply an exercise in vanity, a rebellious gesture by an over-mighty subject who was shortly to be brought down.

Fig. 1: J M W Turner, *Dunstanburgh Castle, c.*1799

The ruins of Dunstanburgh Castle first become visible from a distance. No roads lead up to the castle and anyone visiting must walk the final mile and a half, usually along the sea-shore from the village of Craster to the south. From this side the curtain wall, its turrets and the main gatehouse form an uneven, jagged skyline, standing on a grassy slope which rises gently from the rocky foreshore and the waves of the North Sea; this is the view most famously captured by J M W Turner in a painting of *c.*1799 (Fig. 1). The most striking building is the ruined great gatehouse in the centre, recognisably once containing two drum towers, but now largely reduced to an irregular outcrop of jagged stone pillars; at first sight, it has more in common with natural features like Monument Valley in Utah, than with better-preserved castles elsewhere. As the 19th-century antiquary Cadwallader Bates rhapsodised, 'you … might reasonably conclude that the shattered turrets of the great gatehouse were sustained by the power of enchantment, so much do their fantastic outlines, peering mysteriously over the green slope of the western escarpment, seem to set all known principles of gravitation at defiance'.[1]

The castle's ruined state, its commanding position and particularly its location only 25 miles from the Scottish border, favour an interpretation of Dunstanburgh as a 'military stronghold'. The recent trend in castle studies, tempering this explanation with thoughts of political symbolism, peace-time administration and architectural ornamentalism, seems to have no place here.[2] Yet several new works of scholarship suggest that even at Dunstanburgh, a purely military interpretation is at best incomplete. Historical research into the career of the castle's first lord, Thomas (*c.*1268–1322), second earl of Lancaster, has shown that his reasons for building a castle at Dunstanburgh were closely tied to his immediate political circumstances.[3] In addition, a field survey in November 2003 revealed substantial unrecognised elements of the medieval landscape, almost certainly components of the new castle of the 14th century.[4] The reassessment of the monument is ongoing at the time of writing, but there is already clear potential to reinterpret the castle less as a communal English refuge against the Scots than as a private fortress, show-place and rebellious gesture from one of the most controversial figures of his age.[5] Several of the physical elements of the castle, as revealed during the landscape survey, seem less inspired by the practical considerations of defence or estate

---

1 J Cadwallader Bates, *The Border Holds of Northumberland*, I, Newcastle upon Tyne, 1891, 167.
2 For a recent discussion of this revisionist interpretation, see Matthew Johnson, *Behind the Castle Gate*, London and New York, 2002.
3 Andy King, 'Lordship, Castles and Locality: Thomas of Lancaster, Dunstanburgh Castle and the Lancastrian Affinity in Northumberland', *Archaeologia Aeliana*, 5th ser, XXIX, 2001, 223–35, *passim*; Andy King, 'Bandits, robbers and *Schavaldours*: war and disorder in Northumberland in the reign of Edward II', in M Prestwich, R Britnell

and R Frame (eds), *Thirteenth Century England*, IX, Woodbridge, 2003, 115–29.
4 Alastair Oswald, *Dunstanburgh Castle, Northumberland, Landscape Investigation*, English Heritage Report, unpublished, 2005.
5 It should be noted that the debate about altruism versus self-interest was applied to Dunstanburgh Castle as long ago as 1949 [W D Simpson, 'Further Notes on Dunstanburgh Castle', *Archaeologia Aeliana*, 4th ser, XXVII, 1949, 1–28].

Fig. 2: The great gatehouse of Thomas of Lancaster at Dunstanburgh Castle, from the south

spaces within it. Moreover, the Dunstanburgh gatehouse has several features which are peculiar, if not unique, and which would be inexplicable without the new information about the shape of the castle and the landscape immediately around it. The gatehouse can illuminate the purposes of the castle's builder and the functions he intended the site to perform.

THOMAS OF LANCASTER AND THE CONSTRUCTION OF THE CASTLE

The history of Dunstanburgh Castle began in 1313 with the first documentary references to the construction from scratch of a new castle in the barony of Embleton, belonging to Earl Thomas since his accession in 1296. Its name *Dunstanesburghe* or *Donstanburgh*, seemingly antique, has been dismissed as a medieval confection to rival the nearby royal fortress at Bamburgh, though previous excavations and the recent archaeological survey by English Heritage have hinted at prehistoric occupation. However, it seems likely that at the time of the castle's establishment, the site was laid out to cultivation.

The earl's reasons for building a castle arguably relate less to the Scottish border wars than to the internal affairs of England, particularly actions of Earl Thomas against his cousin Edward II (1307–27) and Edward's unpopular favourite, Piers Gaveston (d.1312). Thomas of Lancaster was the son of Edmund Crouchback, younger brother of Edward I (1272–1307), created earl of Lancaster in 1267. Earl Thomas was thus the grandson of Henry III and, on his mother's side, great-grandson of Louis VIII of France, and to support this honour he was the second-wealthiest landowner in England. In 1312 he headed the faction responsible for besieging Gaveston in Scarborough Castle, seizing him from the safe-conduct of the earl of Pembroke, and ordering his summary execution (on Earl Thomas's own land). Contemporaries certainly interpreted Edward II's later acts against him as belated revenge for his part in Gaveston's death. Earl Thomas's resentment of the excesses of royal purveyors and exasperation about the wars with Scotland fuelled this opposition.[6] However, it has recently been noted that he had little stake in Northumberland, his local affinity being largely restricted to a small (and sometimes unreliable) circle of gentry retainers, including several figures notorious for violence and banditry.[7]

management than by aesthetics or even medieval Arthurian mythology, and it remains for further investigation to test some of the emerging hypotheses.

This paper is concerned with the great gatehouse of Thomas of Lancaster, at the south-west corner of the bailey. All writers on the castle have mentioned the gatehouse and have observed its closest architectural affinities with other castles, though few detailed architectural treatments have been attempted. The gatehouse has been ruinous since the 16th century and its fabric survives in a very incomplete state, but enough remains to show the original form of the building and to suggest functions for the different

6 J R Maddicott, *Thomas of Lancaster*, 1307–1322, Oxford, 1970, *passim*.

7 King, 'Lordship, Castles and Locality … ', *cit.*, 224 and 227.

The small barony of Embleton represented a geographical outlier of his estate, which was mostly concentrated in the north Midlands.

A detailed account preserved in the Duchy of Lancaster papers in the National Archives shows that construction of the castle was under way by May 1313, with references to the excavation of a great ditch (*magnum fossatum*) 16 perches long by 80ft wide, and 18ft deep, 'between the site of the castle and the field of Embleton' (*i.e.* the castle's western side). The castle's buildings were rising at the same time, with purchases of stone and iron (for cramps), Baltic timber for doors and windows, a lodge for the masons, and from the first, the construction by task-work of a gatehouse. The accounts identify the master mason of this last task, a certain 'master Elias the mason', and though the manuscript is badly damaged at this point, indicate that these particular works, at a lump-sum of £224, were procured by indenture made between the mason and the earl. The total value of the surviving account, given at the foot of the roll, was £184 5s 0½d; by Michaelmas 1314 (the end of the first account), £168 10s 3½d had already been spent. Thereafter the progress of the works is imprecisely known, though the assumption is that the basic form of the castle was complete within eight years or so.[8]

In 1322 Thomas of Lancaster was captured by the supporters of Edward II after the battle of Boroughbridge, put on trial in the hall of his own castle at Pontefract (for taking up arms against the king and collusion with the Scots) and summarily beheaded. He had evidently been trying to retreat to Dunstanburgh on the insistence of his supporters, though against his own better judgement; he feared that making his base in Northumberland would fuel rumours that he was conspiring with Robert the Bruce (as is now believed genuinely to have been the case).[9] Dunstanburgh Castle was confiscated by the king and committed to a royal steward in Northumberland, who delivered it forthwith to a keeper, Richard de Emeldon (Embleton). From 1326 onwards, the castle was nominally the property of Earl Thomas's younger brother, Henry, who formally inherited the Lancaster estate in the following year.[10]

THE GREAT GATEHOUSE

The gatehouse at Dunstanburgh Castle presents a particular set of challenges to the archaeologist and historian. The poor survival of its fabric (compared with several of its closest analogues, such as Harlech, Beaumaris, St Briavels or Tonbridge), and limited access to its highest levels, make close inspection impossible and interpretation difficult; moreover, previous survey drawings are few and no plans exist for either of the upper floors or of the front turrets. However, a recent examination has shown that enough survives for its shape to be reconstructed, inferring from the survival of a roof scar, a fireplace or a door on one side of the building that similar features existed on the other side, and so on. Such an interpretation is problematic, since the fabric clearly shows in several areas that the symmetry of the gatehouse was not perfect, particularly on the second floor. However, what follows is a summary of recent observations about the gatehouse's physical form. Combination of this evidence with medieval documents also suggests ways in which the building and the rooms within it were used between the 14th and the 16th centuries.

The essential form of the gatehouse is well understood. The plan of the building, with two large D-shaped towers flanking a central passageway, follows a classic model of great castle gatehouses, particularly associated with English and Welsh castles throughout the 13th century (Fig. 2).[11] Some of the earliest surviving prototypes stand on baronial sites, but the type is also strongly associated with royal works and especially the castles built in Wales for Edward I at Aberystwyth (1277–89), Harlech (1283–90) and Beaumaris (1294–1300). Distinctive features shared by all of them, including Dunstanburgh, are the symmetrical plan of the towers flanking the entrance, their great size, their possession of several upper storeys, and in most cases, their

8 London, National Archives, Public Record Office (hereafter PRO), DL 29/1/3 rot 2 and 2d. This manuscript is badly rubbed, has lost several lines along the frayed bottom edge, and becomes only partly legible even under ultra-violet light. A transcription (made without the aid of UV and demonstrably inaccurate in some details) was published in 1858 and though imperfect, is the only source for several important clauses [The Reverend Charles H H Hartshorne, *Feudal and Military Antiquities of Northumberland and the Scottish Borders,* London, 1858, 135–6]. For evidence that the castle was operational by 1319, see PRO, DL 28/1/13 *passim* and DL 25/3392, indenture of appointment of Richard de Bincestre as keeper in March 1319.

9 F W D Brie (ed), *The Brut or The Chronicles of England,* London, 1906, 217–22.

10 *Calendar of the Close Rolls of Edward II, 1323–7,* London, 1898, 12, 87, 269 and 476.

11 The earliest known example of the type is the main gate at Chepstow Castle, for which dendrochronology has recently suggested a date as early as the 1190s [Richard Avent, 'William Marshal's building works at Chepstow Castle, Monmouthshire, 1189–1219', in J R Kenyon and K O'Connor (eds), *The Medieval Castle in Ireland and Wales,* Dublin, 2003, 50–71, especially 53, 54–62].

Fig. 3 (above): Westward view across the great gatehouse. The original roof level is shown by an off-set in the tower to the left, and by scars in the far wall, showing a very shallow pitch. The door on the left gave access from the roof to one of the frontal turrets that rose two storeys above the main building

capacity for residential accommodation on these upper floors. Such gatehouses protected weak points with massive masonry structures, often incorporating lengthy sequences of gates,

portcullises, murder holes and arrowslits, but scholars have also seen them as compensating for the absence of a true 'keep' by providing accommodation on their upper floors, leading to the term 'keep gatehouses'.[12] It is unarguable that the gatehouses had enormous visual presence and symbolic potency, and in this last capacity, Dunstanburgh fits centrally within the tradition.

No extensive discussion is possible at this time about the identity and background of 'master Elias the mason'. Henry Summerson suggests that he was Elias de Burton, apparently mentioned in accounts for Conwy Castle and town walls.[13] The gatehouse is unusual among the buildings of Dunstanburgh Castle and generally of castles in the north of England in its use of rounded rather than square or rectangular plan-forms, as appear in the Lilburn, Constable's and Egyncleugh Towers at Dunstanburgh, at Pickering Castle (1324–5) and Pontefract Castle (probably 1323–6), both previously owned by Thomas of Lancaster, as well as numerous other examples. This further supports the idea that the Dunstanburgh gatehouse represents the influence of a non-local architectural tradition, doubtless that of the royal works.

---

12 For an outline of gatehouse development, see M W Thompson, *The Rise of the Castle*, Cambridge, 1991, 100–2; F Matarasso, *The English Castle*, London, 1995, 140–3.
13 Henry Summerson, *Dunstanburgh Castle*, London, 1993, 11.

THE LEVEL OF THE ROOF AND THE TURRETS

Although this has been noted before, the arrangements at roof-level in Dunstanburgh are unusual and, in the experience of the writer, unique. The body of the great tower was evidently covered with a low-pitched lead roof immediately above the second floor, indicated by close-set sinkings for horizontal cambered beams below a projecting moulding, and creases for the flashing of the lead covering, surviving in the north-west and north-east corners (Fig. 3). Access onto the roof was possible by doors at the tops of the north-east and north-west staircase turrets. This roof level was protected by a crenellated parapet around the east and west sides of the main drums and a walkway between the main turrets at the south front of the building. Though no battlements have survived, scars show that little height has been lost from these parts of the building, and the medieval merlons can be seen in Francis Place's sketch of 1678 (Fig. 4).

However, the frontal portions of the main turrets, and two projections at the rear corners of the building, stood much higher than this roof level. As early as 1891, Cadwallader Bates realised that parts of the two main towers stood higher than the remainder of the building: 'they formed a sort of false front of two additional storeys'.[14] Modern observation bears this out and suggests ways in which these highest levels were intended to function. These thin tall towers, with flat east, north and west walls, and frontages describing segments of the curvature of the main drums, clearly contained shelters opening from the gatehouse's main roof, so that watchmen stationed on the battlements could take cover in inclement weather. Surviving doorways in the western tower indicate that a further storey was provided above these shelters, running up to the level of the lead roofs of the frontal towers, making five storeys in all. These thin frontal towers also contained spiral stairs which led from the main roof up to the two highest levels and the roofs of thin rectangular turrets, with parapets slightly higher than the crenellations of the towers. Place's 1678 sketch, difficult to interpret in its own right, emerges as a remarkably plausible rendering of this most unusual architectural feature.

Besides these high frontages to the drum towers, the fabric shows that in two further areas, the gatehouse stood higher than the main lead roofs. These were the two rear corners of the building, the north-east and north-west corners, where straight stairs rose from the level of the main lead roof of the gatehouse to form two look-outs,

---

14 Bates, *op. cit.*, 187.

Fig. 4: Francis Place, *Dunstanburgh Castle*, 1678. The main crenellations of the gatehouse were still in place at this date

Fig. 5: A plan showing
Dunstanburgh Castle and the
surrounding landscape,
derived from a survey by
Alastair Oswald

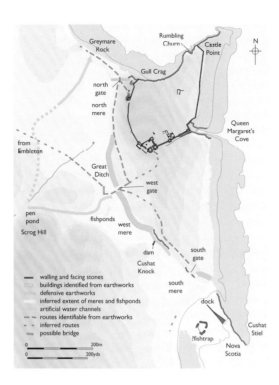

Fig. 5: A plan showing
Dunstanburgh Castle and the
surrounding landscape,
derived from a survey by
Alastair Oswald

only large enough for single watchmen.

Reconstructing the gatehouse with these features is awkward, in that the castle's show south frontage faced neither of the two possible landward approaches. The coastal path from Craster may be as old as the castle, but the historical record confirms that Dunstanburgh Castle was much more closely tied to the inland area to the north-west: its barony was always centred on the village of Embleton (*Emeldone*), lying in this direction, and many of the visitors to the castle would have come this way.[15] The recent archaeological survey has greatly illuminated the western approach to the castle, demonstrating that on this side, the castle was bounded by large fresh-water meres, crossed only by causeways, in whose waters the castle and its hill were reflected (Figs 5 and 6). However, such an approach only reveals the gatehouse from the side, a view which gives little indication of its true architectural form and grandeur; this defect was remedied later in the 14th century when John of Gaunt ordered the construction of a second gatehouse on this side, directly overlooking the Embleton approach.[16] The main frontage of the gatehouse can be seen to better effect from the small Craster trackway. However, what it faces most directly is not a land approach, but the North Sea.

EXPLANATIONS FOR THE FORM AND ORIENTATION OF THE GATEHOUSE

An explanation of this strange orientation, suggested in 1949 by W D Simpson, is that the open ground immediately before the gatehouse's south front was the site of a planned town, perhaps short-lived or unbuilt.[17] This hypothesis remains to be confirmed or refuted by further survey. However, the fieldwork of 2003 has identified a more radical line of interpretation. On the foreshore to the south-east of the castle, archaeologists identified the remains of a stone quay for a harbour, including some of the roughly dressed stone facing of its western flank, and small patches of its cobbled surface. These traces were sufficient to indicate that the main axis of the quay ran directly to the central arch of the gatehouse (and incidentally, through the gatehouse and beyond to the Lilburn Tower on the castle's western flank). There is a strong likelihood that harbour, gatehouse and tower were all planned during a single episode: the initial construction in the second decade of the 14th century.

The harbour would naturally have had great practical utility in the transport of materials during building works, but the more imaginative notion that the castle was specifically designed with direct access to and from the sea, potentially explains some of the gatehouse's most puzzling features. In particular, the massing of the building, apparently unique in a British castle gatehouse, would present an elevation of five storeys only to an onlooker standing on the quay or approaching by boat: from all other sides, the gatehouse is revealed as possessing a (not negligible) three storeys. The designer of the building created a structure which was much more imposing from one direction than the others and this must reflect an expectation that it would be viewed from this side, either by many people, or by a few whose opinion was deemed to matter.

The importance of sea traffic, particularly the transport of the ubiquitous sea-coals from Newcastle, is well-known even in the Middle Ages, and Thomas of Lancaster's household accounts contain numerous references to transporting property by boat along the north-east coast.[18] But there is every likelihood that passengers too would travel to Dunstanburgh by sea. The accessibility of castles from the water has ample

15 Edward Bateson, *A History of Northumberland, Volume 2: The Parishes of Embleton, Ellingham, Howick, Long Houghton and Lesbury*, Newcastle upon Tyne, 1895, 163–83.
16 Malcolm Hislop, 'John of Gaunt's Building Works at Dunstanburgh Castle', *Archaeologia Aeliana*, 5th scr, XXIII, 1995, 139–44.

17 This suggestion had previously been made by Simpson, *op. cit.*, 10.
18 PRO, DL 28/1/13, m 5, account for 1318–19. The account says nothing about Dunstanburgh but makes frequent reference to sea transport, for example, between Kingston upon Hull and Tynemouth.

precedent in the late 13th and early 14th centuries, including several of the still-modern castles of Edward I such as Conwy and Caernarfon (both begun in 1283), and the royal apartments in the Tower of London (begun in 1275). Given the lawlessness of Northumberland in the early 14th century, with the occasional abduction and murder of magnates and officials on the road, it is entirely likely that sea travel would become more appealing.[19]

CONCLUSION

It appears then that the great gatehouse was specifically designed to present its tallest and most impressive front towards the sea. To a distant observer on a ship approaching from the south-east, the twin drum towers would appear as a solid mass of masonry, immensely tall, with its skyline broken by the narrow watch turrets over the gate-passage and with the Lilburn Tower rising directly between the main turrets.[20] Closer in, from the stone harbour on the foreshore, the Lilburn Tower disappears and the form of the gatehouse becomes clearer to appreciate, with the tall frontages revealed as thin slices and the greater part of the towers having their parapets above the third storey.

This form is slightly different from the deceptive 'counter-sunk' roofs of some Romanesque *donjons*, which had high screen walls complete with false windows above roof level on all elevations, leading the onlooker to believe that the towers were a storey higher than was actually the case;[21] but the principle is certainly similar. In this case, however, the matter of direction is crucial. The gatehouse at Dunstanburgh seems to have been sited and orientated to ignore the land approaches from Scotland, the rival castle at Bamburgh, or still more locally from Embleton. The inevitable conclusion is that the builders, under direct instruction from Earl Thomas, aimed to impress a completely different constituency. Important noble visitors to the castle are naturally a good possibility. The other of course is that the gatehouse was an exercise in vanity on the part of the earl himself.

Fig. 6: The great gatehouse and west wall reflected in the water of the 1313 ditch

The case can be made that Dunstanburgh Castle was the whitest of white elephants. Despite lying next to the Scottish border, it lay off to the side of the main roads and played no part in border warfare. Its location, as well as watching over a small estate, was contrived to make the castle visible from the royal castle at Bamburgh along the coast, a veritable two-finger gesture to Edward II's officers, and to reserve its greatest architectural *coup de théâtre* for those arriving by sea. In its great gatehouse, it adapted a distinctive form of royal castles but added two more floors. It is not extravagant to imagine Earl Thomas aiming to communicate his *persona* as the leader of the rebel faction, and at the same time, as more than a king.

ACKNOWLEDGEMENT

The research for this article would not have been possible without the generosity of Alastair Oswald in sharing the results of the 2003 survey and his subsequent researches into many aspects of the site. These and numerous other lines of research will receive much fuller publication in 2007 in a new English Heritage guidebook to Dunstanburgh Castle and its landscape, written by Alastair Oswald and the author.

---

19 King, 'Bandits, robbers and *Schavaldours* … ', *cit.*, 115–18 and *passim*.

20 Both turrets survive in a fragmented condition but will only be accessible by scaffolding: on the next opportunity for inspecting the fabric, the turrets should be checked for sinkings for a flagstaff. They would be natural settings to fly the earl's standard. For comparable examples, see the inner ward at Conwy Castle and the Queen's Tower at Caernarfon, known in the 14th century as *Tour de la Banere*, set over the great hall.

21 Edward Impey and Geoffrey Parnell, *The Tower of London*, London, 2000, 17.

Moreton Corbet Castle

Elain Harwood

Moreton Corbet is a medieval castle that was abandoned in 1680. Between 1578 and 1583 Robert Corbet, humanist and friend of Sir Philip Sidney, built a richly ornamented range facing an ornamental garden. The discovery of a Court Book of 1588 amplifies our understanding of this important piece of Elizabethan architecture, while 18th-century drawings document its progressive decline, and one proposal to rebuild it.

Fig. 14: The west end of the south range of Moreton Corbet Castle from the north-west, *c.*1908

'The last word has certainly not been written about this magnificent ruin', wrote Sir Nikolaus Pevsner in 1958. Moreton Corbet is a medieval defensive site domesticated in the 16th century, first by Sir Andrew Corbet and then more ambitiously by his son Robert in 1579–83. Sadly, the guidebook promised by George Chettle for the Ministry of Works *c.*1956 (and referred to by Pevsner) was never published and a search in 1991 failed to find the text.[1] Instead the present guidebook repeats two frequent assumptions, that Robert Corbet's wing was never finished, and that the house was burned down and left in a ruinous state after it was taken in 1644 by just ten parliamentarians, from a garrison of over a hundred royalists.[2] These claims may make the building more romantic for the visitor, but are untrue. However, much valuable work on the house has been undertaken by local historians, which this article collates, relating its findings more closely to the surviving fabric.

Until 1515 or 1516 Moreton Corbet was called Moreton Toret after a Saxon family of that name, who had acquired the estate by 1110. The Toret family fell foul of King John and in 1215 Bartholomew Toret was imprisoned; he regained his estates in 1217 and his daughter married a Corbet in 1239. The suggested date of *c.*1200 for the earliest surviving masonry corresponds with this one period of unrest in Moreton's medieval history. There is a gateway at the northern apex of the triangular site (Figs 1 and 2), linked by a partially medieval wall to a tower further west,

where an apparently 13th-century fireplace with tall foliate capitals survives on the first floor.

The Corbet dynasty was large and complicated; Moreton Corbet had become the principal seat of the elder branch after Robert Corbet, 'the Pilgrim', had surrendered a larger estate at Caus to his younger brother and joined the Crusades. The 16th century saw the family at the height of their esteem, when Sir Andrew Corbet was three times high sheriff, for three different monarchs. Although Leland described Moreton Corbet as 'a fair castel' *c.*1540, it was typical of the times that Sir Andrew should carry out substantial works of modernisation, perhaps advised by his uncle and former guardian, Richard Corbet, who had had a career at court. His younger brothers Robert and Jerome made additions to their properties at Stanwardine and Beslow from the 1560s onwards.[3] But Sir Andrew's additions were subsumed by those of his eldest son, Robert, who inherited in 1578 and demolished some of them in favour of a new great hall and a three-storey south wing, not completed when he died of plague in 1583 (Fig. 3).

William Camden writes of Moreton Corbet that 'within our remembrance, Robert Corbet, carryed away with the affectionate delight of Architecture, began to build in a barraine place a most gorgeous and stately house, after the Italian modell: But death prevented him, so he left the new worke unfinished and the old castle defaced'.[4] Barbara Coulton shows that the phrase 'after the Italian modell' came into Camden's text of 1607 only with Holland's translation in 1610. But he had special

1 Nikolaus Pevsner, *The Buildings of England Shropshire*, Harmondsworth, 1958, 204; a note dated August 1956 in the red boxes of the National Monuments Record Centre, Swindon, states that 'the Ministry of Works is about to publish a booklet on this building'.
2 Iain Ferris, *Haughmond Abbey, Lilleshall Abbey and Moreton Corbet Castle*, English Heritage, 2000; O J Weaver, 'Moreton Corbet Castle', in *Society of Architectural Historians of Great Britain, Annual Conference notes*, September 1988.
3 Barbara Coulton, 'Moreton Corbet Castle: A House and its Family', *Shropshire History and Archaeology: Transactions of the Shropshire*

Archaeological and Historical Society, LXX, 1995, 185; Augusta Elizabeth Corbet, *The Family of Corbet, its Life and Times*, II, London, [*c.*1919], 276, suggests that the courtier Richard Corbet introduced new heraldic symbols adopted by Sir Andrew. For Beslow see E Mercer and P A Stamper, 'Beslow Hall: The Demolition of a Rival to Pitchford', *Transactions of the Shropshire Archaeological and Historical Society*, LXV, 1987, 56–63.
4 William Camden, *Britannia*, first English edition, translated and enlarged by Philemon Holland, George Bishop and John Norton, London, 1610.

Fig. 1: Moreton Corbet
Castle from the
north, *c.*1700

Fig. 2: Lady Philips
(attributed), *Moreton Corbet
Castle from the north*, *c.*1842,
based on an 18th-century
watercolour, now lost

knowledge of the house from knowing Corbet's widow, and Corbet had certainly visited Italy. Robert Corbet was born *c.*1542 and studied at Cambridge before entering the Middle Temple in 1561. In 1571 he entered the court circle of his distant relation Lord Leicester. Leicester's brother-in-law, Sir Henry Sidney, was lord president of the marches, seated at Shrewsbury. Sidney's son, Philip, attended Shrewsbury School, and in 1566 he stayed part of the year with Sir Andrew Corbet

at Moreton Corbet. Robert Corbet shared Philip Sidney's humanist interests and accompanied him on his continental travels. In 1573–4 they met in Venice, though whether on private or government business is uncertain. Sidney was summoned home by the queen, but Corbet returned via Vienna, Prague and perhaps Nuremberg and Augsburg, and brought Veronese's portrait of Sidney as a gift to Sidney's friend, the diplomat, political thinker and follower of Melanchthon, Hubert Longuet.[5]

5 Malcolm William Wallace, *The Life of Sir Philip Sidney*, Cambridge, 1915, 38, 39–50, 136, James M Osborne, *Young Philip Sidney 1572–1577*, New Haven and London, 1972, 194, 203; Katherine Duncan-Jones, *Sir Philip Sidney Courtier Poet*, London, 1991, 33. I am indebted to Dr Mark Girouard for drawing this to my attention and to Mr Richard Hewlings for following it up.

According to Mrs Augusta E Corbet's history of the family, published *c.*1919, he was

> *endowed with learning and a spirit of roving, had wandered among the olive groves and vineyards of sunny Italy, and amongst the arcades of her marble palaces; and with the enthusiasm of youth sought out ideas and the means for carrying his dreams of art to the Northern home of his Fathers. He went to the famous John of Padua, and fortified with the most elaborate and artistic plans drawn up by that celebrated architect he returned home and the decree went forth that the ancient Castle of Moreton Corbet was to be changed into one of the 'stately homes of England' and after the Italian style. ... Skilled workmen came specially from Italy to carve the marvellous figures on its stones.*[6]

So far was Robert Corbet's life romanticised by the 20th century. Robert subsequently worked for Lord Burghley, and in October 1575 he went as an envoy to Antwerp in a vain attempt to mediate with the Spanish governor Requesens. Thomas Copley wrote to Lord Burghley, 'I shall ever be your servant, and condemn my oversight in forgetting to sign my letter to the Queen, but haste makes waste. I return it signed, by my Lord Ambassador Corbet, a rare man for his years.'[7]

Robert Corbet's work is remarkable not only for the regularity and elegance of its composition, but also for the richness and invention of its sculptural and heraldic decoration (Fig. 4). Anthony Wells-Cole has suggested that the overall character of the new work is 'French, with attached Tuscan columns, but the detail is inclined to the Flemish and two metopes seem to have been derived from Vredeman's designs'.[8] Vredeman de Vries's popular suites of designs based on the orders were published in Antwerp in 1565, with that for Tuscan added in 1578.[9] Moreton Corbet is a very early example in rural England for even these limited Vredeman references, but other motifs from his work subsequently appeared in funerary monuments and decorative sculpture around Shropshire, for example at Condover Hall, where John Richmond of Acton Reynald (another Corbet

estate) was one of the masons working between *c.*1586 and 1595. Vredeman references also appear on monuments to Thomas Scriven (d.1587), also at Condover, and to Sir Richard Lee at Acton Burnell (d.1581).[10] Similar medallions and betassled skulls can also be found in John Shute's example of the Doric order, from 1563.[11]

We have fairly detailed information about just what Robert Corbet left of the previous castle; enough to show that he reduced the medieval fabric to little more than what survives today, but that he retained more of the improvements made by his father. The Moreton Corbet estates could only be passed through the male line, and Robert's only son having died in infancy, they passed to his brother Richard. It was in his ownership when the first Court Book for the estate was begun in 1588. Its opening entry, dated 28 October 1588, is a description of the manor:

> *Upon which site was once situated a certain large castle called Moreton Corbett Castle of which two ancient towers only remain of which one is over the gate of the aforesaid castle facing north, and the other over the old store room of the same castle facing west.*
>
> *Between which towers is a certain great kitchen with two ovens and with a certain large house for storing meat called a larder house adjacent to the kitchen, over which rooms are four chambers, and a cell called Babylon, and a certain porticus over them: which were all newly built by Andrew Corbett.*[12]

Fig. 3 (left): The south range of Moreton Corbet Castle from the south-west in 1991

Fig. 4 (right): The south-west corner of the south range of Moreton Corbet Castle in 1991

6 Corbet, *op. cit.*, 278.
7 *Ibid.*, 293.
8 Anthony Wells-Cole, *Art and Decoration in Elizabethan and Jacobean England*, New Haven and London, 1997, 60.
9 Hans Vredeman de Vries, *Den eersten boeck, ghemaect opde twee Colonnen Dorica en Ionica*, Antwerp, 1565; *Das ander Buech, gemacht auf fide zway Colonnen, Corinthia und Composita*, Antwerp, 1565; *De orden Tuschana*, Antwerp, 1578.
10 Wells-Cole, *op. cit.*, 60.
11 John Shute, *The First and Chief Groundes of Architecture*, London, 1563, fol vii.

12 Shrewsbury, Shropshire Archives, 322, Box 2 (typescript), *Moreton Corbet Court Book*, I, 28 October 1588 (hereafter cited as Court Book), 'Super quem Scitum olim scituabatur quoddam magnum Castrum vocatum the Castell of Moreton Corbett de quo Castro due antique Turres solum nun Remane Quarum una est supra portam predicti castri ex parte Boreali, Et altera supra vetus promptuarium eiusdem Castri ex parte occidentali. 'Inter quas Turres est quedam Magna Coquina cum duobus furnariis in eadem, et cum quadam larga domo carnaria vocata a Larder house eidem adiungente, Supra quibus sunt quatuor Camere, et una Cella vocata Babylon, et quidam porticus supra eisdem: Que omnia, ex novo edificata fuerunt per Andream Corbett'.

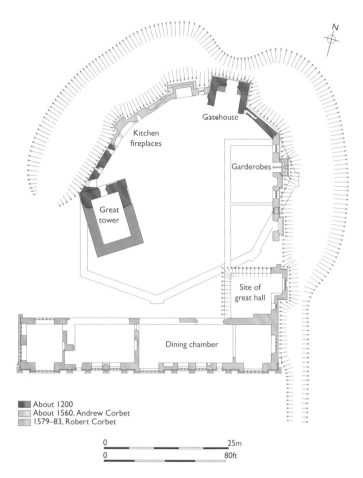

Kitchen fireplaces

Gatehouse

Garderobes

Great tower

Site of great hall

Dining chamber

■ About 1200
▨ About 1560, Andrew Corbet
▨ 1579–83, Robert Corbet

0 — 25m
0 — 80ft

With the benefit of this information, it is easy to identify the remains of Sir Andrew's great kitchen fireplace and stack in the range between the two surviving towers (Fig. 5). A plaque in the principal tower bears the initials SAC and the date 1579. Harder to interpret are a fireplace and garderobes at the north end of the east range, although two- and three-light windows without cusping and with distinctive square stops to their hood moulds suggest that this is Sir Andrew's work. As well as many service buildings, an eastern range, 'formerly new built by the said Andrew Corbett' was described as 'now ruinous having been in part destroyed by the said Robert Corbett who proposed to repair and rebuild them again but sudden death overtook him'.[13]

Robert Corbet evidently rebuilt the south end of the east range and the whole of the south range. At the south end of the east range he built a fine great hall, of which virtually nothing remains today. A drawing of c.1700 in a collection at Shrewsbury School depicts a two-storey oriel, doubtless the high end of the hall (Fig. 6),[14] and a watercolour done between 1767 and 1790 shows another two-storey window north of it (Fig. 7).[15] Four windows at half-landing levels south of the oriel suggest a staircase, leading to Robert Corbet's south wing, which still survives in part, but is

Fig. 5 (above): Plan of Moreton Corbet showing the main phases of the buildings

Fig. 6 (right): The south end of the east range of Moreton Corbet Castle, c.1700

Fig. 7 (facing page top): The south and east ranges of Moreton Corbet Castle from the south-east, between 1767 and 1790

Fig. 8 (facing page bottom): The south range of Moreton Corbet Castle, c.1700

This end is next y meads

13 Court Book, *loc. cit.*, '*Reliqua Edificia ex parte orientali ibidem, quondam noviter faca per predictum Andream Corbett, modo sunt ruinosa, et partim diruta per predictum Robertum Corbett, qui illa iterum reparare et reedificare proposuisset, sed cum mors immature preripult*'.

14 Shrewsbury, Shrewsbury School, Library, S.IX.100, volume of drawings of Moreton Corbet.
15 Shrewsbury, Shropshire Archives, B4295.

Morton Corbett.

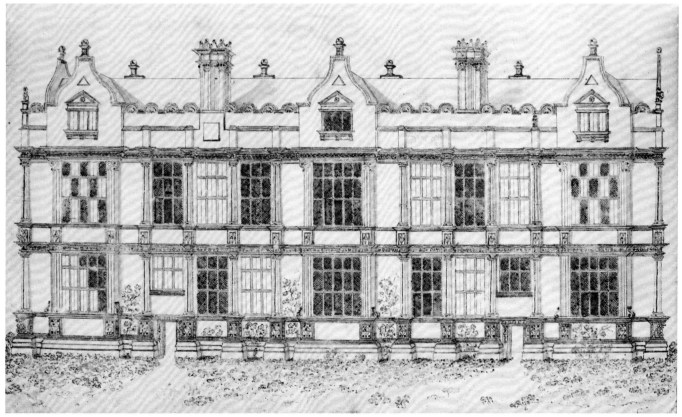

shown complete in another drawing in the Shrewsbury School collection (Fig. 8). The description continues:

> And on the south side and partly on the west side of the said castle are certain high and ample new buildings built of squared and cut stone by Robert Corbett esq. older brother of the said Richard Corbett the present lord, whose windows are not yet glazed apart from one chamber, nor are the other parts of them beyond complete besides their covering with Cornish slates, and the buildings extend in length from east to west (within a wide prospect to the south) sixty paces

together with a certain return towards the north forty paces.

> Within the ambit and circuit of which is a large and ample hall with big windows in the same and a spacious dining room and six other rooms and chambers in the different parts of the said building together with a certain new store house and a new wine cellar beneath them, and upon the uppermost part and top of the said buildings is a certain broad and ample place for walking or gallery stretching the length of the said buildings.[16]

The great surviving southern range retains sufficient of its party walls, of brick behind the stone façades, for it to be clearly composed of a series of chambers, perhaps including a high great chamber and dining chamber, as suggested by an inventory of 1623, but not to have held the great hall.[17] Something of the cellarage survives. The Court Book implies that the range was finished in carcass, and that the topmost floor was an open walkway, or, more probably, a long gallery, given the slate roof. To the south was an extensive formal garden 'with paths and bushes', also described in the Court Book, with a sundial in its centre and an orchard adjoining, together with a gardener's cottage and water supply, and measuring two acres and one rod in total.[18] A survey made in the 1980s suggests that a massive, exactly square platform was created, with gravel paths and a slight mound at its centre, to which Robert Corbet's range was symmetrically aligned on the north side.[19]

Some doubt has remained over the completion of the house after Robert's time, as Richard seems to have lived at Shawbury and to have been more interested in buying land than in architecture. The Ministry of Works noted that the west elevation stops abruptly, and the relationship between Robert's wing and Sir Andrew's service buildings at that end (including a dairy which survived into the 20th century) is unclear.[20] The surviving

16 Court Book, *loc. cit.*, 'Et ex parte Australi, et partim ex parte orientali castri predicti sunt quedam alta et ampla nova edificia ex lapidibus quadratis et sculptilis constructa per Robertum Corbett armigerum seniorem fratrem predicti Ricardi Corbett domini nunc, quorum fenestre adhuc non sunt vitreate preter una Camera, nec cetere partes inde complete preter coeptura eorundem, Tegul Cornubie, Et eadem edificia se extendunt in longitudine ab oriente in occidente (cum amplo prespectu in Austru) as sexaginta passus, unacum quodam diverticulo versus boream ad quadraginta passus.

'In quorum ambitu et circitu est una magna et Ampla Aula, cum largis fenestris in eadem, et unum amplium Cenaculum, et sex alie camere et cubiculi in diversis locis eiusdem structure, unacum quodam novo promptuario et novo vinario cellario suberaneis ibidem, Et in altitudine et summitate predictor edificiorum est quoddam spaciosum et amplum deambulatorium sive Galirium pertendens se ad longitudinem eorundem edificiorum.'

17 Shrewsbury, Shropshire Archives, 322/4/4, Inventory or Sir Vincent

Corbet, 14 May 1623.

18 Court Book, *loc. cit.*, 'Et ex parte Australi novorum edificiorum ibidem scituatur unum gardinum cum uno pomario eidem adiumgente, in medio cuius gardini sunt diversa solaria in uno saxo sculpta et in latere eiusdem gardini est quedam parva domo vocata a kepe pro usu hortulani, simul cum uno fonte pro aquacione gardini predicti, Et sunt ibidem diversa ambulachra et arborea, et predicta gardinum et pomarium content in se dua acra et unam Rodam terrae.'

19 W R Wilson-North, 'Formal garden earthworks at Moreton Corbet Castle, Shropshire', in Mark Bowden, Donnie Mackay and Peter Topping (eds), *From Cornwall to Caithness, Some Aspects of British Field Archaeology*, British Archaeological Reports No. 209, 1989; Paul Stamper, *Historic Parks and Gardens of Shropshire*, Shrewsbury, 1996, 10.

20 London, National Archives, Public Record Office, WORK 14/ 2452 (Ministry of Works, Moreton Corbet Castle, Salop: Report upon its Condition from an Inspection made March 1938).

fragment of the north elevation is much simpler, without the columns, pilasters or sculptural detail that make the south elevation so memorable. However, parish registers for Moreton Corbet suggest that the house was occupied in 1605 by Sir Andrew's sixth son, Vincent, who, having already built a house at Acton Reynald, inherited Moreton Corbet in 1606 and was knighted the next year. An inventory made in 1623, following Sir Vincent's death, shows the house to have been well furnished, with 'a new dining chamber', 'a newe parlour', chambers for Mr Pelham and Sir Vincent, a chamber over the latter and a gallery awkwardly set over the 'new hall', unless, as in the Court Book, there is some confusion between the great hall and the high great chamber. Reference in the south wing to the 'joiners working room', containing a new bed, has encouraged suggestions that the house was not completed.[21] Nevertheless, a sketch of 1627 by John Smythson has a grey wash compatible with Delabole slates (Fig. 9).[22] The pattern of pedimented windows and shaped gables to the front, and alternating pedimented

windows to the rear, prompted Weaver to suggest that the upper parts of the house were re-modelled well after Robert Corbet's death.[23] Yet a second-floor band on the east elevation suggests that Robert Corbet's work reached at least this height, and the same stonework continues in the gables of

Fig. 10 (above): Chimney stack in the eastern part of the south range of Moreton Corbet Castle, *c.*1700

Fig. 11 (below): The Reverend Edward Williams, *The south and east ranges of Moreton Corbet Castle from the south-east*, 16 September 1790

21 Shrewsbury, Shropshire Archives, 322/4/4, Inventory or Sir Vincent Corbet, 14 May 1623.
22 Mark Girouard, 'The Smythson collection of the Royal Institute of

British Architects', *Architectural History*, V, 1962, 144.
23 Weaver, *op. cit.*

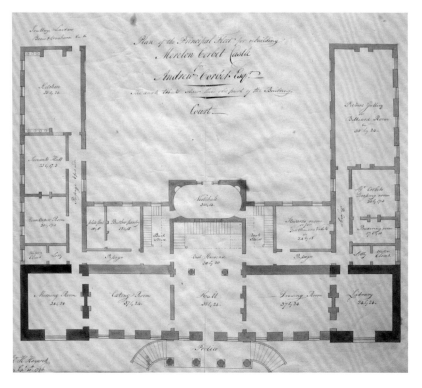

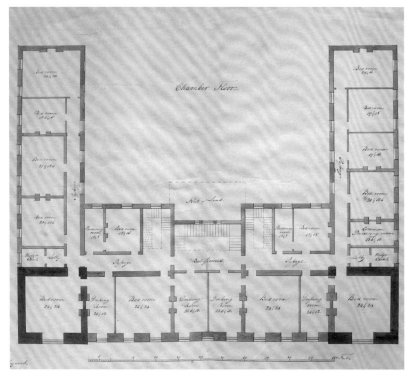

his south façade (Fig. 3). The closest comparison in England is with the remodelling of Longleat in the 1570s by Alan Maynard and Robert Smythson, for which drawings survive showing pedimented gables with scroll decoration.[24]

Sir Vincent was succeeded in March 1623 by his eldest son, another Andrew, who was followed in 1637 by his son Vincent, then still a student. An ardent royalist, he was created a baronet in 1642. Being strategically placed on the River Roden between the royalist stronghold of Shrewsbury and parliamentarian Wem and Market Drayton, Moreton Corbet enjoyed a lively Civil War. In January and February 1644, it was taken by the parliamentarians, but recovered by Sir Vincent. But when Montgomery fell in July, Sir Vincent sent most of his force to try to retake the town. Moreton Corbet was duly attacked on 8 September 1644 by elements of the army of Sir William Brereton, a force of some 110 men against 70 in the castle.[25] Sir Vincent got a back-handed compliment in the size of the heavy composition he had to pay – £1,588 and a yearly payment of £80 – and he never recovered Moreton Corbet, dying in London in December 1656.

The Shrewsbury School drawings record a date stone on a chimney of '1667 SVC' (Fig. 10), a reference to the second baronet, another Sir Vincent, who seems to have lived at Moreton Corbet until his death in 1680. Sadly, however, his heir, another Sir Vincent, died aged 19 when still at Christ Church College, Oxford. The estate passed to the descendants of the first baronet's younger brother, Robert, for whom a new baronetcy was created in the early 19th century and who hold the freehold of Moreton Corbet today.[26] These later Corbets preferred Acton Reynald, and Moreton Corbet was slowly abandoned in the 18th century. In the drawings of c.1700 at Shrewsbury School the great hall is shown unroofed.[27] A painting certainly produced before 1767 and probably by about 1730 shows the south range roofless and the great hall oriel fallen.[28] However, a drawing made shortly after the church's acquisition of pinnacles in 1767–9 shows little further deterioration since 1730 (Fig. 7),[29] and a roof is shown in Girtin's curiously foreshortened

24 Mark Girouard, *Robert Smythson and the English Country House*, New Haven and London, 1983, 5.
25 Paul M Rumfry, *Moreton Corbet Castle 1066–1700, An Open-Day Special*, Worcester, 1999, 24–6.
26 The baronetcy was extinguished by the death of Sir John Corbet, and Moreton Corbet is now held by Mr Christopher Corbet, who was born Russell [I am grateful to Mr James Lawson for this information].
27 Shrewsbury, Shrewsbury School, Library, S.IX.100.

28 Mr James Lawson tells me that the painting is framed in the over-mantel of the dining room of Swan Hill Court, Shrewsbury, built for the second earl of Bath in 1761–2 [Julia Ionides, *Thomas Farnolls Pritchard*, Ludlow, 1999]. A photograph is held at Swindon, English Heritage, National Monuments Record Centre, Y.877/1, made in 1955, when the painting was described as in the possession of Dr C Lawson-Stote.
29 Shrewsbury, Shropshire Archives, B4295.

drawing from the north, known from engravings.[30] But a watercolour by the Reverend Edward Williams of 16 September 1790 shows the house entirely unroofed, most of the centre part of the south elevation fallen, and a brick carriage entrance formed in the western bay of the south front (Fig. 11).[31]

In 1796 another Andrew Corbet commissioned proposals from John Hiram Haycock (1759–1830), the second of four generations of architect-builders of that name who worked in and around Shrewsbury, and who were responsible for many of the town's public buildings in the 1790s and 1800s. Haycock's drawings, dated 10 September 1796, show that he proposed to incorporate part of Robert Corbet's south range, adding wings at either end on the north side (Figs 12 and 13).[32] His design drove a long hall and stairwell through the centre of the range to new staircases and service rooms at the rear. Instead Haycock extended Acton Reynald Hall for Sir Andrew in 1800, ending any intentions that the Corbet family may have entertained of returning to their eponymous seat.[33]

Views of Moreton Corbet in the 19th-century show it as a romantic ruin. W Emans's view, from *Picturesque Views in Shropshire*, of 1831, sets the tone for this more romantic image.[34] In early photographs a farmhouse is shown to the south-west more prominently than in the 18th-century drawings.[35] The 1588 Court Book describes a dairy west of the new range surviving from Sir Andrew Corbet's work.[36] The farmhouse survived until shortly before 1901, when photographs in Manchester Public Library show the south wing in a precarious state, with much fallen stone (Fig. 14, see page 36).[37] The final part of the great hall window seems to have collapsed around the same time. Moreton Corbet was surveyed by the Ministry of Works in 1938 and passed into guardianship in 1949 (Fig. 15); there was briefly a custodian's hut, but from the 1970s the site was no longer manned. The new research, into the landscape in the 1980s and the buildings in the 1990s, has shown that Robert Corbet built a complete country house, with a great hall and formal landscape, as well as the surviving range we see today.

ACKNOWLEDGEMENTS

I am grateful to the Chairman and Governing Body of Shrewsbury School for permission to publish the volume of drawings of Moreton Corbet Castle, and to Mr James Lawson, the Librarian of Shrewsbury School in 1991, for his generous help and advice. I would also like to thank Prof Andrew Saint for his translations from the Court Book, used here, and Mr Richard Hewlings for investigating Robert Corbet's friendship with Sir Philip Sidney.

Fig. 12 (facing page top): John Hiram Haycock, proposed ground-floor plan, Moreton Corbet Castle, 10 September 1796

Fig. 13 (facing page bottom): John Hiram Haycock, proposed first-floor plan, Moreton Corbet Castle, 10 September 1796

Fig. 15 (above): The west end of the south range of Moreton Corbet Castle from the south-west, in 1947, shortly before it was taken into the guardianship of the Ministry of Works

30 Shrewsbury, Rowley's House Museum, SHYMS, FA/1991/184, attributed to Lady Philips, *c.*1842.
31 Shrewsbury, Shropshire Archives, 6001/372/2 (Reverend Edward Williams, *Views of Shropshire Churches*, II), number 66.
32 Shrewsbury, Shrewsbury School, Library, S.IX.100, *cit.*
33 Howard Colvin, *Biographical Dictionary of British Architects 1600–1840*, New Haven and London, 1995, 482.
34 Shrewsbury, Shropshire Archives, 288/14, W Emans, *Picturesque*

Views in Shropshire, 1831.
35 Shrewsbury, Shropshire Archives, 4470/2/34, photograph taken for the *Shrewsbury Journal*, n.d.
36 Court Book, *loc. cit.*, 'Est ibidem ad finem occidentalem novorum edificiorum predicti Roberti Corbett una domus lactearea vocata a dayrie howse dum doubus cameras infra in eadem, et supra est una camera et duo conclavia cum uno portico, in altitudine eorundem.'
37 Copy at Swindon, English Heritage, National Monuments Record.

The Staircase from Anderson Place, Newcastle upon Tyne

Martin Roberts

Anderson Place, Newcastle, demolished for the construction of Grey Street in 1834 or 1835, was in appearance a country house within a town, and a leader of 17th-century architectural fashion in the north-east. This article is the first to analyse its development. In 1980 a letter from the Newcastle architect John Dobson was found, suggesting that the staircase from Anderson Place was reused at Brinkburn Priory, but examination of Brinkburn Priory House failed to identify it. In 2001 the author discovered a magnificent 17th-century staircase in pieces, stored in the roof of the priory stables, doubtless the staircase from Anderson Place, and he has now reconstructed the whole staircase on paper.

Fig. 3: A view of Anderson Place in 1825

ANDERSON PLACE

Anderson Place, probably the largest private house within a walled English town, occupied an open site just inside the northern length of Newcastle's medieval walls (Fig. 1). The site was that of two suppressed religious houses. The eastern part, nearer Pilgrim Street, was that of the Greyfriars, whose buildings were bought by Robert Anderson in 1580; the larger western part, nearer Newgate Street, was that of the priory of St Bartholomew, also bought by Anderson, whose grounds were thereafter known as The Nuns or Nuns' Field.[1] According to Henry Bourne, Newcastle's earliest historian, writing in 1736, Anderson pulled down the priory buildings to prevent them being used as a 'Recepticle for Scots and Unfreemen', replacing them with a garden ('a very pleasant place'), and 'out of the Ruins of the Fryery', he built 'a Princely House, ... very stately and magnificent'.[2] It was evidently princely enough to accommodate the famed Scots commander, the earl of Leven, after the fall of Newcastle to the Scots in 1644, and the captive Charles I for nine months in 1646.[3] On Speed's map of 1610 it is called the 'Newe House'.[4]

Anderson Place was demolished in 1834 or 1835 for the construction of Grey Street. Its architectural history can only be inferred from the graphic evidence, of which the earliest is the view from the east by Leonard Knyff, probably made between 1697 and 1703, and published in 1707 (Fig. 2).[5] Knyff showed the house in the eastern (Greyfriars) part of the 13-acre site, which was divided into a number of parterres. The open Nuns' Field lay to the west. Two ranges of stables and other offices bordered the eastern, Pilgrim Street, edge of the site, either side of a pedestrian gate, which opened onto a path leading to the principal entrance. The ridge of the main roof ran north–south, and we may conjecture that this covered the 'Newe House' built by Robert Anderson after 1580, or even his adaptation of the friary buildings.

The central gable on the east side differed from all the others in being straight-sided, and set some way back from the east elevation, and it may be that it originally roofed a porch, masked by later work. The four other gables on this elevation were shaped, and may belong to a later phase, or even two phases, as the outer pair were narrower than the inner pair. The outer pair rose above two-storey bay windows, mullioned and transomed, whose lights were returned on their side elevations. It is possible that they had originally

---

1 Sydney Middlebrook, *Newcastle upon Tyne: Its Growth and Achievements*, Newcastle upon Tyne, 1950, 46; Richard Welford, *Men of Mark twixt Tyne and Tweed*, London, 1895, I, 55–6; John Brand, *The History and Antiquities of the Town and County of the Town of Newcastle upon Tyne*, Newcastle upon Tyne, 1789, I, 341.
2 Henry Bourne, *The History of Newcastle upon Tyne*, Newcastle upon Tyne, 1736, 50, 85.

3 Welford, *loc. cit.*
4 E[neas] Mackenzie, *A Descriptive and Historical Account of the Town and County of Newcastle upon Tyne*, Newcastle upon Tyne, 1827, I, 178.
5 Leonard Knyff and Jan Kip, *Britannia Illustrata ...* , London, 1707, pl 54. Reprint, edited by John Harris and Gervase Jackson-Stops, Bungay, 1984, 116–17: Knyff's drawings were probably begun in 1697, and handed to Kip for engraving in 1703.

Fig. 1: Thomas Oliver, *Plan of the Town and County of Newcastle upon Tyne and the Borough of Gateshead and their respective Suburbs Shewing the Buildings and different Properties contained therein from an Actual Survey by T Oliver, Architect and Surveyor*, 1830, detail. Anderson Place lies on the west side of Pilgrim Street

terminated wings which would have given the house the typical Elizabethan E-plan, evident in Northumberland at Ford Castle by 1589[6] and at Chipchase Castle in 1621,[7] and in the variant H-plan type at Westholme Hall, County Durham in 1606.[8] A two-storeyed porch, some way in advance of the central gable, also had a mullioned and transomed window, a balustraded parapet, and a door flanked by pairs of columns on high bases (Fig. 3, see page 46), comparable to those at Belsay Castle, Northumberland, dated 1614, and Gibside, County Durham, dated 1620.[9] It had a small flat

roof, reached by a door in the central gable.

It may be that the end wings and the porch represent a second phase, distinguished (in the former case) by the gable shape, but, from the details of the windows and doors, hardly any later than the first quarter of the 17th century. If, on the other hand, wings and porch were all part of the first phase, the dissimilarity of the gables would suggest that those on the wings were later rebuilt in conformity with the inner pair of gables. The latter surmount windows of a different shape from the others, later shown sashed, and possibly even sashed at the time of Knyff's view; they are evidently no earlier than the second half of the 17th century. The fabric surmounted by the inner gables is likely to have been an infill of the two small courts left by the E-plan. A similar development can be seen at Middridge Grange, Shildon, County Durham, where the forecourt of a single-pile house with end wings, built in 1578, was filled in in the later 17th century, giving the same unequal gable widths as at Anderson Place.[10] At the latter it produced a flat elevation with widely spreading gables linked at their bases, unrelated to the bay rhythm of the lower storeys. In this and in the particular gable shape it resembles Norton Conyers, near Ripon, although the Anderson Place gables had a more complex profile than those of Norton Conyers, and they were further embellished by dwarf obelisks and ball finials (Figs 3 and 4).[11] Norton Conyers may have been rebuilt by Sir Richard Graham, who died in 1653.[12] Its affinity with Anderson Place suggests that this phase of the latter may be due to Sir Francis Anderson (1614–79), whose likely descent from Robert Anderson cannot be verified. Sir Francis, like Sir Richard Graham, was a zealous royalist, who fled abroad after the fall of Newcastle in 1644, and was imprisoned for plotting a rising in 1655. He was MP for the city in the Convention, Cavalier and first Exclusion Parliaments, and mayor in 1662–3.[13] He may have owned the house when he was knighted (as sheriff) in 1641, but he certainly did so in 1665, by which time it was

6 Christopher Hussey, 'Ford Castle, Northumberland–I', *Country Life*, LXXXIX, 11 January 1941, 34.
7 Gordon Nares, 'Chipchase Castle, Northumberland–I', *Country Life*, CXIX, 14 June 1956, 1293, and 21 June 1956, 1362.
8 Nikolaus Pevsner (revised Elizabeth Williamson), *The Buildings of England County Durham*, Harmondsworth, 1983, 500.
9 Christopher Hussey, 'Old Belsay Castle, Northumberland', *Country Life*, LXXXVIII, 19 October 1940, 350; Richard Hewlings and Stephen Anderton, *Belsay Hall Garden and Castle Northumberland*, London, 1994, 42; Christopher Hussey, 'Gibside, County Durham', *Country Life*, CXI, 8 February 1952, 354.
10 A J Arnold, R E Howard and C D Litton, *Middridge Grange Co Durham, Scientific Dating Report*, English Heritage Research Department Report Series No. 9/2006; Martin Roberts, draft report on

Middridge Grange for the North East Vernacular Architecture Group.
11 These details are not visible in Knyff's view, but are in views of *c.*1780, 1812 and 1825 [A W Purdue, *The Ship That Came Home: The Story of a Northern Dynasty*, London, 2004, frontispiece, 27, 28, and 30].
12 Gervase Jackson-Stops, 'Norton Conyers, Yorkshire–II', *Country Life*, CLXXX, 9 October 1986, 1095; R T Spence, 'The First Sir Richard Graham of Norton Conyers and Netherby, 1583–1653', *Northern History*, XVI, 1980, 120.
13 Basil Duke Henning, *The History of Parliament: The House of Commons 1660–1690*, London, 1983, I, 532–3; Welford, *op. cit.*, 56; Roger Howell, *Newcastle upon Tyne and the Puritan Revolution*, Oxford, 1967, 160; C H Hunter Blair, 'The Mayors and Lord Mayors of Newcastle upon Tyne 1216–1940 and the Sheriffs of the County of Newcastle upon Tyne 1399–1940', *Archaeologia Aeliana*, 4th ser, XVIII,

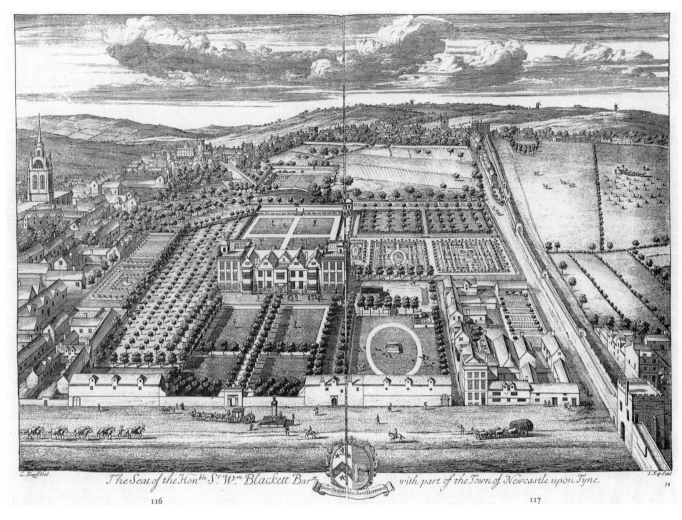

The Seat of the Honble S^r. W^m. Blackett Bar^tt. *with part of the Town of Newcastle upon Tyne*

116 117

Fig. 2: Leonard Knyff, *The Seat of the Honble S^r. W^m. Blackett Bar^tt.* [Anderson Place], engraved by Jan Kip, by 1707

called Anderson Place.[14] However, he was in chronic financial difficulty from 1646 until his death, so this phase may have preceded this date.

Symmetrically placed blocks at the north and south ends of the house, in a different style again, are evidently further additions. They were three storeys high, and had flat parapeted roofs and small roof pavilions. The Queen's House at Greenwich, designed by Inigo Jones in 1616–19,[15]

may have set the fashion for flat roofs with parapets and roof pavilions, and the fashion was maintained by ostentatious houses such as Thoresby House, Nottinghamshire, designed by Wren or Hawksmoor *c.*1685–7.[16] At least nine country houses in Yorkshire had adopted the fashion by the time Samuel Buck recorded them in 1719–20.[17] Five of these can be dated to between 1676 and 1704, three of them in the 1690s.[18]

1940, 66, 72, 75; C H Hunter Blair, 'Members of Parliament for Northumberland and Newcastle upon Tyne 1559–1831', *Archaeologia Aeliana*, 4th ser, XXIII, 1945, 143–4, 145.

14 Middlebrook, *op. cit.*, 299; Henning, *loc. cit.*

15 John Harris, Stephen Orgel and Roy Strong, *The King's Arcadia: Inigo Jones and the Stuart Court*, London, 1973, 155, Fig. 287; Giles Worsley, *Classical Architecture in Britain: The Heroic Age*, New Haven and London, 1995, 7.

16 Colen Campbell, *Vitruvius Britannicus*, I, London, 1715, 91; Howard Colvin, *Biographical Dictionary of British Architects 1600–1840*, New Haven and London, 1995, 951.

17 Ivan Hall, *Samuel Buck's Yorkshire Sketchbook*, Wakefield, 1979, illustrates seven, namely Wheatley Hall [66], Sprotborough Hall [69], Cannon Hall [128], Hunmanby Hall [337], Acklam Hall [350], Sedbury Hall [357], and Swinton Hall [387]. To these Newby Park [John Cornforth, 'Designs for Newby', *Country Life*, CLXVI, 19 July, 1979, 173] and Myton Hall may be added. Buck recorded another seven with flat roofs, but without roof pavilions, namely Middlethorp

Hall [43], Burn Hall [50], Stainborough Hall [100], Aldwarke Hall [116], Kippax Hall [218], Newbiggin Hall [330] and Yorke House, Richmond [380]. To these Halnaby Hall [Christopher Hussey, 'Halnaby Hall, Yorkshire–I', *Country Life*, LXXIII, 1 April 1933, 334–5] can be added. Aldwarke and Kippax Halls both had such substantial chimneys as to produce an effect similar to that of roof pavilions.

18 The dated examples are Newby, begun after 1676, but before 1690 [Newcastle upon Tyne, Northumberland Record Office, Blackett of Matfen MSS, ZBL 273]; Myton, 1693 [*The Victoria History of the Counties of England, Yorkshire North Riding*, London, 1923, 157]; Swinton, 1695–7 [John Cornforth, 'Swinton, Yorkshire–I', *Country Life*, CXXXIX, 7 April 1966, 790]; Sprotborough, 1696–1700 [Colvin, *op. cit.*, 354]; Cannon Hall, 1700–4 [Sheffield Archives, Sp. St. 60674/1]. Two of those without roof pavilions can also be dated, namely, Middlethorp, before 1702 [Giles Worsley, 'Middlethorpe Hall, Yorkshire', *Country Life*, CLXXVIII, 12 December 1985, 1896]; Stainborough, 1709 [John Harris, 'Bodt and Stainborough', *Architectural Review*, CXXX, July 1961, 34].

Fig. 4: Anderson Place in 1812

Locally, Newcastle Mansion House, built in 1692 in a conspicuous position between The Close and the river front, had roof pavilions and a large, flat, parapeted roof.[19] The terminal blocks of Anderson Place are therefore likely to fall into this date range.

The windows in the two blocks at either end were sashed. The earliest documented sash windows in the north-east were at Croxdale Hall, County Durham (1704), although Tullie House, Carlisle (1689) may have been sashed from the start.[20] But the distinctive feature of the windows of Anderson Place is that they were vertically linked by masonry panels slightly

proud of the remaining wall face. Ornamental panels between ground and first-floor windows were a feature of Althorp House, Northamptonshire, built by Anthony Ellis in 1666–8.[21] Panels in that position, slightly proud of the wall face, occur at Cliveden House, Buckinghamshire, designed by William Winde c. 1676–8, Petworth House, Sussex, c. 1688–90, and Dyrham Park, Gloucestershire, designed by William Talman in 1698.[22] Although otherwise unusual in the south, this detail appeared on 16 country houses in Yorkshire, three houses in York, one country house in Cumberland, one in Northumberland, and one other house in Newcastle itself.[23] Eight of these northern houses can be dated to between 1674 and 1700.[24] The other Newcastle example, at 53 Westgate Road, still survives, but, although illustrated on Corbridge's map of 1723 (as Lady Clavering's house), its date is not known.[25] One of the Yorkshire houses was Newby Hall, begun before 1690, and the Northumbrian house was Wallington Hall, begun after 1689.[26]

This is no coincidence, for in 1675 Anderson Place was sold to Sir William Blackett (1621–80), first baronet, MP for the city from 1673 to 1680, a merchant with extensive coal- and lead-mining interests, and its name reverted to Newe House.[27] He left Anderson Place to his third son, William (1647–1705), who was also created a baronet in 1685, and was MP for the city from 1685 to 1690, 1695 to 1700, and 1705. The second Sir William bought the Wallington estate in Northumberland from Sir John Fenwick in September 1689, and evidently built Wallington

19 The Mansion House was illustrated from the south by Samuel Buck in 1745 [Ralph Hyde, *A Prospect of Britain: The Town Panoramas of Samuel and Nathaniel Buck*, London, 1994, pl 48], and from the north by Mackenzie, *op. cit.*, I, opposite page 229. Its date comes from Newcastle, Tyne and Wear Archives, Newcastle upon Tyne Chamberlain's Accounts, 543/69. Heaton Hall, just north-east of the city, built at an unknown date before 1745, may also have had a flat parapeted roof, not necessarily with roof pavilions [Hyde, *loc. cit.*].
20 Durham, Durham County Record Office, D/Sa/E 631; Nikolaus Pevsner, *The Buildings of England Cumberland and Westmorland*, Harmondsworth, 1967, 100.
21 Colen Campbell, *Vitruvius Britannicus*, II, London, 1717, pls 96–7; Colvin, *op. cit.*, 341.
22 Kerry Downes, *English Baroque Architecture*, London, 1966, pls 170, 135, 137, 149; Colvin, *op. cit.*, 341, 1067 and 953.
23 Hall, *op. cit.*, illustrates 12 of the Yorkshire examples, Bell Hall [45], Camblesforth Hall [51], Norton Priory [63], Sprotborough Hall [69], Banks Hall [126], North Bierley Hall [155], Ryshworth Hall [158], Ness Hall [306], Hunmanby Hall [337], Acklam Hall [350], Sedbury Hall [357] and Swinton Hall [387]. Knyff and Kip, *op. cit.*, illustrate another two, Ribston Hall [pl 61] and Whixley Hall [pl 78]. To these can be added Myton Hall and Newby Hall [John Cornforth, 'Newby Hall, North Yorkshire–I', *Country Life*, CLXV, 7 June 1979, 1802], although the panels at Newby are, like those at Althorp, not proud of the wall face. The three houses in York are Cromwell House, Ogleforth [Royal Commission on Historical Monuments (England), *City of York*, V, London, 1981, 172 and pl 144], The Red House, Duncombe Place

[*ibid.*, 130–1 and pl 139] and No. 2 Pavement, although in the last case the panels are as at Newby. The Cumberland house is Hutton-in-the-Forest [John Cornforth, 'Hutton-in-the-Forest, Cumberland–I', *Country Life*, CXXXVII, 4 February 1965, 232–3].
24 The dated examples are Ribston, 1674 [Gervase Jackson-Stops, 'Ribston Hall, Yorkshire', *Country Life*, CLIV, 11 October 1973, 1051]; Bell, 1680 [*The Victoria History of the Counties of England, York East Riding*, III, Oxford, 1976, 78]; Acklam, which has the date 1684 in the plaster ornament [Nikolaus Pevsner, *The Buildings of England Yorkshire: The North Riding*, Harmondsworth, 1966, 55]; Hutton-in-the-Forest, c. 1685, but certainly before 1700 [Colvin, *op. cit.*, 66]; Myton, 1693 [*The Victoria History of the Counties of England, Yorkshire North Riding*, London, 1923, 157]; Swinton, 1695–7 [Cornforth, 'Swinton ...', *loc. cit.*]; and Sprotborough, 1696–1700 [Colvin, *op. cit.*, 354]. Newby was begun after 1676, but before 1690 [Newcastle, Northumberland Record Office, Blackett of Matfen MSS, ZBL 273].
25 Raymond Frostick, 'James Corbridge and his Plan of Newcastle upon Tyne 1723', *Archeologia Aeliana*, 5th ser, XXXII, 2003, 172; Middlebrook, *op. cit.*, between 82 and 83.
26 For Newby, see Northumberland Record Office, Blackett of Matfen MSS, ZBL 273. For Wallington, see John Cornforth, 'Wallington, Northumberland–I', *Country Life*, CXLVII, 16 April 1970, 854–8. Wallington was only bought by Sir William Blackett, its builder, in September 1689 [Henning, *op. cit.*, I, 663–4].
27 Henning, *op. cit.*, I, 662–3; Hunter Blair, 'Mayors ... ', *cit.*, 71, 73; Hunter Blair, 'Members ... ', *cit.*, 144–5; J R Boyle, *Vestiges of Old Newcastle and Gateshead*, Newcastle upon Tyne, 1890, 126.

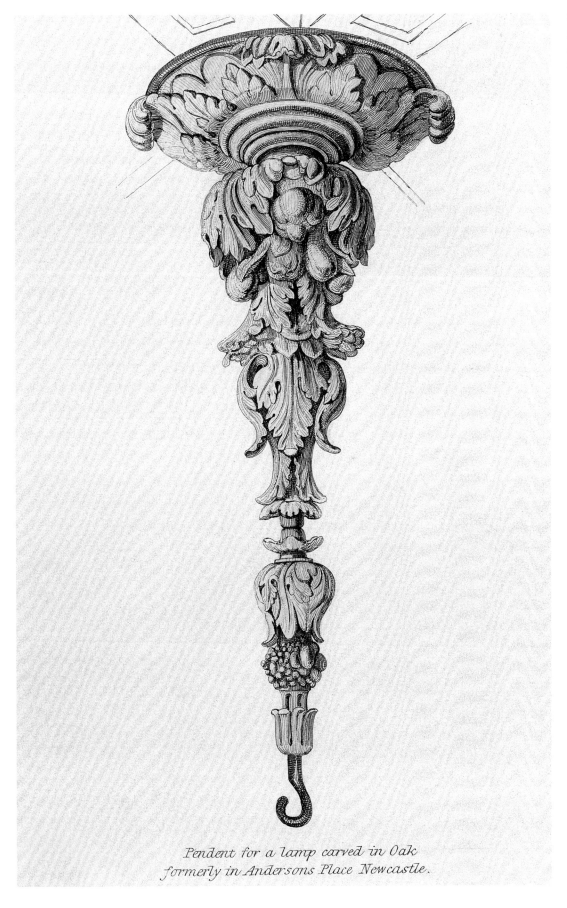

Fig. 5: William Scott Bell, pendant finial from Anderson Place, drawn in 1851

Pendent for a lamp carved in Oak formerly in Andersons Place Newcastle.

Fig. 6: Chimneypiece
formerly at Anderson Place

Hall shortly thereafter.[28] The eldest son, Sir Edward Blackett (1649–1718), who had inherited their father's baronetcy, bought the Newby estate, near Ripon, after his marriage to a Yorkshire heiress in 1676, and had begun to build Newby Hall before his brother had bought Wallington.[29] Their resemblance to Newby and Wallington therefore suggests that the terminal blocks at Anderson Place are therefore most likely to have been built by the second Sir William Blackett, owner from 1680 to 1705; indeed Bourne, writing in 1736, named him as the builder.[30] Sir William may also have been responsible for other features apparently of this date. A remarkably carved or modelled pendant finial, recorded in 1851, but whose whereabouts are now unknown, came from the hall and appears to belong to this phase (Fig. 5).[31] Not recorded, however, were 'the curious and well-painted ceilings … in the interior of this spacious mansion', noted by Mackenzie in 1827; but such ceilings were the fashion of Sir William Blackett's day.[32]

Knyff shows that the gate giving onto Pilgrim

Street, east of the house, was in a different style again. It had a round-headed door, with moulded voussoirs, but below the imposts the jambs were horizontally channelled, and all of this was recessed in an unmoulded rectangular panel. Doors and windows recessed within unmoulded panels were an introduction of Hawksmoor's, proposed by him, for instance, for the gatehouse arch of Ravensdowne Barracks, Berwick upon Tweed, in 1717.[33] Horizontally channelled jambs with moulded voussoirs is a combination devised either by Hawksmoor or by Vanbrugh; its earliest appearance is on the first floor of the north front of Castle Howard, begun in 1700.[34] In Northumberland it occurs on the office arcades of Seaton Delaval, begun in 1719,[35] and at Eglingham Hall, which has a date stone of 1704 and a rainwater head dated 1728.[36] It seems unlikely that Hawksmoor or Vanbrugh would have designed the gate of Anderson Place, but, if not, it must have been designed by someone who had been in contact with them, such as William Etty, mason at Castle Howard, and executant architect of Seaton Delaval and Morpeth Town Hall (begun by 1716).[37] The gate at Anderson Place was apparently earlier than these, and is evidently the earliest instance of Hawksmoor's or Vanbrugh's influence in the north-east. If Etty designed it, it would be his earliest known work.

Behind it were four lawns, with statues in the centres of two of them, and there were four more lawns with central statues on the west side of the house. There may have been more statues in the elaborate parterres north of these last. Bourne noted that 'that Part of it which faces the Street, is thrown into Walks and Grass Plats, beautified with images', and 'The other Part of the ground on the West Side of it, is … adorned with many and the most beautiful Statues, and several other Curiosities', either of which could be the lead garden statues now at Wallington.[38] If so, they may have been Sir

28 Henning, *op. cit*., I, 663–4; Hunter Blair, 'Mayors … ', *cit*., 78–9, 82; Hunter Blair, 'Members … ', *cit*., 146–8.

29 Eveline Cruickshanks, Stuart Handley and D W Hayton, *The House of Commons 1690–1715*, Cambridge, 2002, III, 221–2.

30 Bourne, *op. cit*., 85, 'House … built out of the Ruins of this Friery; except the North and South ends of it, which were built by Sir Wm. Blackett, Bart., the Grand Father of the present possessor Walter Blackett, Esq.'. This was repeated by Brand, *op. cit*., in 1789, 'The two wings were added by Sir William Blackett, Bart. whose grand-daughter married its late lamented owner and inhabitant, Sir Walter Blackett, Bart.'

31 Simon Swynfen Jervis, 'Antiquarian Gleanings in the North of England', *Antiquaries Journal*, LXXXV, 2005, 331 and 347, pl 17. The finial masked a hook to hold a lantern; it is not clear whether it was carved wood or modelled plaster. In 1851 it belonged to G Rippon Esq, of South Shields.

32 Mackenzie, *op. cit*., I, 179.

33 Richard Hewlings, 'Hawksmoor's "Brave Designs for the Police"', in

John Bold and Edward Chaney (eds), *English Architecture: Public and Private*, London and Rio Grande, 1993, 223.

34 Downes, *English Baroque Architecture, cit*., pl 227; Charles Saumarez Smith, *The Building of Castle Howard*, London, 1990, 44.

35 Downes, *English Baroque Architecture, cit*., pl 272; Kerry Downes, *Vanbrugh*, London, 1977, 103, and pls 119–20.

36 Gervase Jackson-Stops, 'Eglingham Hall, Northumberland', *Country Life*, CLVIII, 27 November 1975, 1458, 1460.

37 Colvin, *op. cit*., 354–5. Morpeth Town Hall was built by the third earl of Carlisle, the builder of Castle Howard, and is thus attributed to Vanbrugh, but the building accounts do not confirm this. Instead they record payments to William Etty between September 1717 and November 1718 [Durham, University of Durham, Department of Palaeography and Diplomatic, Howard of Naworth MSS, Northumberland Estates, 108/13].

38 Purdue, *op. cit*., 61. The provenance of these statues is not explained.

Fig. 7: G Sonander, *The mansion of the late Sir Walter Blackett Bart.* [Anderson Place], published by Armstrong and Walker, presumably shortly after 1777, when Sir Walter died

William Blackett's additions to the gardens.

By 1745 the flat roofs of the end blocks had been replaced by double-pitched roofs.[39] A finely carved chimneypiece, apparently of *c.*1740 (Fig. 6), and a mid-18th-century wooden stair, which still survive *ex situ*, suggest that internal alterations were also made at that date.[40] By *c.*1777 the house had been extended by high garden walls flanking the outermost wings, each pierced by 18th-century Gothic doorways (Fig. 7). Also by that date two-centred arched doors with hood moulds had been formed in the two outer projecting bays on the east front, giving that elevation a total of three porches.[41] This perplexing arrangement, and the internal changes which it must reflect, may relate to a subdivision of the house, not otherwise known.[42] All this may have been done for Sir Walter Blackett (1708–77), second baronet, MP for the city from 1734 to 1777, who had inherited the estate from his uncle in 1728.[43] Sir Walter was a considerable patron of architecture, altering Wallington Hall between 1735 and 1753 (to the designs of Daniel Garrett), building St Nicholas's church library, Newcastle, in 1736 (to the design of Gibbs), and endowing Newcastle Infirmary

(built to Garrett's designs in 1751–2).[44]

In 1782, five years after the death of Sir Walter, Sir John Trevelyan, his nephew and heir, sold the house to George Anderson, a wealthy builder, not known to be a descendant of the earlier Andersons. His son Major George Anderson, a popular local philanthropist with an interest in improving the visual amenities of the town, renamed it Anderson Place.[45] By 1827 'the present spirited proprietor' had replaced the wooden gate which had concealed the view of the 'grand and noble mansion', presumably from Pilgrim Street, by 'an ornamental iron one, which exposes the beauties of this agreeable place'.[46] The iron gates formerly at Hermitage, Sheriff Hill, Gateshead, are also alleged to have come from Anderson Place, and may have been these.[47] In 1831, Major Anderson left it to his cousin Thomas Anderson, who sold it to the developer Richard Grainger in 1834.[48]

RICHARD GRAINGER AND JOHN DOBSON

By the mid-1820s 'the spirit of improvement was flourishing as never before' in Newcastle upon Tyne.[49] The area outside the walls to the north had

39 They are shown in the distance in Samuel Buck's view of Newcastle, 1745 [David Heslop, Brian Jobling and Grace McCombie, *Alderman Fenwick's House*, Newcastle upon Tyne, 2001, 28; Hyde, *loc. cit.*], and more explicitly in views of the house of *c.*1777, 1812 and 1825 [Purdue, *op.cit.*, 26, 28, 30].
40 Purdue, *op.cit.*, 36, 38.
41 *Ibid.*, 30.
42 I am grateful to Mrs Grace McCombie for this suggestion, and the possibilities which it suggests of research in the Blackett family papers.
43 Romney Sedgwick, *The House of Commons 1715–1754*, London, 1970, 464; Hunter Blair, 'Mayors ... ', *cit.*, 90, 93, 95, 97, 98; Hunter Blair, 'Members ... ', *cit.*,150–2. Sir Walter, who changed his name from Calverley, did not inherit either of the Blackett baronetcies, but that of his father, Sir Walter Calverley, first baronet. The third Sir William

Blackett (1689–1728), second baronet, from whom he inherited Anderson Place and Wallington, was his father-in-law as well as his uncle on his mother's side.
44 Colvin, *op. cit.*, 402, 393 and 395.
45 Boyle, *op. cit.*, 147; Welford, *op. cit.*, 59–61.
46 Mackenzie, *op. cit.*, I, 178–9.
47 Boyle, *op. cit.*, 126. But they had been removed by April 2006, so it was not possible to confirm this.
48 T E Faulkner, 'Early Nineteenth-century Planning of Newcastle-on-Tyne', *Planning Perspectives*, V, 1990, 149–67; Ian Ayris, *A City of Palaces: Richard Grainger and the Making of Newcastle-on-Tyne*, Newcastle upon Tyne, 1997; Welford, *op. cit.*, 61.
49 Thomas Faulkner and Andrew Greg, *John Dobson: Architect of the North East*, Newcastle upon Tyne, 2001, 43.

Fig. 8: Plan of Brinkburn Priory, showing the church and house, with the approximate position of the stair wing proposed in 1833

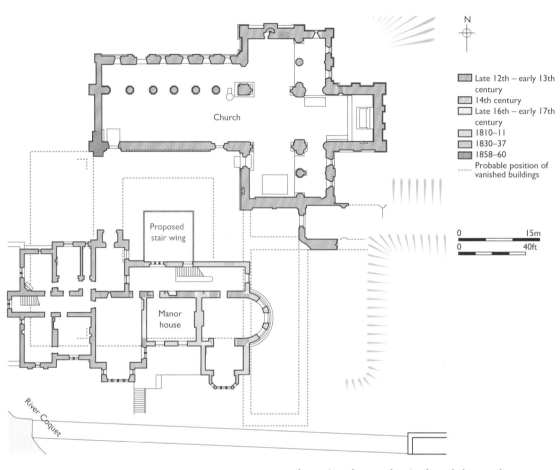

Fig. 9 (below): John Dobson, *North-west View of Brinkburn Priory*, as proposed in 1833

long since been urbanised, and the northern stretch of the wall had been demolished by 1827.[50] The 13 undeveloped acres of Anderson Place were thus by that time at the centre of the town, and an obvious attraction to all improvers. As early as 1783 the elder George Anderson had offered the estate to the Corporation, who were unable to accept it because of their own initiatives elsewhere in the town.[51] In the years that followed, the failure of the Corporation to purchase the estate disappointed many. Amongst them was the young architect John Dobson who published proposals for the land *c.*1825, with a new civic mansion house, a market place, square and central streets. The plans came to nothing but the aspiration remained in town maps of the period, marked with 'projected streets' through the Anderson Place estate.[52]

---

50 The wall is shown on a survey by John Dobson, dated 14 February 1815 [Newcastle, Northumberland Record Office, Blackett of Matfen MSS, ZBL 62/4], but not on the *Plan of Newcastle upon Tyne and Gateshead made by John Wood 1827* [Frank Graham, *Town Atlas of Northumberland and Durham by John Wood 1820–1827*, Newcastle upon Tyne, 1991]. I am grateful to Grace McCombie for this information.
51 Faulkner and Greg, *op. cit.*, 43.
52 *Ibid.*, 44. The projected streets were shown on John Wood's map of 1827 and Thomas Oliver's map of 1830, illustrated here as Fig. 1.

Thomas Anderson, however, evidently keen to leave Newcastle for the life of a country gentleman,[53] reached an agreement with the developer Richard Grainger in 1834, and Grainger presented his own plans to the Common Council of the town at the same time. When the council signed its agreement with Grainger and Anderson on 15 July, Grainger's workmen, assisted by the populace, took possession of Anderson Place that afternoon, and began levelling the ground for the New Market, designed by John Dobson, in the Nuns' Field.[54] Two watercolour views of the house are dated 1835, so it is possible that it survived a little longer, but not much, as it stood on the line of the centrepiece of the proposals, Grey Street, which was completed in 1837.[55] A number of features of the old house were salvaged and were incorporated into other properties. Amongst them was the staircase, the subject of this paper, recently discovered in pieces at Brinkburn Priory.

BRINKBURN PRIORY

Brinkburn Priory was an Augustinian monastery, whose early 13th-century church still survives. Its refectory in the south range and probably the neighbouring west range became a house in the 16th century (Fig. 8), later extended to form a rambling pile, sketched, in its partially ruined state, by Turner c.1801.[56] In 1810–11 Richard Hodgson, who had acquired it through marriage in 1809, rebuilt the upper floors on the surviving medieval basement, imposing a symmetrical plan, with simple Gothic detailing which successfully acknowledged the style of the great church beside it.[57]

In 1830 Hodgson's son, Major William Hodgson Cadogan, fortified by marriage to an heiress from Barbados, commissioned John Dobson to rebuild the western half of the building, on a much larger scale and in a severe Tudor Gothic style, redeemed by its picturesque composition. A view by Dobson, dated 1833, shows a square wing, wide enough to have accommodated an open well stair, projecting

north into the cloister garth (Fig. 9).[58] This wing was not built, and the rebuilding, completed by 1837, only included a modest dogleg service stair.[59] But the discovery of correspondence between Dobson and Major Hodgson Cadogan, reveals that Dobson negotiated the sale of a presumably more pretentious staircase from Anderson Place for reuse at Brinkburn.[60]

The covering letter from Dobson to Cadogan, then in London, was written in 1841, seven years after the demolition of Anderson Place. His professional relationship with Grainger had become increasingly strained, following the latter's ill-fated acquisition of the Elswick estate west of Newcastle in 1838–9.[61] In the letter Dobson calls Grainger 'a strange man', and hopes to 'bring him to act honestly in this transaction by preventing him from being a Rogue'. In the letter which Dobson enclosed he writes of Grainger's 'want of feeling', 'want of prudence', and 'strange behaviour', and complains that he has been treated 'so shamefully'. The Elswick enterprise proved financially disastrous for Grainger, and the 'present purpose' alluded to and emphasised in the

Fig. 10: Fragments of the staircase at Brinkburn Priory in 2003

53 He had bought the Kirkharle and Little Harle estates in 1833 [Welford, *op. cit.*, 62].
54 Faulkner and Greg, *op. cit.*, 46–8.
55 The two views were sold by Messrs Anderson and Garland, Newcastle upon Tyne, 23 March 2006, Fine Art Auction (135). The date is on the *verso* and may indicate the presentation or gift of the paintings, even after the demolition of the house. Mr David Heslop tells me that Lloyds Bank in Grey Street stands on the site of the house.
56 London, British Museum, Turner Bequest, J M W Turner, *Dunblane Abbey* (incorrectly endorsed), pencil drawing, c.1801; Newcastle upon Tyne, Laing Art Gallery, J M W Turner, *Brinkburn Priory*, pencil drawing, c.1801.
57 Graham Fairclough, 'Brinkburn Priory', *Archaeologia Aeliana*, 5th ser, VIII, 1980, 143–52.
58 Newcastle, Laing Art Gallery, Prints, H9458, J9135, John Dobson

(1787–1868), *North-west View of Brinkburn Priory*, 1833. An engraving by M J Starling is published in Thomas Rose, *Cumberland, Westmorland, Northumberland and Durham Illustrated*, London, 1832. This enigmatic illustration has avoided explanation until now. The substantial north wing shown, which might have been interpreted as a lost wing, can now be seen as Dobson's proposal.
59 Faulkner and Greg, *op. cit.*, 169. The terminal date is taken from the list of Dobson's works published in *The Newcastle Daily Journal* on 16 January 1865, shortly after his death.
60 Newcastle, Northumberland County Record Office, ZFE 158, 159, printed in full in the appendix. The correspondence was discovered by Richard Hewlings in 1980, drawn to the attention of Graham Fairclough, who noted it in *op. cit.*, 151, n.5, and thereafter filed. It was brought to the present author's attention by Grace McCombie.
61 Faulkner and Greg, *op. cit.*, 135.

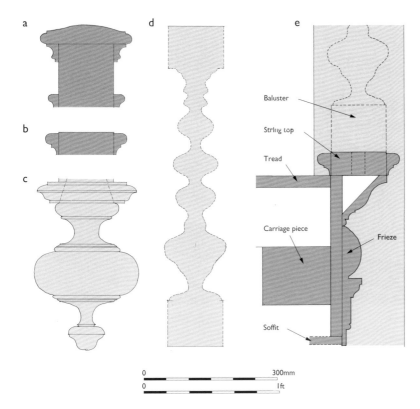

Baluster

String top

Tread

Carriage piece

Frieze

Soffit

0   300mm
0   1ft

Fig. 11: The Anderson Place staircase:

a. handrail

b. top of string

c. drop finial or pendant drop

d. ghost of half-baluster on side of newel

e. a reconstructed section through the string

enclosure, may have been some means of reducing his debts, particularly a debt to Dobson, by £250, which he alleged Dobson owed him for the acquisition not just of a staircase, but also of a ceiling from Anderson Place. But its result was to get Dobson to instruct his solicitor to 'proceed without delay against him so that I may not be further imposed upon by him'.

Dobson enclosed a copy of a letter sent by him to Percival Fenwick, his solicitor. First he dismissed the idea that he had acquired, or was responsible for, any ceiling. Thomas Anderson had apparently let Grainger have a ceiling by 'written agreement', which Dobson knew that Anderson still held, and which a Mr Joseph Anderson would show Fenwick the next day. The ceiling had been removed to Anderson's coach manufactory, where it was 'unfortunately burnt'.[62]

As for the staircase, Dobson implied that it had never been Grainger's property. Anderson had first given it to his uncle, George Anderson. Cadogan had then bought it for £35, the price expressed (and perhaps set) by Wardle, Grainger's clerk.

The financial arrangements between Atkinson, his uncle and Grainger may have been more involved than is made clear, but if Thomas had 'given' it to his uncle it must have been the latter, not Grainger, who sold it to Major Cadogan, Wardle only acting as a valuer. Dobson also implied that he was not the beneficiary, so it 'was quite unnecessary to trouble me about it'.

Dobson did, however, admit to being Cadogan's agent ('I only agreed to purchase the Staircase for the Major'), and that Cadogan had not yet paid ('the Major will pay'). The reason for this was that Grainger's workmen had 'injured the balusters', although Grainger had promised to restore them 'at any time'. Before selling it, however, 'Mr. Anderson', one of them, had removed the remaining unbroken balusters, which went to Benwell Tower, presumably sold to Thomas Crawhall, who had built it in 1830–1.[63] Cadogan had expressed 'disappointment ... in not getting the Balusters [and would] return the whole unless a considerable deduction [was] made from the £35'.

In setting out the bones of his case Dobson also revealed some details of the staircase's removal. Grainger's workmen did not injure the balusters in the course of dismantling it, because it was not they who did so. It was taken down by 'Mr Robert Wallace now the Town Surveyor ... employed by the Major'.[64] The injury took place before the stair had been given to Anderson's uncle, and if Cadogan had purchased it from the latter, Grainger's men must have damaged it some time before the stair was dismantled. Wallace had made a plan of the stair before dismantling it, 'to assist the workmen in putting it up', but 'the Staircase [had] not been put up'.

The material evidence confirms this. There are two stairs at Brinkburn Priory. The plain doglegged service stair in the western part, designed by Dobson, evidently dates from 1830–7, and cannot have come from Anderson Place. The main staircase, a long straight flight running along the north wall of the entrance hall of 1810–11, is designed in the same classical manner as the work around it, and is unlikely to have been reused.[65] In the absence of any sign of a stair from Anderson Place, the presumption might

62 By deduction it must have been impressive if one can assume that its value far exceeded that of the staircase. If the total cost of the transaction was £250, and the staircase was only valued at £35, even allowing for labour and transport charges, the ceiling commanded a significant price.

63 Colvin, *op. cit.*, 313.

64 Robert Wallace was initially a builder and joiner, and was employed by Dobson as clerk of works on Lilburn Tower in 1828–9. He later became town surveyor for Newcastle upon Tyne [Faulkner and Greg, *op. cit.*,145–6].

65 Aware of Hewlings's discovery of the correspondence, Fairclough, *op. cit.*, 151, n.5, presumed that this was the stair from Anderson Place. One of its windows was blocked by Dobson, and Fairclough thought that this was evidence that the stair was inserted in 1830–7. However,

be that Cadogan and Grainger did not resolve their disagreement over the balusters and that Cadogan returned the stair. However, in 2001 the stair was found.

Brinkburn Priory house was vacated *c.*1950 and in 1965 the present owners entered into a guardianship agreement with the Ministry of Public Buildings and Works, which became English Heritage in 1984. In early 2001, the owners of the Brinkburn estate, Mr and Mrs Hugh Fenwick, were planning to convert a stable block close to the priory. In the course of inspecting the stable the author and David Sherlock, then inspector of ancient monuments in English Heritage's north-east region, discovered lengths of oak handrail and newel posts resting on the tie beams of the roof trusses of the main coach house. It appeared to be the Anderson Place staircase, which had evidently not been re-erected. In 2003 the Fenwicks agreed to the transfer of the fragments into the care of English Heritage and in September of that year over 300 pieces were placed in store in the priory house (Fig. 10), completing the journey begun in 1834.

THE ANDERSON PLACE STAIRCASE –
A RECONSTRUCTION

The four handrails and their associated strings give the rake of the stair and enable a reconstruction of the complete balustrade, including the spacing of the missing balusters, but not their detailed design. That information comes from the corner newels, which provide both the ghosts of the missing baluster design and the full string section and alignment (Fig. 11). The constructional mortices on the newels confirm that the staircase had an open well, and the top landing section of handrail gives some dimensions to the space of the staircase hall once the dimensions of the surviving steps are added to the equation. The steps confirm the rake of the stair, the pendant drops add further detail, while the numerous pieces of dado wainscot confirm that the rising ramped balustrade was reflected against the wall of the staircase hall (Fig. 12).

The three handrail sections are not of equal length. If at least two sections matched it would be possible to determine a precise shape to the central well and so the whole hall. The anomaly can be accommodated if one flight is the lowest

Fig. 12: The Anderson Place staircase: reconstructed balustrade

0   1m
0   3ft

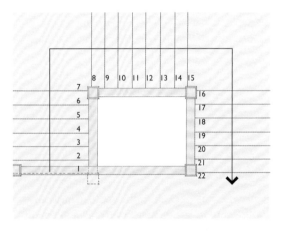

0   2m
0   6ft

Fig. 13: The Anderson Place staircase: reconstructed plan

flight, rising from the ground floor. If this was slightly shorter or longer than the flight on the opposite side of the well, it need not matter as only the latter's length controls the geometry of the staircase (Fig. 13). The fragments comprise a staircase rising from ground to first floor, terminating in the long landing section (Fig. 14). Evidently it cannot have risen to the roof.

The reconstruction gives a floor to floor height

---

the blocked window is not cut by the stair, and close examination shows that it was blocked by Dobson to provide a fireplace in the unheated small room at the top of the stair. This room lay above the unheated ground-floor entrance lobby and must have been one of the coldest spots in the house [Faulkner and Greg, *op. cit.*, 62, followed Fairclough]. However, John Grundy, Grace McCombie, Peter Ryder and Humphrey Welfare, *The Buildings of England Northumberland,* London, 1992, 202, make no such assumption.

of 11ft, enough to allow for a low ground floor at Anderson Place, but inadequate to rise through the 14ft of the ground floor of the house at Brinkburn. It is surprising that Robert Wallace's survey of the staircase *in situ* had not alerted both architect and client to the difficulties before it was actually moved up to Brinkburn. Changing the angle of the staircase or introducing longer flights were impossible, given the strict constraints dictated by the joinery. But this may explain why the staircase was never installed.

THE ANDERSON PLACE STAIRCASE IN CONTEXT
Other staircases in the North-East provide some dated comparisons. The use of stained or painted oak, the closed string and the panelled risers are found in 17th-century examples. But the plan form, the section of the handrail, the ramping and the pendant drops are found in examples dated just after 1700. The baluster type may be regionally unique.

Black stained and painted oak and pine were commonly used in Durham staircases, and are documented at Durham Castle in 1662 and Auckland Castle in 1663.[66] There are painted stairs in Durham, pine at Abbey Cottage, Dun Cow Lane (*c.*1665–70) and at 59 Old Elvet (*c.*1695–1700), and oak at 12 South Bailey.[67]

The closed string with a pulvinated frieze is found in 17th-century Durham, though there they are usually deeper, and sometimes carved. At Abbey Cottage and at Sir John Duck's House, 39 Silver Street, also of *c.*1665–70, the stairs had vigorously carved pulvinated friezes, which crudely imitated the Black Stair in Durham Castle.[68] The late 17th-century stair at 22 North Bailey had a shallow pulvino the full width of the string.[69] By 1709 at the latest, the open string had appeared at the important staircase at Ryton Rectory, County Durham, a few miles west of Newcastle.[70]

The panelled risers on the stair itself are also found in Durham Castle (1662), whereas in Alderman Fenwick's House, Pilgrim Street,

Newcastle (*c.*1670) the risers have mouldings on their top and bottom edges, which are not returned at the ends to form panels.[71]

The staircase had an open well and rose round four sides of a staircase hall, lined with a panelled dado. If the delivered fragments are the complete staircase it only rose to the first floor, which would either suggest an 18th-century date or offer a very early example of the 18th-century form in the region. Bishop Cosin's Black Stair in Durham Castle, and the stairs in Bessie Surtees House (*c.*1658) and Alderman Fenwick's House, both in Newcastle, all rise to the roof.[72] The staircase at Acklam Hall, Yorkshire, largely of 1684, does the same, though the top flights are introductions of the early 20th century.[73] But in the 18th century, at the Eden House, 3 South Bailey, Durham (*c.*1730)[74] and 55 Westgate Road, Newcastle upon Tyne (*c.*1740–50),[75] the staircases only rise to the first floor.

The handrail section is large, broad and flat, unlike the upstanding and grippable rails of the late 17th-century examples at Alderman Fenwick's House, Bessie Surtees House and Durham Castle.

17th-century staircases in the region are not generally ramped, whereas 18th-century ones invariably are; the precise date of the introduction of this feature in the North-East has yet to be defined. The usual 18th-century model has balusters that are extended to take up the raised ramping. The solid spandrel in the ramping is always transitional, and is found at Arden Hall, Hawnby, Yorkshire (*c.*1700),[76] and at Judge's Court, Coney Street (early 18th-century), Cumberland House, 9 King's Staith (*c.*1710) and 70 Walmgate (early 18th-century), all in York.[77] Further south it is found at Belton House, Lincolnshire (1684–8) and Brickwall, Northiam, Sussex (*c.*1685). Closer, however, the interesting staircase at Ryton Rectory has a similar ramped and flat handrail, with pendant drops below the newels. But, differently, it has double bine twist

66 'The correspondence of John Cosin, D D, Part II', *Surtees Society*, LV, 1872, 90 (letter XXXVI), 362 (contract no. 6). The outer stonework of the stair tower at Durham Castle was under construction in February 1662, and may be coeval with the stair. A contract was let for painting the stair at Auckland Castle in 1663, presumably the *terminus ante quem*. There the bottom rail was 'painted traile work shadowed'. Although the stair at Durham castle gained the appellation 'The Black Stair' at some time, it is not clear that that was the original colour. But the use of oak for main members and pine for finer mouldings of the stair at the Old Hall, West Auckland, stylistically dated to *c.*1660–90, would have necessitated some unifying paint finish.
67 Francis F Johnson, *Historic Staircases in Durham City*, Durham, 1970, 24, 37, 32.
68 *Ibid.*, 24, 35.
69 *Ibid.*, 270.

70 Pevsner, *County Durham, cit.*, 394; D Higdon, *Notes on Holy Cross Rectory*, unpublished guide, [*c.*1990].
71 David Heslop, Brian Jobling and Grace McCombie, *Alderman Fenwick's House*, Newcastle upon Tyne, 2001, pls 2, 5 and 6.
72 Pevsner, *County Durham, cit.*, 215 and pl 65; Grundy, McCombie, Ryder and Welfare, *Northumberland, cit.*, 470; Heslop, Jobling and McCombie, *op. cit.*, 11–12 and 16–17.
73 Nikolaus Pevsner, *The Buildings of England Yorkshire: The North Riding*, Harmondsworth, 1966, 55 and pl 38b.
74 Johnson, *op. cit.*, 36.
75 Grundy, McCombie, Ryder and Welfare, *Northumberland, cit.*, 479.
76 Pevsner, *Yorkshire: The North Riding, cit.*, 185.
77 Royal Commission on Historic Monuments of England, *York Historic Buildings in the Central Area*, London, 1981, pls 190–1.

Copy letter from John Dobson to Percival Fenwick, undated

Mr Fenwick

I have this morning received Mr Clayton's letter to you inclosing Mr Grainger's charge against me of £250 for a Staircase & painted Ceiling taken from the mansion of the late Major Anderson and sent to Brinkburn Priory. I really cannot imagine how Mr G could have the confidence and want of feeling to have made such an attempt to impose on me by such a transaction as this, and of his want of prudence in doing so, as he must be well aware that I must know that Mr Anderson hold his written agreement to let him have the painted ceiling, etc and that Mr Anderson had the ceiling removed to Mr Anderson's Coach Manufactory where it remained until it was unfortunately burnt.

Mr Grainger must also know that Mr Anderson gave the Staircase to his uncle George Anderson after Mr Grainger's workmen had injured the balusters. Mr G expressed his regret to him that such had taken place, but that he would restore the balusters for him at any time.

I have just seen Mr Joseph Anderson who has promised to call on you tomorrow morning and let you see the agreement and will explain the facts above stated. I have also seen Mr George Anderson who will state to you the facts as regards the Staircase after the injury had been done to the staircase. Major H Cadogan purchased it for £35, and before it was taken away Mr Anderson had all the Balusters removed which were unbroken, and which are now at Benwell Tower, a right I did not know he had at the time when the Major purchased it, therefore the Staircase was reduced much in value.

Mr Robert Wallace now the Town Surveyor was employed by the Major to take the staircase down, who also made a plan of it, to assist the workmen in putting it up, and who must have a correct knowledge of the value of the Fragments sent, and of the whole transaction. His brother James Wallace also will tell you that Mr Wardle (Mr G's Clerk) told him that the price of the Staircase was £35.

Now as the Staircase most fortunately has not been put up it may be valued at any time. Should Mr Grainger refuse taking Mr Wallace's valuation of it, and I am quite certain the Major will pay it when ever called upon to do so, and that Mr G might have paid long ago had he sent in his charge for it. From the disappointment the Major expressed in not getting the Balusters he will return the whole unless a considerable deduction is made from the £35. It is quite clear that I only agreed to purchase the Staircase for the Major, and that was quite unnecessary to trouble me about it, unless to answer Mr Grainger's 'present purpose' therefore after such strange behaviour as this I cannot longer entertain that feeling of anxiety to serve a person in the manner I have striven and wished to do, that would treat me so shamefully if he could, I have therefore to request you will proceed without delay

against him so that I may not be further imposed upon by him.

I am

Dear Sir

Yours respectfully

John Dobson

Percival Fenwick Esq

APPENDIX B
THE STAIRCASE FRAGMENTS

All the fragments are of oak, except for concealed packing pieces and structural carriage pieces in softwood, some of the latter bearing Baltic sawmill or cargo batching marks. The exposed surfaces have remains of dark brown-black staining. The fragments may be grouped as follows.

1 Three ramped handrails, of slightly varying lengths for a gently rising stair, with a fourth handrail ramped for a landing. The heavy rail has a flat, wide, gently rolled top, impossible to grip, and each ramped section has a solid spandrel beneath it. The handrails are tenoned and mitred for junction with the newels. The soffits of the handrails have markings for the balusters.

2 Four newels and some half newels to the wall, with sunk panels and moulded bands. The main newels are morticed for handrails, with matching mitres. The newels have some ghost marks for the absent half balusters left by the staining of the exposed woodwork.[89]

3 There are no balusters, but the ghost marks reveal that they had three evenly spaced wide bulbs thinning to narrow necks, with no discernible bowl or urn.

4 Varying lengths of closed string. Fragments of four lengths remain to match the four handrails. The string was composed of an upper base for the balusters, whose markings are identifiable, and three or more elements, including a pulvinated frieze.

5 Twelve oak steps, with generous treads and low risers with two recessed panels per step. The undersides are cut and shaped in places to rest on the supporting carriage pieces.

6 Rough-cut softwood carriage pieces and other structural supports, some carriage pieces notched to accommodate the steps.

7 Two wicker baskets with a variety of oak blocks, packing pieces and tread supports, small mouldings, and various quarter, half and whole pendant drops for fixing beneath the newels on the well side and against the wall.

8 Substantial fragments of dado wainscot, including framing, bolection mouldings, and dado rail ramped to match the handrail.

9 Bolection-moulded architraves to door openings, with two two-panelled doors with decorative H-hinges.[90]

10 Splayed soffit panels to line window heads.

---

89 The dismantled newel posts from Anderson Place did not retain the fixed half baluster that survived on other *ex situ* staircase fragments recorded at Bradley Hall, Wolsingham (*c.*1660–80) and St Helen's Hall, St Helen's Auckland (*c.*1630), both in County Durham [reports of both these buildings by the author are in course of preparation for publication by the North East Vernacular Architecture Group].

90 The precise fitting of doors to architraves has not yet been investigated.

The Later Stuart Portraits in the Suffolk Collection

Anna Keay

The Suffolk Collection is an important group of some 50 paintings originally from Charlton Park, Wiltshire, famous for its early 17th-century portraits of the earls of Suffolk and Berkshire. It also includes a less well-known collection of late Stuart royal and court portraits, whose apparently anomalous presence was explained in 1878 as an addition, given from the royal collection by William III. This article argues that this story is highly implausible, and reveals that after the Restoration the Berkshire Howards, usually dismissed as nonentities, in fact occupied important positions at court, and had every reason to have acquired portraits of their royal patrons.

Fig. 5: Sir Peter Lely, *Mary of Modena*, 1673–80

The Suffolk Collection is a group of some 50 paintings, mostly portraits of members of the family of the earls of Suffolk and Berkshire. It hung at their seat, Charlton Park, Wiltshire (Fig. 1), until it was given to the Greater London Council by Mrs Greville Howard in 1974. Thereafter it hung at Ranger's House, Blackheath, until 2002, when it was moved to Kenwood House, Hampstead. Its fame is due principally to the early 17th-century portraits in the collection. Since 1873 it has been believed that the mid- to late 17th-century paintings were additions, a gift from the Stuart royal collection. This exciting attribution was first made in 1878, in F E Paget's work on the houses of the Howard family. In the chapter on Charlton Park, Paget describes a series of 'pictures that, evidently, once formed part of the Royal Collection of James II, being portraits of his kinsfolk, and of others whose names are familiar to us in the Court records of his own, and his brother's, reign'. In the footnote the attribution is expanded upon, Paget explaining that William III gave to Colonel James Grahme 'a number of packages ... containing a collection of pictures from James's private apartments, in one or more of the royal palaces. ... They remained in their packing cases for many years ... and when the late Lord Suffolk fitted up the gallery at Charlton, he unpacked them and placed them in it.'[1]

James Grahme was a prominent figure of the late Stuart court, and his advantageous marriage to Dorothy Howard, niece of the second and third earls of Berkshire, in 1675 contributed substantially to his rise (Fig. 6). He served in the household of James, duke of York, and was appointed keeper of the privy purse when the duke became king. Grahme was a political survivor and, instead of following his master into exile, he remained in England after the Glorious Revolution and even managed, occasionally, to win the favour of William III. His last years were spent partly at Levens, the estate he had purchased in Westmorland, but largely at his wife's family home of Charlton Park. It was through this connection, Paget's argument went, that these paintings found their way from the royal palaces to Charlton.[2]

When, in the early 1970s, John Jacob wrote his catalogue of the collection, he tentatively supported the provenance given by Paget. Though Jacob was frustrated at being unable to find the source for Paget's story, it did at least solve the great mystery of why the Howards acquired paintings of the quality and subject matter of this part of the collection. As Jacob explained, 'Neither the Berkshires nor the Suffolks were prominent in the service of the Crown after the Restoration and so it is surprising to find so many portraits of this period [in the collection]'.[3] This view has remained unchallenged, and in Julius Bryant's *London's Country House Collections*, for example, the

---

1 F E Paget, *Some Records of the Ashstead Estate*, Lichfield, 1873, 156.
2 Julian Munby, 'The Early Career of James Grahme of Levens, 1650–1692', *Transactions of the Cumberland & Westmorland Antiquarian & Archaeological Society*, XCVIII, 1998, 183–205; *Historical Manuscripts Collection: 10th Report, Part V*, MSS of Capt J F Bagot,

327–9; Eveline Cruickshanks, 'Grahme, James (1650–1730)', *Oxford Dictionary of National Biography*, Oxford, 2004, XXIII, 255–6.
3 John Jacob, 'The royal portraits', in *The Suffolk Collection: Catalogue of Paintings*, London, 1974.

Fig. 1: Unknown artist, *Charlton House from the north-west,* late 18th or early 19th century

likelihood of their coming from the royal collection is again rehearsed.[4]

This article takes another look at this fascinating attribution. It does so, first, by asking whether any more light can be shed on Paget's account of their provenance and, second, by examining John Jacob's assertion that the Berkshire Howards were so poorly connected at the later Stuart court, that an alternative explanation of the family collection of late Stuart dignitaries must be found.

A ROYAL PROVENANCE

Unfortunately no trace has yet been found of the source for Paget's story. The footnote suggests that Paget himself had not seen a documentary source; in fact he acknowledges that his own 'researches'

at Levens had not brought to light a date or more details. Julian Munby's recent extensive work in the Levens papers has also not revealed any corroborating evidence, and no information about such a gift has yet come to light from other manuscript sources.[5] The likelihood is, perhaps, that the provenance which Paget describes was a family tradition rather than the result of his own documentary research. The flooring and fitting out of the long gallery by the 'late' Lord Suffolk (Thomas, the sixteenth earl, who succeeded in 1820 and died in 1851), during which, according to Paget, the Stuart paintings had been unpacked, had taken place some 50 years before, so even this he may well not have heard of from an eye-witness.[6] Though not, in itself, a reason to dismiss

---

4 Julius Bryant, *London's Country House Collections,* London, 1993, 14.
5 I owe this to a personal communication from Julian Munby, September 2005.

6 Paget, *op. cit.,* 156; J Alfred Gotch, *Architecture of the Renaissance in England,* London, 1894, II, 4ff, pls 69, 70.

Paget's story, it does mean that we need to look to other aspects of this supposed provenance to seek verification.

Paget is quite clear that the paintings which William III gave to Grahme were from James II's privy lodgings in the royal palaces. Happily two relatively detailed inventories survive of the pictures in James II's collection.[7] In carrying out a close comparison of these to the Suffolk Collection, it becomes clear that the works which James II had in his privy apartments were rather different in character from those in the Suffolk Collection. The pictures in James's own rooms were, on the whole, a mixture of biblical and classical scenes, with a smattering of portraits of European princes, Tudor monarchs, and, occasionally, his own family. So, for example, the king's bedchamber at Whitehall was hung with a Madonna, a Venus and Cupid, and a cupid crowning a female figure, while the privy gallery was hung with dynastic pieces, including the painting of the meeting of Henry VIII and the Emperor Maximilian, now at Hampton Court. To find, among the many hundreds of works listed in James II's picture inventories, pieces which could be paintings now in the Suffolk Collection is not easy.

The inventory describes one piece as 'the kings picture when he was Duke', which could, perhaps, be the studio of Lely in the Suffolk Collection (Fig. 2), but this work is listed as among Princess Anne's paintings, not those hung in James II's apartments.[8] There is in the 'yellow bedchamber', 'King Charles the first his Children', but this is not that now in the Suffolk Collection (Fig. 3), but the iteration of this composition showing the sitters with a large dog, now hanging at Windsor.[9] In fact it is striking how hard it is, even when working simply on the sitter alone, to identify paintings in James II's collection with those in the Suffolk Collection. In an additional list, two further paintings in the king's bedchamber at Whitehall are noted, 'the late king at length' and 'the queen at half length'.[10] The former could be the Kneller of Charles II in the Suffolk Collection (Fig. 4), but this is made unlikely by the fact that the work listed in

Fig. 2: Studio of Sir Peter Lely, *James, Duke of York*, c.1670

Fig. 3 (below): Studio of Sir Anthony Van Dyck, *The Three Eldest Children of Charles I*, c.1635

Fig. 4: Studio of Sir Godfrey Kneller, *King Charles II*, c.1680–5

---

7 London, British Library (hereafter BL), Harleian MS 1890 (hereafter Harl. 1890); Glasgow, Glasgow University Library, Hunter MS 238 (hereafter GUL). A further inventory is held by the royal collection at St James's Palace. I am very grateful to Andrew Barclay and Simon Thurley for their assistance in relation to these inventories.

8 GUL, fol 83, listed 'In the Princesses Presence' at Windsor Castle.

9 GUL, fol 71, listed 'In the Yellow Bed Chamber' at Whitehall Palace. See also Oliver Millar, *The Tudor, Stuart and Early Georgian Pictures in the Collection of Her Majesty the Queen*, London, 1963, text volume, 98–9.

10 GUL, fol 93, listed 'In the Kings Bed Chamber' at Whitehall Palace, as pictures 'that were not the Late Kings'.

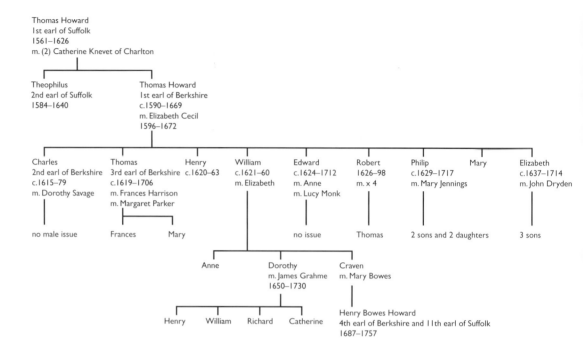

Fig. 6 (above): Genealogy of the early earls of Suffolk and Berkshire

Fig. 7 (facing page): After 'The Comet Master', *The Countess of Berkshire*, née *Lady Elizabeth Cecil*, 17th century

the inventory was still in the royal collection well into the 18th century and by the rather poor quality of the Charles II in the Suffolk Collection.[11] The 'queen at half length' could be thought at first glance to refer to the Lely *Mary of Modena* now at Kenwood (Fig. 5, see page 62), but this work is in fact, as Oliver Millar pointed out, the portrait of Mary in riding habit still at Windsor Castle.[12]

It is worth noting that the inventories were probably made by William Chiffinch, closet keeper to both Charles II and James II, who was well acquainted with all the figures of the Restoration court, and though he might have struggled with the more obscure 16th-century European princes, he could have had no problem identifying sitters known to him personally.[13] In short, of the dozen or so mid- to late Stuart paintings in the Suffolk Collection, it would only be possible even to suggest a case for perhaps two being among those that hung in James II's apartments, and it is my contention that none ever formed part of that collection.

THE BERKSHIRE HOWARDS
John Jacob believed that the family of the earls of Berkshire were not prominent at Court between the Civil War and the Glorious Revolution (Fig. 6). In fact many members of the family were significant figures at Restoration Whitehall. Thomas Howard, first earl of Suffolk, was succeeded in that title, and in his principal seat, Audley End, by his eldest son Theophilus in 1626. His second son, Thomas, inherited his mother's estate at Charlton, where he had been settled since at least 1620.[14] Thomas was a central figure at the court of the future Charles I: from 1614 he had been the prince's master of the horse, in 1623 he travelled with Charles and the duke of Buckingham to Madrid to woo the Spanish infanta, and on the prince's accession Thomas was a prominent recipient of his favours. He was elevated to the peerage, as Viscount Andover in 1622, and as earl of Berkshire in 1626, and in 1625 he was created a knight of the Garter.[15]

In 1644, now in his 50s, Berkshire was appointed to the post of governor to another prince of Wales, the future Charles II. In this capacity he was constantly at the side of the young prince, and was one of the small band of men hand-picked by Charles I to accompany his eldest

11 Millar, *op. cit.*, 141. I am grateful to Andrew Barclay for pointing this out to me.
12 *Ibid.*, 132.
13 Chiffinch's signature appears on BL, Harl. 1890. For Chiffinch and his career, see D Allen, 'The Political Function of Charles II's Chiffinch', *The Huntingdon Library Quarterly*, XXXIX (3), May 1976, 277–90.
14 *The Victoria History of the Counties of England, Wiltshire*, XIV,

London, 1991, 41; Pauline Croft, 'Howard, Thomas, first earl of Suffolk (1561–1626)', *Oxford Dictionary of National Biography*, Oxford, 2004, XXVIII, 436–9.
15 James Anderson Winn, *John Dryden and his World*, New Haven and London, 1989, 121; G E C[okayne], *The Complete Peerage of England, Scotland and Wales*, II, London, 1912, 150–1.

Fig. 8: Cornelius Johnson,
King Charles I, after 1632

son, and act as his council.[16] In April 1646 the prince and his councillors landed in Jersey at the start of what would be a long exile. The earl of Berkshire was described by one island onlooker as first among the prince's entourage, and it was noted that he and the prince, alike, sported their Garter stars proudly on their left breasts.[17]

In 1614 the earl of Berkshire had married Lady Elizabeth Cecil, daughter of the second earl of Exeter (Fig. 7). The union produced several daughters and seven sons who lived to adulthood. The eldest two, Charles and Thomas, in due course succeeded their father to the earldom, as the second and third earls of Berkshire, respectively.[18] At the Restoration the first earl was nearly 70. Nonetheless his family's loyalty and his personal attendance on Charles II in the dark days of the 1640s were not forgotten. The aged earl and at least three of his sons rode in the great entry parade into London on 31 May 1660, and he was appointed to Charles II's closest service, as a gentleman of the king's bedchamber. This post came with high prestige, as it was only granted to the greatest men in the kingdom (his fellow gentlemen included General Monck and the second duke of Buckingham), but also with considerable financial reward, as it carried an annual salary of £1,000.[19] Despite his advanced age, the earl actively undertook his duties as a gentleman of the bedchamber throughout the 1660s. In July 1666 Samuel Pepys was among the crowd who watched the king dine, and he noted in his diary that 'it astonished me to see my Lord Barkeshire, waiting at table and serving the king [his] drink', one of the duties of the office.[20]

It was not just the old earl who found favour and position at court at the Restoration. His sons and daughters also profited. His eldest son, Charles, named presumably for the Stuart kings whom his father served, travelled with the king in exile and had been part of his household in the Low Countries in the late 1650s. However, his

and his wife's catholicism was to be an obstacle to court positions, and when the Test Act was passed soon after Charles succeeded to the earldom in 1669, he was forbidden from holding any such post.[21]

Thomas Howard, who succeeded as third earl in 1679, served Charles I with great distinction during the Civil War, commanding a regiment of horse. He seems not to have held a court position at the Restoration, but clearly moved in the highest political circles: in the 1680s he corresponded with the king's erstwhile first minister, Lord Danby, reminiscing fondly of the friendship the two men formed, 'when I had the Honnor to live with you att court'.[22]

William Howard, the fourth son, was dead by the Restoration, but both his wife and daughters were well-connected. Elizabeth, his widow, was part of the duke of York's household, serving at one point as his housekeeper, and his daughters, Dorothy and Anne, had court positions as maids of honour: Dorothy to the duchess of York in the later 1660s and, it seems, both Dorothy and Anne to the queen, Catherine of Braganza, in the 1670s.[23]

Robert, the first earl of Berkshire's sixth son, had been a distinguished soldier in the royalist service during the Civil War and was knighted for gallantry on the battlefield in 1644. He was briefly imprisoned at Windsor Castle in 1658, at the time of the famous trial of his friend and cousin, the royalist ringleader, John Mordaunt. At the Restoration he accumulated an impressive collection of lucrative offices: he was sergeant painter, a post in the Office of Works responsible for all aspects of the painted and gilded decoration of the royal palaces, and was a clerk of chancery, which brought in the hefty salary of £3,000 a year. Sir Robert would have had a distinguished career as an MP, but enjoyed equal fame in the world of Restoration theatre, as a playwright and theatre owner. The king, a theatre enthusiast himself, knew him well, and helped to arrange his second,

16 Edward Hyde, earl of Clarendon (ed W Dunn Macray), *History of the Rebellion and Civil War in England*, Oxford, 1888, II, 318, 258–9, 451, 533; Ronald Hutton, *Charles II*, Oxford, 1989, 6; Eva Scott, *The King in Exile*, London, 1905, 8.

17 J Elliot Hoskins, *Charles II in the Channel Islands*, London, 1854, I, 354; Winn, *op. cit.*, 562.

18 G E C[okayne], *Complete Peerage*, II, 1912, 150–1.

19 Edward Chamberlayne, *Angliae Notitia or the Present State of England, Together with Divers Reflections upon the Ancient State Thereof*, London, 1669, 262–3. Although at least two contemporary sources clearly record that Berkshire was a gentleman of the bedchamber, he is strangely absent from John Sainty and Robert Bucholz's *Office-Holders in Modern Britain, XI: Officials of the Royal Household 1660–1837. Part 1: Department of the Lord Chamberlain and Associated Offices*, London, 1997, 8; Winn, *op. cit.*, 119. Berkshire also served on the committee for reassembling the royal art collection: see Jerry Brotton, 'The

Art of Restoration: King Charles II and the Restitution of the English Royal Art Collection', *The Court Historian*, X (2), December 2005, 115–35, 116.

20 Robert Latham and William Matthews (eds), *The Diary of Samuel Pepys*, London, 1970–6, VII, 217. A month before his death, the old earl was to be found dining at the house of Henry Bennet, earl of Arlington, who was now virtually the king's first minister [E S de Beer (ed), *The Diary of John Evelyn*, Oxford, 1955, III, 529].

21 Winn, *op. cit.*, 121; G E C[okayne], *Complete Peerage*, II, 1912, 151; London, The National Archives, Public Record Office (hereafter PRO), PROB 11/360, 4 June 1679.

22 G E C[okayne], *Complete Peerage*, II, 1912, 151; BL, Add MS 28,053, fol 184r; PRO, PROB 11/488, fol 254.

23 De Beer, *op. cit.*, III, 529–30; IV, 69–71; Latham and Matthews, *op. cit.*, XI, 468; Chamberlayne, *op. cit.*, 1673, 235; Paget, *op. cit.*, 75–8.

Fig. 9 (right): Attributed to Jacob Huysmans, *Catherine of Braganza*, 1660s

Fig. 10 (far right): Studio of Sir Godfrey Kneller, *Laurence Hyde, Earl of Rochester*, c.1685

Fig. 11 (facing page): William Wissing, *Queen Mary II*, c.1685–8

advantageous, marriage. He would marry twice more, finally, in 1693, marrying Anabella Dives, one of Mary II's maids of honour. Like his brother Philip, Sir Robert's early political sympathies gradually faded, and, come the 1680s, he supported the exclusion of James, duke of York, from the succession. He was one of the movers in bringing about the Glorious Revolution and served in William III's Privy Council.[24]

The first earl's seventh son, Philip Howard, also travelled abroad during the Commonwealth, and entered the service of Charles II's sister, Mary, in the Orange court in Holland. He acted as one of the go-betweens in the negotiations in 1660 between the exiled king and the House of Commons which were to bring about the Restoration. His service was acknowledged when he was made a gentleman of the duke of York's bedchamber in December 1660, a post which he would hold for the next 22 years. He continued, despite the turbulent politics of the reign, to enjoy the king's favour, as is demonstrated by the fact that in 1681 Charles II agreed to stand as godfather to Philip Howard's young son. Like many, his loyalties changed during the reign, and

though a long-standing member of the duke of York's household, he lost his court position when his support for the duke of Monmouth became public in 1682.[25]

It was not just the Howard sons who had promoted the royalist cause during the Commonwealth. The first earl's daughter, Lady Mary Howard, suffered imprisonment, like her brothers Robert and Philip, as a consequence of her efforts for the king: she was held in the Tower for several weeks in 1659, during which time Charlton was closely searched by parliamentary troops.[26] Similarly, the Howard women were also part of the London court world at the Restoration. Lady Elizabeth Howard married the young poet John Dryden in 1663, and in 1665 they escaped the plague at Charlton Park, where Dryden wrote *Annus Mirabilis*, one of his most famous works, and Elizabeth gave birth to their eldest son. Dryden's great success at court was sealed when in 1668 Charles II created him poet laureate. Like his brother-in-law, Dryden was drawn to catholicism, though his conversion at just the time of the duke's accession to the throne was regarded by

24 Basil Duke Henning, *The History of Parliament: The House of Commons 1660–1690*, London, 1983, II, 595–604; Eveline Cruickshanks, Stuart Handley and D S Hayton, *The History of Parliament: The House of Commons 1690–1715*, Cambridge, 2002, IV, 404–8; J P Vander Motter, 'Howard, Sir Robert (1626–1698)', *Oxford Dictionary of National Biography*, Oxford, 2004, XXVIII, 412–13; H J Oliver, *Sir Robert Howard (1626–1698): A Critical Biography*, Durham, North Carolina, 1963, *passim*.

25 Henning, *op. cit.*, II, 594–5. Philip Howard was closely associated with Sir Charles Berkeley, James II's groom of the stole, and the two petitioned the king together for court places in 1660 [Mary Anne Everett Green, F H Blackburne Daniell and Francis Bickley (eds), *Calendar of State Papers, Domestic Series of the Reign of Charles II*, London, 1860–1938, I, 1660–1, 386].

26 *Calendar of the Clarendon State Papers in the Bodleian Library*, Oxford, 1872–1970, IV, 365; Oliver, *op. cit.*, 5.

Fig. 12: Sir Godfrey Kneller,
Charles Mordaunt,
Earl of Peterborough and
*Monmouth, c.*1689–97

many as a political rather than a religious act.[27]

Thus the suggestion that the Berkshire Howards were not well connected in the later 17th century is quite wrong. Despite the advanced age of the three earls of this period, the family was very much part of the Restoration court world. Perhaps a dozen of its members were acquainted with the king himself, and the Berkshire Howards were among the ranks of those holding the most honoured court positions in the households of Charles II, of Queen Catherine of Braganza and of the duke of York. As was the case with so many families during this period, some of the family were to support James II and others William III, and some switched loyalties between the two.

A FAMILY COLLECTION

It is therefore suggested that we no longer need to look to Paget's unsourced story about gifts to James Grahme *via* William III to explain the presence of the mid- and late 17th-century paintings in the Suffolk Collection. There was every reason why a family like the Berkshire Howards should have acquired such paintings. If we remember that it is an accumulated family collection, rather than that of one person, we may explain its inclusion of prominent Jacobite and Williamite figures, which commentators have struggled with in the past.

Thus, connections between the sitters of those paintings for which we have a reasonably firm

27 Winn, *op. cit.*, 414ff.

identity and the Berkshire Howards are easily made.[28] Charles I (Fig. 8) gave the family its titles and was fought for by almost all the Howard brothers. The first earl was appointed governor to Charles, prince of Wales (Fig. 3). Charles II was served in exile and at the Restoration by Berkshire Howards; in 1681, at about the time when the studio of Kneller portrait was painted (Fig. 4), he stood as godfather to Philip Howard's son, and the painting may have been connected with that event. William Howard's two daughters were maids of honour to Queen Catherine of Braganza (Fig. 9), and a Catholic queen would have been a significant figure to the Catholic second earl. Philip Howard had been gentleman of the bedchamber to the duke of York (Fig. 2) for a decade *c.*1670 and would be so for another before his political allegiances changed. Mary of Modena (Fig. 5) was a highly significant figure to Philip Howard, and was probably looked to for patronage, as Dorothy Howard, his niece, had been a maid of honour to her predecessor as duchess of York. Laurence Hyde, earl of Rochester (Fig. 10), was a prominent court figure during Charles II and James II's reigns. As master of the robes to Charles II, he would have been a close associate of the bedchamber staff in the daily rituals of dressing. Perhaps more importantly, in the context of a painting, he was also a patron of Elizabeth Howard's husband, John Dryden; in 1683 Dryden had dedicated *The Duke of Guise* to Hyde and he continued to look to him as a patron in the years that followed, with another dedication, *Cleomenes*, in 1691. Mary II (Fig. 11) was a key figure for Whigs like Sir Robert and Philip Howard, as the hereditary link that justified the Glorious Revolution. Furthermore, Sir Robert, in particular, had close connections to her; his fourth and final wife was one of her maids of honour, and the queen even dined with him at Ashstead on at least one occasion in the early 1690s.[29] Carey Frazier, who married the earl of Peterborough (Fig. 12), was, with the Howard daughters, one of the maids of honour in the 1670s. Like Robert Howard, Peterborough was one of the major contributors to the Glorious Revolution; he was the first member of the House of Lords openly to propose that William of Orange

be asked to take the throne, and Robert Howard echoed this vociferously in the Commons. The two families had long-standing ties: Peterborough's grandmother had been a Howard; and his father was the royalist conspirator with whom Robert Howard had corresponded in the 1650s, and whose arrest and trial in 1658 were probably the causes of Robert's own imprisonment in Windsor that year.[30] Every known sitter in these paintings had a connection to the Howards of Charlton Park that could comfortably explain the addition of his or her portrait to their collection.

The Suffolk Collection today is only a portion of the paintings that once hung at Charlton Park. An inventory of 1697, which lists the paintings in the great hall there, includes a number now gone, among them a full length of King Edward VI, the 'pelican' portrait of Queen Elizabeth I and a half-length of Queen Henrietta Maria.[31] These paintings passed from the collection over the following 200 years or so. But, had they and other works which once formed part of it remained, the Suffolk Collection would contain portraits of almost every king and queen of England from the Reformation to the mid-18th century.[32] The works that hung most prominently over the high table at Charlton in 1697 were the royal portraits, with family full-lengths hanging below. In this context we should stop viewing these paintings, and the royal sitters among them, as a perplexing anomaly, a strange epilogue to the story of the great Jacobean portraits of the family circle. We need to realise, instead, that royal portraiture had always been an integral part of the collection and does not require special explanation. On the contrary, it is with the later Stuart paintings alone that something of the Suffolk Collection's original character still remains.

ACKNOWLEDGEMENTS

This paper was prepared for a seminar on the Suffolk Collection held at Kenwood House on 25 November 2005. I am especially grateful to Laura Houliston, who organised the conference, for sharing her own research on the collection with me. I would also like to thank Andrew Barclay, Diana Dethloff, Louise Mitchell, Julian Munby and Simon Thurley.

28 Paintings for which there is not a firm or convincing identification have been omitted from this list. Those are the works described by John Jacob as Susan Armine, baroness Bellasis (cat. no. 41), the unknown lady (cat. no. 42), a lady as St Catherine (cat. no. 43), and unknown man called William III (cat. no. 44).
29 Oliver, *op. cit.*, 280.
30 *Ibid.*, 11–12; John B Hattendorf, 'Charles Mordaunt, third earl of Peterborough and first earl of Monmouth (1658?–1735)', *Oxford Dictionary of National Biography*, Oxford, 2004, XXXIX, 13–21.

31 Trowbridge, Wiltshire Record Office, MS 88/9/10, 'The Earl of Berkshires deed of gift for the Pictures at Charlton Hall &c August 19 1697'.
32 Chelmsford, Essex Record Office, D/DBY Z41–43, Inventory of the Suffolk Collection, *c.* 1830. The sovereigns whose portraits are recorded at Charlton were: Edward VI, Elizabeth I, James I, Charles I, Charles II, James II, William III (if the portrait called William III is indeed William III), Mary II, George I.

Three Drawings by John James at Audley End

Richard Hewlings

Three architectural drawings of an unexecuted building in the collection at Audley End have recently been found to be by the architect John James, surveyor to the Fifty New Churches Commission, and architect of St George, Hanover Square. This article describes them and considers which of James's unexecuted projects they illustrate, concluding that they most resemble his unaccepted designs for the Foundling Hospital in London.

Left: John James, principal elevation of a proposed public building (detail from Fig. 1)

Three scaled elevation drawings in ink of a monumental public building, in the collection at Audley End House, Essex, can now be identified as works by the architect John James (*c.*1673–1746).[1] What they represent is less certain; this article reviews the possibilities. The drawings are not signed or dated, but the verso of one has the inscription 'Mr. James', and those of the two others have evidently been cropped, leaving the letters 'mes' on each. 'Mr. James' was doubtless the architect of that name, as the scale bars at the bottom of each drawing are of a type which John James used on other drawings, for instance, on drawings of the Queen's House at Greenwich,[2] for Westminster Bridge[3] and for Welbeck Abbey.[4] But the inscriptions were unseen until recently, as the drawings were mounted, and, although the mounts had open panels to allow the verso to be inspected, the inscriptions did not align with the panels, and were thus hidden.[5]

Although the three elevations are to the same scale, 1in to 12ft (1:144), and illustrate a building of the same general form, there are enough differences of detail to indicate that all three are variant designs. The general form is a building, 60ft (or 66ft) high, of two storeys (or two storeys with an attic), its roof hidden behind a balustraded parapet; it has two long wings running forward at each end of the principal elevation, forming a three-sided courtyard, which is closed by an iron screen held by masonry piers. The basement storey has horizontally channelled rustication, with an arcade (or a blind arcade in which round-arched windows are set concentrically). The other storey (or two storeys) is ornamented by an applied Composite pilastrade. The only internal arrangements which the drawings reveal are those in the central range, where the first floor is occupied by a single high room with a coved ceiling 35ft above the floor.

The principal elevation (Fig. 1) shows two main storeys and a low attic storey with square windows.[6] Its centre, the elevation towards the court, is five bays wide; the centre three bays break forward on all floors and columns are substituted for the pilasters. Its wings are four bays wide. The attic windows are placed immediately below the frieze in the centre, but below capital level on the end elevation of the wings. The arcade is not blind in the centre range, but open, and the principal door must have been within it. A door is shown, asymmetrically, in the left-hand bay of the left-hand wing. The screen appears to be detached from the building, and may be some way in front of it. It has a carriage gate in the centre and pedestrian gates at each side. The design of the iron work is shown precisely, so this detail, unusually, was not to be left to the smith.

The two other elevations are marked 'A' and 'B', and both show the main, central range in section at their left. They must therefore represent alternative treatments of the side elevation of the right-hand wing, the elevation which faces the courtyard. 'A' has two storeys and nine bays (Fig. 2).[7]

1 Audley End House (hereafter AE), 88096401-3 (formerly bound in a volume entitled 'Miscellany Prospects').
2 John Brushe, 'Some Designs by John James', *Georgian Group Journal*, IV, 1994, 4 and 7.
3 Chatsworth, Devonshire Collection, Boy. Coll. [14] 2.
4 Peter Smith, 'Lady Oxford's Alterations at Welbeck Abbey', *Georgian Group Journal*, XI, 139, 143, 144 and 145.

5 The skilled connoisseurship of Mr John Brushe has to be acknowledged here. Mr Brushe, who was already convinced that the drawings were by James, encouraged me to re-examine them in his company, while they were still mounted. We found the inscriptions by shining a torch through the mount.
6 AE, 88096402.
7 AE, 88096401.

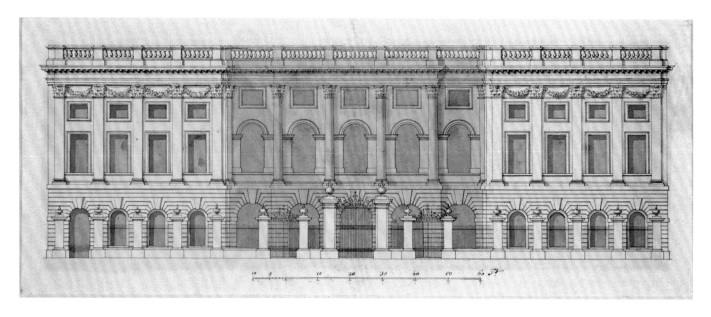

Fig. 1: John James, principal elevation of a proposed public building

The round-arched openings in the basement are deeply shaded, suggesting that a cloister ran under the full length of the wing. In the central three bays the pilastrade is transformed into an applied colonnade, and, although the entablature breaks forward over the columns, the basement does not break forward beneath them. There must therefore have been a substantial shelf under the pilasters.

The ornament is richer than on the other two elevation drawings; the ground-floor keystones have human masks, the frieze is ornamented with festoons of flowers suspended from lions' masks, and the parapet has four standing female figures over the four columns and urns over the six pilasters. The drawing indicates that the central range was to have a timber floor, a plaster cove to the first-floor room, and a strutted kingpost roof with an iron strap clasping the feet of the posts to the tie. It shows the open ground floor arcade in section.

Elevation 'B' has two storeys and an attic, like the central range, and the attic storey is partly within the level of the capitals (Fig. 3).[8] It is ten bays wide, with an arcade under the two right-hand bays only. In the other bays the ground-floor arcade is blind, with segment-headed windows set in it. It has pilasters only, and therefore no breaks forward. It has no sculpture, and is clearly intended to be a cheaper or less festive alternative, though bigger. The drawing indicates that the central range was only to have two storeys, although the first-floor room was additionally to

be lit by attic windows. It was to have the same type of ceiling and roof as shown in elevation 'A', but the open ground floor was to have had both spinal and lateral brick or masonry arcades to provide additional support to the floor.

The proposal represented in elevation 'A', with two storeys, clearly differs from that represented in the two other drawings, with two and a half storeys. But elevation 'B' also differs from the principal elevation. The arcade under its two right-hand bays does not occur in the drawing of the principal elevation, which shows a blind arcade in which round-arched windows are set concentrically. Evidently the three drawings illustrate three variant proposals. Since neither plans nor drawings of the remaining elevations are included, the three are survivors of a larger set, which may have included other proposals.

The drawings do not represent any building known to have been designed by James, nor do they give any indication of what it was. It might be a proposed rebuilding of Audley End, but it does not look like a country house. An arcade would have been unusual at that date and unnecessary on a site with unlimited space.[9] It could be a proposed town house, on as palatial a scale as that built for the duke of Buckingham at the end of Pall Mall,[10] or that intended to house the duke of Chandos on the north side of Cavendish Square.[11] James claimed to have 'served [the duke of Buckingham] in the business of [his] buildings'

8 AE, 88096403.
9 Shotover Park, Oxon., is a rare example of an 18th-century country house with a ground-floor arcade [James Lees-Milne, *English Country Houses Baroque 1685–1714*, London, 1970, 252–7].
10 John Cornforth, 'The Sheffields at Buckingham House', *Country*

Life, CXXXII, 12 July 1962, 86–8.
11 C H and M I Collins Baker, *The Life and Circumstances of James Brydges, Duke of Chandos*, Oxford, 1949, 265–95, especially plate opposite 272.

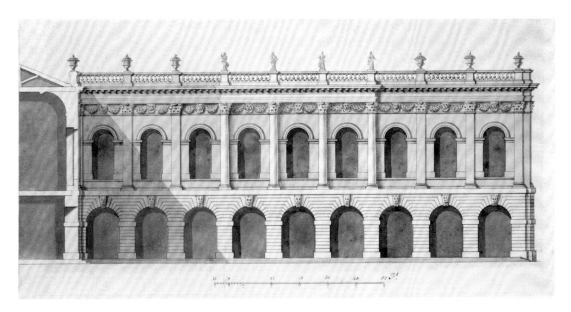

Fig. 2 : John James, alternative side elevation 'A' of a proposed public building

before 1711, and he worked for the duke of Chandos after 1714, so both these buildings might be the subjects of these drawings. But, although tall, even two-storey, rooms were not unusual in early 18th-century private houses, few were on the first floor.[12] It is more likely that the drawings represent a proposed royal palace or public building, although in or at the edge of a town.

James could have submitted designs for any of the numerous public buildings proposed in his lifetime.[13] As the son of a clergyman and schoolmaster he may have had clerical connections; he was involved with more charitable institutions, including colleges, schools and hospitals, than most architects of his time.[14] There are, however, six public buildings for which James is known to have submitted proposals which were not accepted, and the Audley End drawings may be considered as these. Three may be eliminated immediately since they are known from drawings by James which bear no resemblance to the Audley End designs. They include his proposal for the Mansion House, solicited by the City of London in March 1735.[15]

James's plans for this were solid rectangles like that of the building which was eventually erected to George Dance's design.[16] Its principal elevation was 95ft wide, half the width of the principal elevation in the Audley End drawings.[17] But in October 1735 James wrote that he had also made a plan for another site which the City were considering, in Leadenhall Street.[18] This plan has not survived and it might be that the Audley End drawings represent it. Its site was L-shaped, but James wrote that his plan was 'much upon the Dimensions that piece contains, if there were room to make it Square'.[19] However, the widest part of that site was 166ft, appreciably less than the 190ft 6in of the principal elevation in the Audley End drawings, and, as its depth was 228ft, if James had really meant square, rather than rectangular, its principal elevation would have been longer than that in the Audley End drawing.[20]

A proposal for rebuilding the north quadrangle of All Souls' College, Oxford, under consideration *c.*1709, is represented by another group of drawings attributed to James.[21] If the Audley End

12 Two-storey rooms on the ground floor are found at Beningbrough Hall (1714–16), Barnsley Park (*c.*1720), Moor Park (1721), Grimsthorpe Castle (1723), Towneley Hall (1724) and Hainton Hall (1735). They are found over a low basement at Easton Neston (1702), Kimbolton Castle (1707–9), Castle Howard (1709), Bramham Park (1709), Duncombe Park (1713), Blenheim Palace (1716, 1720 and 1722–5), Seaton Delaval (1718) and Gilling Castle (*c.*1719). I am only aware of them on a *piano nobile* over a full basement storey, as in these drawings, at Wanstead (1715) and Wentworth Woodhouse (*c.*1735).
13 Mr Brushe has suggested that they might be proposals for The Queen's College, Oxford; on the basis of their plan alone they could equally be for Worcester College. And many institutions may have considered rebuilding without leaving any record.
14 Richard Hewlings, 'The School and Almshouses at Sevenoaks', *Georgian Group Journal*, XI, 2001, 234. James was also a governor of Bethlem Hospital [Beckenham, Bethlem Royal Hospital, Archives, Minutes of the Court of Governors]; and he designed Codrington

College, Barbados, for the Society for Propagating the Gospel in 1718–25 [Howard Colvin, 'A Biographical Dictionary of British Architects 1600–1840: Corrections and Additions to the Third Edition (Yale University Press 1995)', *Architectural History*, XXXIX, 1996, 238. I am indebted to Sir Howard Colvin for drawing this to my attention].
15 Sidney Perks, *The History of the Mansion House*, Cambridge, 1922, 163–4; Sally Jeffery, *The Mansion House*, Chichester, 1993, 9.
16 Jeffery, *op. cit*., pls 17 and 19.
17 Perks, *op. cit*., 167.
18 Jeffery, *op. cit*., 12.
19 *Ibid.*, 9, 12, 23.
20 *Ibid.*, 8.
21 H M Colvin, *A Catalogue of Architectural Drawings of the 18th and 19th Centuries in the Library of Worcester College Oxford*, Oxford, 1964, nos. 14, 15, 16, 30 and 31; 1709 is the date of the drawings by other architects under consideration [*The Victoria History of the County of Oxfordshire*, III, London, 1954, 190].

drawings were an alternative proposal, the double-height room in the central block could only have been the hall, chapel or library, and the open side of the courtyard would thus have had to have been the north or south sides, which was never envisaged at All Souls'.

Another drawing attributed to James is among proposals by other architects for the University Press building in Oxford.[22] It shows a single-block, two-storey building like that which was built in 1712–15, and the Audley End drawings are evidently not an alternative proposal for this site either.

Another Oxford proposal is not known from a drawing; indeed there is no evidence that a drawing was made. In 1720 the trustees of Dr Radcliffe's will minuted their intention to ask seven architects, of whom James was one, for designs for a new library in Oxford.[23] When, in 1734, they eventually did so, they only approached Hawksmoor and Gibbs, who produced designs which were rectangular, T-shaped or circular.[24] The plan represented in the Audley End drawings, three ranges which would have obscured the fine buildings all around, might have been regarded as unsuitable for the site, and it seems unlikely that he would have submitted this unsolicited design in the intervening 14 years. The Audley End drawings therefore do not appear to correspond with any of these Oxford proposals, nor did the owners of Audley End in James's lifetime have any connection with Oxford to account for the drawings' presence in the Audley End collection.

By contrast, the owners of Audley End enjoyed a patronal relationship with the University of Cambridge. They were visitors of Magdalene College *in perpetuum*, the vice-chancellor and the heads of houses had waited on Elizabeth I and James I at Audley End,[25] and in John James's lifetime four owners of Audley End (the sixth, seventh, eighth and tenth earls of Suffolk) were members of Magdalene.[26] James also had a more positive connection with Cambridge. He had rebuilt the chapel of Gonville and Caius College, Cambridge, in 1718–26,[27] and in 1720 he was asked to pay a visit to the master of St John's College, possibly in connection with the proposed rebuilding of that chapel, but he had no time to do so.[28] The syndicate responsible for building the new university buildings included the masters of both these colleges,[29] and thus it is not surprising to find that James submitted a proposal for the new buildings, probably shortly after 15 July 1720, when William Edmundson, fellow of St John's, wrote to Matthew Prior, 'Last week Mr James came down to take a view of the ground for the Theatre and King's College'.[30] In March 1722 the syndics chose the proposals of James Gibbs,[31] but Gibbs's proposal was a three-sided courtyard like that in the Audley End drawings (Fig. 4).[32] James had made drawings, which were seen, although not accepted; in January 1724 the syndics paid 'Mr. James ye Architect for trouble in surveying & drawing plans (tho' not proceeded on)'.[33] Could they be the drawings now at Audley End?

The history of the development of the site suggests not. Only the Senate House in the north wing of Gibbs's design was built. In August 1726 contracts for digging the foundation trench for the central block were let by James Burrough, amateur architect, fellow of Caius, and a syndic since March 1721,[34] but in the following May Dr Thomas Gooch, the master of Caius, wrote to the vice-chancellor objecting to the 'attachment' of the three blocks, as Caius, which lay immediately to the north of the site, would lose the 'View of that noble fabrick Kings-chapell' on the south.[35] In the suit which followed Dr Gooch advocated the 'detachment' of the three blocks, to allow for the view, the air, and the preservation of the right of way from Caius to the Schools.[36] Gibbs wrote in support of his 'one united Building' in May 1728, in part because it would 'skreen the Inferior Building of Cajus College, which being seen

22 Howard Colvin, *Unbuilt Oxford*, New Haven and London, 1983, 60–1.
23 [H F Alexander and S G Gillam], *Bibliotheca Radcliviana 1749–1949*, Oxford, 1949, 11–12.
24 Colvin, *Unbuilt Oxford, cit.*, 64–73; Suzanne Lang, 'By Hawksmoor out of Gibbs', *Architectural Review*, CV, April 1949.
25 William Addison, *Audley End*, London, 1953, 20–1, 29, 143, 216–22, explains the relationship between Audley End and Cambridge.
26 G E C[okayne], *Complete Peerage*, XII, London, 1953, 472, 473, 475.
27 R Willis and J W Clark, *Architectural History of the University of Cambridge*, Cambridge, 1886, *op. cit.*, I, 195; III, 44.
28 Historic Manuscripts Commission, *Calendar of the Manuscripts of the Marquis of Bath*, III (Prior Papers), London, 1908 (hereafter HMC, Bath), 484; Bryan D G Little, *The Life and Work of James Gibbs, 1682–1754*, London, 1955, 58, suggests that James supplied a design for St John's College chapel, but, although there is an 18th-century

design for a chapel in the College archives [Cambridge, St John's College, Archives, MPSC 1.1–2], there is no indication that it is by James.
29 Willis and Clark, *op. cit.*, III, 44.
30 HMC, Bath, 484.
31 Willis and Clark, *op. cit.*, III, 44.
32 *Ibid.*, 45; Terry Friedman, *James Gibbs*, New Haven and London, 1984, 227–8.
33 Cambridge, Gonville and Caius College, Library, MS Caius Coll. 621/457, fol 202; Cambridge, Cambridge University Library, UAc. 2, p.506.
34 Willis and Clark, *op. cit.*, III, 49, note 2; and *ibid.*, 44, for the date of Burrough's admission to the syndicate.
35 *Ibid.*, 50–1.
36 *Ibid.*, 51–2.

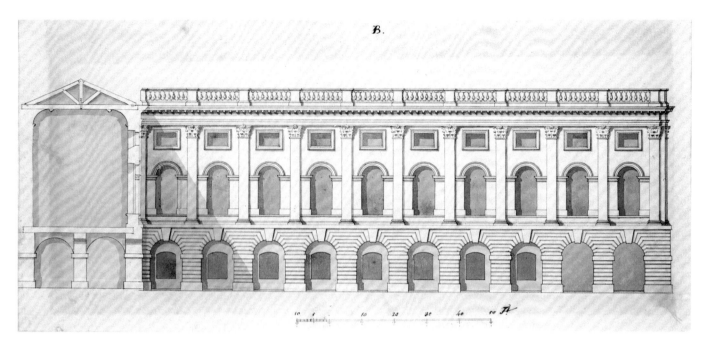

between the detach'd Buildings will have a disagreeable look and a very bad effect, which must be allowed by all impartial Judges'.[37] James, responding to a letter from Gooch, wrote in August 1729 in support of the 'Detachmt. of the Senate house on the north, and the Consistory &c on the South, from the front of the Building wch. is the Library' on the grounds that it would be 'altogether as beautiful as the conjunction of the West Ends of those buildings wth. The Library', and he added, rather lamely, that it would prevent the spread of fire.[38] As a compromise he suggested 'porticos of Columns only ... to make some Communications' between the detached buildings. His advocacy of the detached scheme might therefore suggest that the attached proposal shown in the Audley End drawings was not intended for the Cambridge University buildings.

However, this assumes sincere and consistent opinions from all parties. James wrote to Gooch, master of the college which had formerly employed him, and whom he had no cause to disoblige. Even so, his letter is rather half-hearted. The college may not have been of one mind; it was Burrough, a fellow, who had let the contracts for

the foundation trenches of the attached scheme, and Burrough was not disinterested, as he had submitted a design of his own which had been given to Gibbs to improve.[39] Gooch himself may have changed his mind; when vice-chancellor in 1717–19, he had purchased the property on which the attached scheme would have been built.[40] And it is possible that James had also changed his mind by 1729. He had surveyed the site nine years before, and his proposal could have been envisaged even earlier; he could have been the author of a proposal rumoured 'to front ye present schools on either side the Regent walks with an arch in the middle' as early as October 1715;[41] if the arcade under the central building in the Audley End drawings could have been described as an arch, this description could refer to them. Nonetheless the case for the Audley End drawings being proposals for Cambridge University buildings is not very strong.[42]

The sixth of James's known unaccepted designs for a public building was for the Foundling Hospital, to whose General Committee he presented proposals on 22 June 1742.[43] The hospital was eventually built to the design of

Fig. 3: John James, alternative side elevation 'B' of a proposed public building

---

37 *Ibid.*, 53.
38 Cambridge, Gonville and Caius College, Library, MS Caius Coll. 635/532. James's letter begins 'Revd. Sir I was from home on Saturday last that I could not acknowledge the ffavour of yours by the last post', which indicates that his letter was solicited.
39 T P Hudson, 'James Gibbs's designs for University Buildings at Cambridge', *Burlington Magazine*, December 1972, 844.
40 Willis and Clark, *op. cit.*, III, 50.
41 Hudson, *op. cit.*, 843.
42 Their dimensions are not indicative. They are not the same as

Gibbs's designs. Gibbs's drawings show the open side of the courtyard 172ft wide in one design, 220ft wide in another; the principal elevation in the Audley End drawings falls between these, at 190ft 6in. Gibbs's drawings show the courtyard elevations of the side wings 100ft long in one design, 110ft long in another; the elevation marked 'A' in the Audley End drawings is 162ft long, and that marked 'B' is 163ft 6in. But the size of the site may not have been determined at the time when James made his drawings.
43 Alan Borg, 'Theodore Jacobsen and the Building of the Foundling Hospital', *Georgian Group Journal*, XIII, 2003, 18.

Fig. 4: James Gibbs, perspective of the proposed university buildings at Cambridge, 1721

Theodore Jacobsen, similar in general form to the drawings at Audley End (Fig. 5). It had a U-shaped plan with far projecting wings, and a forecourt closed by a screen at a distance from the ends of the wings. The wings and the central block had open arcades on the ground floor. The central block had a single room, equivalent to two storeys in height, with a coved ceiling. The secretary's room was in the south-west corner of the west wing (on the left as seen from the front), and had a secondary door (although on the north side) which allowed the secretary direct access, as the door on the left of James's front elevation appears to do.[44]

The appearance of James's designs for the Foundling Hospital is not accurately known. But they would have had to satisfy the same general requirements as Jacobsen's, and must have been similar in general form. Having seen James's drawings for the hospital, the General Committee of the Foundling Hospital minuted that both 'Mr. James & Mr. Jacobsen's Plans are a Quadrangle open to the side next Red Lyon Street; on the opposite side is proposed the Chapel, the two other sides are proposed for the Hospital ... '.[45]

The committee had instructed the competing architects to design a building of 'Two stories & an Attick Story, The Wards to be twenty four feet wide. And that there be an Arcade to each Wing the whole length of the Building.'[46] Two of the drawings at Audley End satisfy the first of these requirements, and the elevation marked 'A' satisfies the last of them. The outside width of the wings as

shown on the principal elevation drawing is 55ft 6in., which would accommodate two 24ft wide wards, with one central and two outer walls each 2ft 6in. wide.

The Audley End drawings therefore conform to the general form of James's designs for the Foundling Hospital, but unfortunately they do not conform to them in detail. The committee recorded the dimensions of both Jacobsen's and James's proposals. In the latter 'The Front to Red Lyon Street extends ... 222 feet'; the principal elevation of the Audley End drawing extends for only 190ft 6in. 'The side front vizt. The front of the proposed Wing' was 292ft long; the elevation marked 'A' at Audley End is 162ft long, and that marked 'B' is 163ft 6in. The length of the arcade was also 292ft, the same as the wing itself; the arcade in the elevation marked 'A' at Audley End is the same length as the wing, a mere 162ft. The committee also gave their 'Opinion that Double Wards as proposed by Mr. Jacobsen are more convenient than single as proposed by Mr. James, as they will be warmer in winter, cooler in summer, and easier kept clean'.[47] If James had adhered to his brief, wards which fitted into the wings shown in the Audley End drawings would have been 'double'. It was therefore not the Audley End drawings which the committee saw. But, as suggested above, the differences between the drawings suggest that they were not a definitive version, and the committee may have seen another, presumably bigger, and with a different plan.

Most of the 253 architectural drawings at Audley End were made for Sir John Griffin Griffin (Lord Howard de Walden from 1784), who owned the house from 1762 to 1797, and of the remainder, most were made later. The three by John James, who died in 1746, are among only eight which appear to pre-date Sir John's ownership. Of these some were evidently brought to Audley End by the previous owner, Sir John's aunt, Elizabeth, *née* Griffin, who married the first Viscount Lymington in June 1741. One of these, for instance, is a drawing of a garden ornament at Hurstbourne Park, Hampshire, Lord Lymington's country house, which must have been made before April 1743, when he was created earl of Portsmouth.[48] Lady Portsmouth bought Audley End in September 1751.[49]

John James was the son of the vicar of

44 Borg, *op. cit.*, 19, Fig. 3.
45 London, London Metropolitan Archives, A/FH/A/3/2/1, Foundling Hospital General Committee Rough Minutes 20 Nov 1739–25 July 1744 (hereafter FHGC Minutes), fol 455.
46 *Ibid.*, fol 437.

47 *Ibid.*, fol 456.
48 AE, 88096456, captioned ' ... in Lord Limintons Park ... ', and thus made between June 1741 and April 1743.
49 Addison, *op. cit.*, 86.

Basingstoke, had an estate at Eversley in Hampshire, and had a small but distinct group of gentry from that area among his patrons.[50] Lord Lymington, lord lieutenant and vice-admiral of Hampshire from 1733 to 1742, may have known him through these connections.[51] Lord Lymington was also governor and vice-admiral of the Isle of Wight from 1734 to 1742;[52] he is unlikely to have been ignorant of Appuldurcombe House, the largest house on the island, which was probably built to James's design c.1701–13.[53] As no other connection between James and Audley End is known, it is likely that the three James drawings were brought to Audley End by Lord or Lady Portsmouth.

Lord Portsmouth was a loyal Whig politician, not a very successful one. His elevation to the peerage was compensation for the loss of his seat on the Treasury Board in 1720; the earldom came as compensation for the loss of his local offices in 1742.[54] Among the few other public offices which he held was a governorship of the Foundling Hospital from its foundation in 1739.[55] He was not among the eleven members of the building committee,[56] but there are further connections between the builders of the Foundling Hospital and those of Audley End, which suggests that he might at least have taken an interest. James Horne supervised the building of the Foundling Hospital gratuitously between 1742 and 1751, making designs for details and drawing up agreements with some of the builders.[57] Some time after 1751 Horne sent Lady Portsmouth an estimate for pulling down the east wing of Audley End.[58] John Phillips and George Shakespear were the carpentry contractors for the west wing of the Foundling Hospital, beginning in 1743, and of the chapel, beginning in 1748.[59] In 1753 they demolished the east wing of Audley End, as Horne had advised, and replaced it with a library and two servants' rooms.[60] William Wilton was the plasterer of the Foundling Hospital chapel in 1749, and of the east wing in 1751.[61] In 1753 he worked at Audley End.[62] Edward Ives was the plumber of the west wing of the Foundling Hospital in 1743, of the chapel in

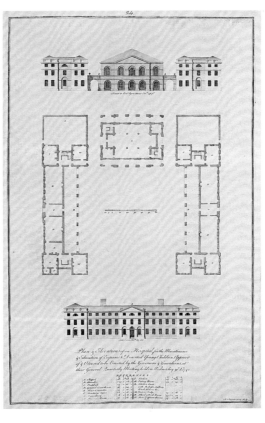

Fig. 5: Paul Fourdrinier, engraving of Theodore Jacobsen's plan and elevations of the Foundling Hospital, London, made between June 1742 and July 1746

1748–9, and of the east wing in 1751–3.[63] He stripped the lead off the roof of the east wing at Audley End in 1753 and tried to sell it to the duke of Bedford for use at Woburn; when the duke decided to have a slated roof instead of a lead flat, Ives managed to sell three and a half tons of it to Admiral Byng for use at Wrotham Park.[64] Horne, Phillips, Shakespear, Wilton and Ives may have owed their employment at Audley End to the knowledge which Lord Portsmouth had of the Foundling Hospital.

So the three drawings by John James at Audley End, although evidently not the drawings which he presented to the General Committee of the Foundling Hospital, may be earlier proposals for it, and were evidently of interest to the new owners of Audley End in 1751.

50 Howard Colvin, *Biographical Dictionary of British Architects 1600–1840*, New Haven and London, 1995, 538–40; Sally Jeffery, 'John James', Ph.D. thesis, University of London, 1986, 131–57.
51 Romney Sedgwick, *The House of Commons 1715–1754*, London, 1970, 507.
52 *Idem.*
53 L O J Boynton, *Appuldurcombe House*, London, 1986, 26–7.
54 Sedgwick, *loc. cit.*
55 R H Nichols and F A Wray, *The History of the Foundling Hospital*, London, 1935, 346.
56 Borg, *op. cit.*, 16.
57 Borg, *op. cit.*, 17, 20, 21 and 30; Richard Hewlings, 'The Builders of

the Foundling Hospital', *Georgian Group Journal*, XIII, 2003, 38.
58 Chelmsford, Essex Record Office (hereafter ERO), Pt. Accn. 5859, Lady Portsmouth's letter book, 'Mr Horn's estimate'.
59 Hewlings, ' … Foundling Hospital', *cit.*, 36, 39 and 42.
60 Paul Drury, ' … Audley End', *Architectural History*, XXIII, 1980, 27; ERO, D/DBy, A364.
61 Hewlings, ' … Foundling Hospital', *cit.*, 41 and 44.
62 Drury, *op. cit.*, 33, n.68.
63 Hewlings, ' … Foundling Hospital', *cit.*, 37, 41 and 44.
64 ERO, D/DBy, A364; *ibid.*, Pt. Accn. 5859, Lady Portsmouth's letter book, John Phillips to Lady Portsmouth, 18 August 1753.

Painting Like Devis: Edward Haytley

Hugh Belsey

A portrait, probably of the dowager countess of Burlington, was recently acquired for Chiswick House, and was at that time attributed to Arthur Devis. This article reattributes it, by stylistic comparison, to Devis's Lancastrian contemporary, Edward Haytley. The article attributes a number of other important portraits to Haytley and adds the first-ever checklist of his work for the benefit of future scholars.

Fig. 1: Edward Haytley, *Juliana, Dowager Countess of Burlington, in the Garden of Chiswick House*, late 1740s (checklist 12)

Before the time of public exhibitions and newspaper reports, the fame of an artist fell on the shoulders of the artist's family. If a painter had no children or had descendants who considered him an artisan rather than an artist, it was unlikely that sitters' books or accounts would have survived. To the disadvantage of historical fact, the common classification for documents is clutter and their usual fate is to be thrown out. Frequently the art historian is forced to depend on an inscription for author and date. In the 18th century at least, the artistic world appears to have been divided between those who signed and those who did not.

Prominent among the former is Arthur Devis. His family were long-established residents of Preston in Lancashire and he was himself a town councilman from 1729 to 1744, and from 1753 until 1761, but documentary evidence about him is limited and the means by which art historians have reconstructed his career and artistic development has been through the careful reading of the inscriptions that appear on so many of his works. For example, in the modest but stylish hand complementing his style of painting, 'Artr Devis fe. 1749', appears on the double portrait nicknamed *The Duet* in the Victoria and Albert Museum.[1] Did he always sign his work? Is the notion of signers and non-signers a credible way of describing artists? Without a signature can we be sure that Devis painted any canvas?

Devis's success, replacing the energetic unease of Hogarth's conversation pieces with refined country elegance, appealed to the gentry of provincial England and was adopted by other artists. His style, so polished, with the satin folds showing no trace of brushwork, was evidently a characteristic of artists working in the North-West. Christopher Steele's work and the early work of George Romney both reveal the same myopic taste for detail and surface.[2] Closer to Devis than either of these artists was Edward Haytley. Most of his work consists of small-scale full-length figures in the Devis mould, but there are notable exceptions and they raise Haytley to the status of a minor master. In a clutch of paintings his delight in landscape all but eclipses his abilities as a figure painter. These canvases, all dating from the 1740s, have been attributed to various artists, including the figure painter Joseph Highmore and the landscapist George Lambert, until they were correctly identified by references in the papers of Elizabeth Montagu (1718–1800), famous as the original blue-stocking.[3] In them Haytley combined delicate topographical landscapes with portraiture. There are two splendid groups of the Drake-Brockman family (checklist 8 and 9), who proudly pose around the newly built Temple Pond at Beachborough Manor, near Folkestone (*c.*1744; both Melbourne, National Gallery of Victoria).[4] Edward and Elizabeth Montagu and their family (checklist 19) are shown at Sandleford Priory, Berkshire (1744; private collection, United States).[5] Sir Roger and Lady Bradshaigh are shown outside Haigh Hall in Lancashire (late 1740s). This design is known in two versions; the one which belonged to the Bradshaighs is now in the collection of Wigan Metropolitan Borough Council (checklist 6).[6] The other, in a private collection

1 Ellen G D'Oench, *The Conversation Piece: Arthur Devis and His Contemporaries*, exhib. cat., Yale Center for British Art, New Haven, 1980, x, 56 (no. 22).
2 Mary E Burkitt, *Christopher Steele 1733–1767 of Acre Walls, Egremont*, Kendal, 2003, *passim*; Alex Kidson, *George Romney 1734–1802*, exhib. cat., Walker Art Gallery, Liverpool and National Portrait Gallery, London, February–August 2002, especially 7–10, 41–68.
3 David Posnett, *Exhibition of English Eighteenth Century Paintings*, exhib. cat., Leger Galleries, London, June–July 1978 (no. 7).
4 Emma Devapriam, 'Two Conversation Pieces by Edward Haytley', *Apollo*, CXIV, August 1981, 85–7; Ursula Hoff, *European Paintings Before 1800 in the National Gallery of Victoria*, 4th edn, Melbourne, 1995, 143–4.
5 Posnett, *op. cit.*
6 *National Art Collections Fund Report*, 1981, 61–3; Devapriam, *op. cit.*, 87.

(checklist 7), was the version requested by the novelist and printer Samuel Richardson in a letter dated 6 March 1750, asking Sir Roger to 'take a copy of the picture that hangs over your chimney in New Bond Street. You know the pleasure I shall have in looking upon it, when you are at that seat, which is there drawn in so lively a manner, and is so very delightful.'[7]

This article provides a checklist of works attributable to Haytley, adding a number of larger works to Haytley's *oeuvre* that date from the last years of his career. In particular it examines a portrait, until recently attributed to Arthur Devis, which belongs to English Heritage and is exhibited at Chiswick House.

It is not known when or where Edward Haytley was born, but it seems probable that, like Devis, he was a Lancastrian. Some of his works painted for Lancashire clients, including the group commissioned by Lord Derby in 1746, are inscribed 'Heatly Pinx'.', which may have been his name at birth. When the artist travelled south a phonetic spelling of the north-country vowels may have transformed his name to Haytley, just as Devis may be a southern transliteration of Davis.

In a letter dated 21 August 1740 we learn that Haytley was drawing flowers for Anne Donnellan and that the author of the letter, Elizabeth Robinson, the future Mrs Montagu, wanted to use some of them as designs for an apron she was embroidering for her friend the duchess of Portland.[8] The same author, who married Edward Montagu in 1742, wrote to her daughter on 28 December 1743:

> *Mr. Haytely is come back from my Neighbours where he has been drawing a landskip from ye life it is a view of his pond & his Temple that is to be built & ye neighbouring fields & hills, with some figures to adorn it the principle of which are ye Squire & Miss Molly. She is sett on a stool and drawing & he is fishing near her, then at some distance is Miss Hymore and ye Parson and Miss Betty and Miss Henkle.*[9]

The description is of one of the Beachborough

landscapes that are now in Melbourne (checklist 9).

William Hogarth identified Haytley as one of the up-and-coming artists of the day and asked him to submit two roundels of hospitals at Bethlem and Chelsea for the court room at the Foundling Hospital (checklist 39 and 40). Haytley supplied them in about 1747 and, like the companion canvases by Samuel Wale, Richard Wilson and Thomas Gainsborough, they hang between the great biblical histories painted by their older mentors, Hayman, Highmore, Hogarth and Wills. Highmore, perhaps already known to Haytley through the Drake-Brockmans, included Haytley's view of the Bradshaighs of Haigh Hall in the background of his famous portrait of Samuel Richardson (London, National Portrait Gallery).[10]

In September 1754 Haytley visited the Montagus at Sandleford Priory, where he painted 'a very pretty landskip with Eloisa' (untraced) and a portrait of Sarah Montagu which was 'a good likeness … with a spirit in the countenance and attitude that is very uncommon, that you will say whenever you see it, it is one of the best pictures that have been done by a modern hand' (checklist 24).[11] There is an unexplained gap in Haytley's biography in the second half of the 1750s, but in 1760 he reappears, contributing to the first exhibition of the Society of Artists at Spring Gardens. As numbers 26 and 27 he exhibited *A boy giving a bunch of grapes to his brother*, perhaps anticipating the design of Devis's 1762 portrait of the Edgar sisters (National Trust, Upton House),[12] and *A lady's portrait with a letter in her hand*, which may have been a reworking of Haytley's portrait of ten years earlier (checklist 35). In the following year three further portraits, all of which have escaped identification, show a gentleman (no. 39) and a lady (no. 41), both presumably small-scale full-length portraits, together with a *Portrait of a gentleman, three-quarters* (no. 40).[13] For whatever reason, Haytley did not exhibit again. In 1764 he signed and dated a likeness of Sir William Milner, second baronet (checklist 18), which was painted as a pendant to one of Lady

7 A L Barbauld (ed), *Correspondence of Samuel Richardson*, London, 1804, VI, 13–14.
8 Emily J Climenson (ed), *Elizabeth Montagu: The Queen of the Blue-Stockings*, London, 1906, I, 57.
9 San Marino (California), Henry E Huntington Library, Montagu papers, 4682, quoted by Hoff, *op cit*., 143. 'Miss Hymore' is convincingly identified as Susanna Highmore, daughter of the artist.
10 Highmore included the privately owned version of the painting which, like the other version owned by the Bradshaighs, was set in the panelling above the chimneypiece [J Kerslake, *Early Georgian Portraits*, London, 1977, 232–3, pls. 689, 689a].
11 Posnett, *op. cit*., citing a letter from Elizabeth Montagu to her sister Sarah, 6 November 1754. The landscape is untraced. In *Realism through Informality*, exhib. cat., Leger Galleries, London, October–November

1983, 11, Posnett identifies a triple portrait of a husband, wife and child as Mr and Mrs Matthew Robinson with their daughter Sarah, and a seated woman in an interior as a portrait of Sarah (the reproduction of the group portrait is reversed). Checklist 23.
12 Stephen V Sartin, *Polite Society by Arthur Devis 1712–87*, exhib. cat., Harris Museum and Art Gallery, Preston, and National Portrait Gallery, London, October 1983–January 1984, 49. Devis's portrait was probably exhibited at the Free Society in 1763 [*ibid*., 55].
13 Only two other standard head-and-shoulder portraits are recorded, sold from the Farington Collection in 1948 (checklist 5 and 15). The portrait of the Reverend William Farington (checklist 13) shares the same provenance and was purchased by the Harris Museum and Art Gallery, Preston, at the same sale.

Milner that Devis had painted four years earlier.[14] The Milner portrait is his last recorded work and, in the absence of definitive information, it is assumed he died soon afterwards.

The portrait at Chiswick House (Fig. 1, see page 82) shows an elderly woman seated in what is evidently the garden of Chiswick House, identifiable from the Ionic temple in the background (checklist 12). The temple, completed by 1727 at the latest, is the focus of an amphitheatre constructed by the third earl of Burlington in the grounds of his famous villa.[15] Orange trees in tubs are arranged on the terraces and are used to close the composition on the right of the painting, and an obelisk at the centre of the amphitheatre is cut by the left-hand edge of the canvas. The sitter poses beneath another tree, providing a focus for the composition. In her right hand, which rests on her lap, she holds an orange sprig, giving a delicate foil to the white of her muslin apron. She wears a plain open robe with a stomacher held by ribbon ties and deep-cuffed sleeves with white elbow ruffles. Over her white hair she wears a mob cap with lappets tied beneath her chin.[16] The style of her dress suggests a date in the 1730s or the early 1740s, and it might be supposed that the sitter was the third countess (1699–1758), formerly Lady Dorothy Savile, and wife of the builder of the villa and developer of the garden in which she is portrayed. But she appears to be a woman in her seventies and may therefore be Lord Burlington's mother, formerly Juliana Noel (1672–1750), widow since 1704 of the second earl of Burlington, whom she had married in 1688. In view of the setting it is likely that the portrait was commissioned by her son, whom she was to pre-decease by only three years on 17 October 1750.[17]

But why attribute this little canvas to Edward Haytley? In 1746 Haytley painted six small-scale full-length portraits of the Stanley family of Knowsley in Lancashire (checklist 11, and 25 to 29). He inscribed them with the names of the sitters, the Lancastrian form of his signature, and dates for five of them. The sitters were all children of Edward, eleventh earl of Derby (1689–1776). The commission appears to have been prompted by the clandestine marriage at Dr Keith's Chapel in London of Derby's son, James, Lord Strange (1717–71) to Lucy Smith on 17 March 1746. The portrait group comprises likenesses of Lord

Strange and his new wife, and Derby's daughters, Ladies Mary, Isabella, Margaret and Charlotte. The female portraits show a variety of poses and fancy costumes with the sitters shown in contrasting interiors and landscapes. To ring the changes yet further, they lean on tables or garden ornaments and hold musical instruments.

The portrait of Lady Margaret Stanley (checklist 26) shows her in fancy dress standing before a pedimented classical temple, with a landscape

Fig. 2: Edward Haytley, *Lady Margaret Stanley in a landscape,* signed and dated 1746 (checklist 26)

14 Cambridge, Fitzwilliam Museum, PD.25–1997.
15 Richard Hewlings, *Chiswick House and Gardens*, English Heritage, 1989, 28, 44.
16 London, English Heritage, Properties Presentation Department, Curators' Files, Chiswick Correspondence, Paintings and Engravings,

Edward Haytley, e-mail from Jane Clark to Cathy Power, 1 July 2001, citing opinions of Prof Aileen Ribeiro, Miss Elizabeth Einberg and Miss Joanna Marschner.
17 *Burke's Peerage Baronetage and Knightage*, London, 1959, 906 (s.v. Gainsborough), 538 (s.v. Cork and Orrery).

Fig. 3: Edward Haytley,
Francis Popham fishing in
the River Kennet, c. 1760
(checklist 22)

view opening up the left of the composition
(Fig. 2). The relationship of the figure to the
building is as ambivalent in this painting as it is in
the portrait of the dowager Lady Burlington, and
the treatment of the light across the folds in the
skirt is exactly the same. If Devis had painted the
Chiswick canvas the elements in the composition
would have been more mathematically placed.
It would resemble a computer desktop after the
command to tidy it.

The portrait of the dowager Lady Burlington is
indicative of the influential connections which
Haytley enjoyed in the middle of the century but
it is a painting that cannot be ranked amongst his
finest. However, a portrait at Upton House in
Warwickshire of a man fishing (Fig. 3), here (but
not previously) attributed to Haytley, is a major
addition to the artist's *oeuvre* (checklist 22).[18]
Assuming that the painting originally conformed
to one of the prescribed sizes for portrait canvases,
a 4in strip has at some time been cut from the
bottom edge. In the original painting the tree on
the right, designed as a compositional anchor and
a frame for the figure, would have been shown
firmly rooted in the ground.[19]

When the canvas was bought by Lord Bearsted
from the dealers Knoedler's in 1922 it was
attributed to George Stubbs, and shortly afterward
Arthur Devis's name was associated with it.[20] The
identity of the figure, Francis Popham (1734–80),
is confirmed when it is compared with Mason
Chamberlain's portrait of about the same date.[21]
He is shown casting his line from the tidy bank of
a millpond dammed from the waters of the River
Kennet on the Littlecote estate between Chilton
Foliat and Ramsbury in Wiltshire.[22] The angler has
already shown some aptitude, as the picture
includes two fine trout lying beside a wicker basket,
and at his feet are his hat, a book and a circular
box, presumably for flies. Close examination of the

18 I am grateful to Dr Brian Allen, who first suggested Haytley as the
author of the painting.
19 R St John Gore first made the suggestion that the painting had been
cut [*Upton House: The Bearsted Collection: Pictures*, 2nd edn, The
National Trust, 1964, 12, (15)].
20 Stubbs was proposed by W S Sparrow, *British Sporting Artists*,
London, 1922, 144. In the following year he noted that some had
attributed the canvas to Arthur Devis, and that others had thought that
the figure was by another artist [W S Sparrow, *Angling in British Art*,
London, 1923, 182–5]. The attribution to Devis was rejected by Sydney
Pavière [Gore, *loc. cit.*].
21 It last appeared at Sotheby's on 25 November 1998 (25).
22 The topography is difficult to identify. John Andrews and Andrew
Drury, *A Map of Wiltshire*, 1773, no. 12, show How Mill at Ramsbury
and Chilton Mill at Chilton Foliat, but neither mill appears to
correspond with the buildings in Haytley's painting. It is also worth
noting that the map includes a fishpond and elaborate gardens
immediately to the north of Littlecote and a fence and trees backed by
rising land (Elm Down) upstream and to the west of the house.

Fig. 4: Edward Haytley, *Lady playing an English guitar in a garden, c.*1760 (checklist 37)

painting shows that Haytley originally painted the hat, book and box nearer the edge of the canvas and at some point during the painting moved them further into the composition. The figure is drawn with particular elegance, its left leg straightened at a complementary angle to the fishing rod, and the face concentrating on the task in hand. Always conscious of the prescribed poses dictated by contemporary dance masters, Haytley adapts the classic pose of a man standing for his own purposes.[23] To the left twin mills straddle the river, with two undershot water wheels suspended between the buildings. Further downstream two similar wooden structures are no doubt part of the same complex of industrial buildings. On the right a decorative white paling fence with a higher gate leads to an orchard with fields rising up the chalk slope of Elm Down beyond.

It is tempting to think that the book protected by the sitter's hat from the dampness of the grass may be the two parts of the 1760 edition of Izaac Walton's *Compleat Angler*, bound together as one volume. The book, published by T Hope, was financed by Francis Popham's father, Edward (1709–72) and edited by the musicologist and lawyer, Sir John Hawkins (1719–89). Hawkins's edition includes a letter to his patron Edward Popham which notes that 'those for whose instruction and delight the book was written none who has ever seen or heard of the waters of Chilton can be ignorant of the care and expense with which they are preserved'.[24] The Kennet valley appears to have remained well-tended for at least 60 years; in 1825 John Britton described the river, 'a branch of which passes through the garden and forms a preserve for trout'.[25] Haytley has recorded

23 The best-known manual is F Nivelon, *The Rudiments of Genteel Behaviour*, London 1737, republished with notes by Paul Holberton and Hugh Belsey, London, 2003.
24 Frederick W Popham, *A West Country Family: The Pophams from 1150*, [Sevenoaks], 1976, 68–9.
25 John Britton, *Beauties of Wiltshire*, London, 1801–25, III, 259.

the same manicured landscape that was described by both Hawkins and Britton.

The attribution of the Popham portrait to Haytley also provides stylistic similarities with other portraits that have been variously attributed to Arthur Devis, his contemporary Edward Penny (1714–91), and even, in one case, to Johan Zoffany (1733–1810). One shows Sir Peter Leicester greeting his wife; another represents a lady playing an English guitar in a garden landscape (Fig. 4); the third shows two gentlemen standing before a backdrop of the falls of Tivoli (checklist 16, 37 and 38). The fourth painting, previously attributed to Zoffany, shows a woman walking on a terrace, with an ornamental canal in the background. It bears an inscription identifying her as Jane, Mrs Carew Mildmay of Shawford, Hampshire (checklist 17). The costume and the setting are so similar to the unidentified woman playing an English guitar that the relationship may be familial; perhaps they are sisters or sisters-in-law. All of them show a new complexity in the artist's work that is mirrored in the title of the double portrait of two boys exhibited in 1760.

Despite his modest demeanour Edward Haytley provides an archetypal mirror to 18th-century Britain, so much so that Sir Ellis Waterhouse chose his view of Sandleford Priory for the dust jacket of his *Dictionary of British Eighteenth Century Painters*. This short article is intended to add another building block in his rehabilitation as one of the most charming artists of the mid-18th century.

ACKNOWLEDGEMENTS

I am grateful to Brian Allen for suggesting improvements to the text and expansion of the scope of this article. I should also like to thank Cathy Power of English Heritage for giving me the opportunity to examine the portrait of the dowager Lady Burlington at Chiswick House.

APPENDIX
A CHECKLIST OF WORKS ATTRIBUTED TO EDWARD HAYTLEY

This checklist consists of paintings that are known through photographs and reproductions. It omits the five paintings exhibited by Haytley in 1760 and 1761, as none has been identified. It adds a number of paintings to the first rudimentary list of paintings by or attributed to Edward Haytley which appeared in Leger Galleries' catalogue of 1978, and includes portraits that have been attributed in the past to a number of other artists including Arthur Devis, Joseph Highmore, Edward Penny and Johan Zoffany. It does not claim to be exhaustive; other canvases by Haytley will appear disguised as works by other artists. Its intention is to record a coherent group of works that provides a definition of Haytley's style and shows a stylistic development during a career of 20 years.

The present location of paintings is given, and when this is unknown reference to the painting's most recent appearance on the art market is provided instead. Generally there has been no attempt to refer to the earlier provenance of the works. Citations to reproductions have been given but there has been no attempt to list references in literature or appearances of the works in exhibitions, unless the accompanying catalogue provides the most accessible and best illustrations.

PORTRAITS

1 *Atherton, ?Rev Richard, posing before a group of wild animals*, c. 1758.
Oil on canvas, 50.1 x 35.6cm (19¾ x 14 inches).
Sotheby's, 12 March 1980 (131), repr.; Lawrence of Crewkerne, 26 October 1989 (101), repr. col.
Private collection, Dorset.

2 *Austin, Rev Daniel, vicar of Berrington, Shropshire*, after 1743.
Oil on canvas, 50 x 34.5cm (19½ x 13½ inches).
Sotheby's, 19 July 1978 (22), repr.

3 *Austin, Mrs Daniel (née Anne Sandford)*, after 1743.
Oil on canvas, 50 x 34.5cm (19½ x 13½ inches).
Sotheby's, 19 July 1978 (22), repr.

4 *Bouverie, Hon Mrs (née Harriot Pleydell), at Coleshill, Berkshire*, late 1740s.
Oil on panel, 49.5 x 34.3cm (19½ x 13½ inches).
London, Courtauld Institute of Art, Photographic Survey, neg. no. B88/177.
Private collection, Wiltshire.

5 *Bradshaigh, Sir Robert*, signed and dated 1750.
Oil on canvas, 76.2 x 63.5cm (30 x 25 inches).
E J Reed and Sons, Preston, Henry Nowell Farington sale, Worden Hall, Lancashire, 28 January 1948.

6 *Bradshaigh, Sir Roger, with his wife Dorothy at Haigh Hall, Wigan, Lancashire*, signed and dated 1746.
Oil on canvas, 67 x 87cm (26¼ x 34¼ inches).
Stephen V Sartin, *Polite Society by Arthur Devis 1712–87*, exhib. cat., Harris Museum and Art Gallery, Preston, and National Portrait Gallery, London, October 1983–January 1984, (54),

repr.; Hayes, *Portraits in British Art: Masterpieces Bought with the Help of the National Art Collections Fund*, exhib. cat., National Portrait Gallery, London, November 1991–February 1992, (18), repr. col.
Metropolitan Borough of Wigan.

7 *Bradshaigh, Sir Roger, with his wife Dorothy at Haigh Hall, Wigan, Lancashire, c.* 1746.
Oil on canvas, 68.5 x 111.8cm (27 x 44 inches).
John Harris, *The Artist and the Country House: a History of Country House and Garden View Painting in Britain 1540–1870*, London, 1979, 219, repr.
Private collection.

8 *Brockman, James, and his family in the rotunda at Temple Pond, Beachborough Manor, Kent, c.* 1744.
Oil on canvas, 52.7 x 65cm (20¾ x 25½ inches).
Harris, *op. cit.*, 220; Elizabeth Einberg, *Manners and Morals: Hogarth and British Painting 1700–1760*, exhib. cat., Tate Gallery, London, October 1987–January 1988, (128), repr. col.; Ursula Hoff, *European Paintings Before 1800 in the National Gallery of Victoria*, 4th edn, Melbourne, 1995, 143–4, repr. col.
Melbourne, National Gallery of Victoria, 1246/5A.

9 *Brockman, James, and his family beside Temple Pond, Beachborough Manor, Kent, c.* 1744.
Oil on canvas, 52.7 x 65cm (20¾ x 25½ inches).
Harris, *op. cit.*, 220; Einberg, *op. cit.*, (127), repr. col.; Hoff, *op. cit.*, 143–44, repr. col.
Melbourne, National Gallery of Victoria, 1246/5B.

10 *Burgoyne, John, in hussar's uniform, c.* 1746.
Oil on canvas, 50 x 34cm (19¾ x 13¼ inches).
Sotheby's, 30 June 2005, (74), repr. col.

11 *Burgoyne, Lady Charlotte, in a landscape*, signed and dated 1746.
Oil on canvas, 48.3 x 34.4cm (19 x 13½ inches).
Posnett, *op. cit.*, fig. 6; Sotheby's, 30 June 2005, (64), repr. col.
Private collection.

12 *Burlington, Juliana, dowager countess of, in the garden of Chiswick House*, late 1740s (fig. 1).
Oil on canvas, 51 x 36.8cm (20 x 14½ inches).
English Heritage, Chiswick House, 88278800.

13 *Farington, Rev William, vicar of Leigh and rector of Warrington, Lancashire*, early 1740s.
Oil on canvas, 50.8 x 35.6cm (20 x 14 inches).
Sartin, *op. cit.*, (7), repr.
Preston, Harris Museum and Art Gallery, P2237.

14 *Granby, John Manners, marquess of, in a landscape with Belvoir Castle*, signed and dated 1751.
Oil on canvas, 50.8 x 35.3cm (20 x 13¾ inches).
Christie's, 20 September 2004, (548), repr. col.

15 *Heywood, Nathanial, Captain in the First Regiment of Dragoons*, signed and dated 1750.
Oil on canvas, 76.2 x 63.5cm (30 x 25 inches).
Posnett, *op. cit.*, fig. 10.
E J Reed and Sons, Preston, Henry Nowell Farington sale, at Worden Hall, Lancashire, 28 January 1948, (680).

16 *Leicester, Sir Peter, greeting Lady Leicester at the door of Tabley House, Cheshire, c.* 1760.
Oil on canvas, 100.3 x 125.7cm (39½ x 49½ inches).
London, Courtauld institute of Art, Witt Library mount.
Christie's, 20 July 1951, (88).

17 *Mrs Carew Mildmay, c.* 1760.
Oil on canvas, 74.9 x 62.2cm (29½ x 24½ inches).
Inscribed, lower right: *Jane, wife of Carew Mildmay of Shawford, 1760.*
London, Courtauld Institute of Art, Photographic Survey, neg. no. B75/2311.
Private collection.

18 *Milner, Sir William, second baronet*, signed and dated 1764.
Oil on canvas, 50.8 x 38cm (20 x 15 inches).
Cambridge, Fitzwilliam Museum PD.26–1997.

19 *Montagu, Edward, with his wife, Elizabeth, and sister-in-law, Sarah Robinson, on the terrace of Sandleford Abbey, Berkshire, with an extensive landscape*, before July 1744.
Oil on canvas, 89.5 x 152.4cm (35¼ x 60 inches).
Posnett, *op. cit.*, (7), repr. col.; Harris, *op. cit.*, 267.
Private collection, United States.

20 *Montagu, Elizabeth, in a landscape, c.* 1750.
Oil on canvas, 51 x 34.3cm (20 x 13½ inches).
Philips, 12 December 1989, (35), repr.
With Ackermann, London, April 1991.

21 *Newenham, Thomas, posing in a landscape with a telescope, c.* 1758.
Oil on canvas, 49.5 x 34.3cm (19½ x 13½ inches).
J H Plumb, *The Pursuit of Happiness*, exhib. cat., Yale Center for British Art, New Haven, April–September 1977, (96), repr.
New Haven, Connecticut, Yale Center for British Art, B1981.25.230.

22 *Popham, Francis, fishing in the River Kennet, c.* 1760 (fig. 3).
Oil on canvas, 90.2 x 124.5cm (35¾ x 49 inches).
The National Trust, Upton House, Bearsted Collection.

23 *Robinson, Matthew, with his wife, Elizabeth, and daughter Sarah at Mount Morris, Hythe, Kent*, signed and dated 1746.
Oil on canvas, 63.5 x 76.2cm (25 x 30 inches).
Posnett, *op. cit.*, fig. 9, repr.
With Ehrich Galleries, New York, 1929.

24 *Robinson, Sarah, in an interior, c.* 1744.
Oil on canvas, 76.2 x 63.5cm (30 x 25 inches).
Posnett, *op. cit.*, (11), repr. col.
With Leger Galleries, 1983.

25 *Stanley, Lady Isabella, in a landscape*, signed and dated 1746.
Oil on canvas, 48.3 x 34.4cm (19 x 13½ inches).
Posnett, *op. cit.*, fig. 4.
Private collection.

26 *Stanley, Lady Margaret, in a landscape*, signed and dated 1746 (fig. 2).
Oil on canvas, 48.3 x 34.4cm (19 x 13½ inches).
Posnett, *op. cit.*, fig. 5.
Private collection.

27 *Stanley, Lady Mary, in a landscape*, signed and dated 1746.
Oil on canvas, 48.3 x 34.4cm (19 x 13½ inches).
Posnett, *op. cit.*, fig. 3.
Private collection.

28 *Strange, James, Lord, in a landscape*, signed and dated 1746.
Oil on canvas, 48.3 x 34.4cm (19 x 13½ inches).
Posnett, *op. cit.*, fig. 1.
Private collection.

29 *Strange, Lady, in an interior*, signed and dated 1746.
Oil on canvas, 48.3 x 34.4cm (19 x 13½ inches).
Posnett, *op. cit.*, fig. 2.
Private collection.

30 *Wandesford, Miss Elizabeth, wearing Van Dyck dress and standing beside an obelisk*, signed and dated 1753.
Oil on canvas, 49.5 x 34.3cm (19½ x 13½ inches).
Julius Bryant, *London's Country House Collections*, London, 1993, 78, repr. col.
English Heritage, Marble Hill, MH69.

31 *Woffington, Peg, as Mistress Ford in 'The Merry Wives of Windsor'*, before 1751.
Oil on canvas, 50.8 x 35.6cm (20 x 14 inches).
Engraved by T Faber, mezzotint, 1751.
Leger 1978, fig. 11.
Private collection.

32 *Unknown gentleman wearing a blue grey coat and red waistcoat, leaning on the pedestal of an urn*, early 1740s.
Oil on canvas, 53.4 x 40.6cm (21 x 16 inches).
Christie's, 18 November 1988, (119), repr. col.
With Mallett, London, 2006.

33 *Unknown sportsman with a gun*, signed and dated 1752.
Oil on canvas, 51.7 x 36.5cm (20¼ x 14¼ inches).
Posnett, *op. cit.*, fig. 12.
New Haven, Connecticut, Yale Center for British Art, B1976.7.37.

34 *Unknown woman seated in her dressing room*, late 1740s.
Oil on canvas, 50.8 x 39.4cm (20 x 15½ inches).
London, Courtauld Institute of Art, Photographic Survey, neg. no. B90/72. Private collection.

35 *Unknown woman holding a sheet of music and leaning against a fountain*, c.1750.
Oil on canvas, 49 x 35cm (19¼ x 13¾ inches).
Sotheby's, 17 March 1982, (20), repr.
Sotheby's, 21 July 1982, (18).

36 *Unknown woman holding bonnet and leaning against a rock*, c.1750.
Oil on canvas, 50.8 x 36.6cm (20 x 14 inches).
Apollo, XCVI, October 1972, advertising section p.56, repr.
With Old Hall Gallery Ltd, Rye, 1972.

37 *Unknown woman playing an English guitar on the steps of a garden pavilion*, c.1760 (Fig. 4).
Oil on canvas, 67.2 x 89.5cm (26½ x 25¼ inches).
Christie's, 26 April 1985, (92), repr. col.

38 *Two gentlemen standing on a terrace with a view of Tivoli in the background*, c.1760.
Oil on canvas, 88.5 x 131cm (34¾ x 51½ inches).
Sotheby's, 20 November 1985, (45), repr. col.

LANDSCAPES

39 *Bethlem Hospital*, c.1747.
Oil on canvas, 53.3cm (21 inches) diameter.
Einberg, *op. cit.*, (165), repr. col.
London, Foundling Museum.

40 *Chelsea Hospital*, c.1747.
Oil on canvas, 53.3cm (21 inches) diameter.
Harris, *op. cit.*, 311; Einberg, *op. cit.*, (164), repr. col.
London, Foundling Museum.

Thomas Hyde Page and Landguard Fort, 1778–1803

Paul Pattison

This article outlines the career of the military engineer Sir Thomas Hyde Page, and describes the improvements which he made to Landguard Fort at Felixstowe in Suffolk between 1778 and 1785, when Britain found itself isolated and vulnerable to attack during the American War of Independence. The article reveals the temporary transformation of this coastal fort into a defensible camp for a small field corps capable of meeting an invasion force.

Fig. 6: *A New Survey of part of the Peninsula of Landguard Fort Showing the Fort and New Works with Sections and References explaining the parts Finished, Unfinished and Proposed. Taken and Drawn by Thomas Cubitt, Draftsman January 1st 1784*

This brief article addresses an episode during a time of national emergency, when extensive preparations were made for the defence of the British Isles. It is centred on a significant military engineer, (Sir) Thomas Hyde Page, who was commissioned to improve the defences of Landguard Fort at Felixstowe in Suffolk, as well as many other locations on the east and south-east coasts.

It was inspired by the re-emergence of Page's portrait in the collection of the National Trust at Tyntesfield House, Somerset (Fig. 1).[1] The artist was Sir Thomas Northcote, who may have painted it between 1778, when Page was appointed as engineer to the Eastern Coastal District and 1782, when the red uniform he wore for the portrait was superseded by a blue one.[2] Alternatively, it may mark his knighthood on 23 August 1783.[3] It is a noble painting whose composition symbolically illustrates part of Page's notable story. A thoughtful and uniformed Page is looking out to sea. In his left hand he holds a plan of the Landguard Peninsula with a design for new fortifications drafted on it; his sword and gloves rest on warrants signed by Lord Amherst as general on the staff (commander-in-chief of the army 1778–82) and Lord Townshend as master-general of the Board of Ordnance (1772–82 and 1783), the latter responsible for all permanent work on fortifications.[4] In the left background is Landguard Fort, in particular Chapel and Harwich bastions, the north-west curtain and the principal internal buildings (Fig. 2). Beyond the fort can be

seen the masts and sails of a ship coming into Harwich Haven, the important anchorage which the fort protected. The proximity of fort and ship is not simply artistic licence, as the deep water channel of the haven lies close under the fort wall. Of particular interest to this article is the plan in Page's left hand, several copies of which are preserved in national repositories, enabling us to reconstruct exactly what his intentions were for new defences at Landguard.

Northcote captured Page as a lieutenant in the engineers at a significant moment in his career: in 1783 he was both knighted and elected a fellow of the Royal Society. Page was born in 1746 in Harley Street, Westminster to Elizabeth (*née* Morewood) and Robert Hyde Page, also a military engineer. Thomas followed his father's profession and attended the newly founded Royal Military Academy at Woolwich, where from 1741 the Board of Ordnance trained its artillery and engineer officers in their respective disciplines. Page was a student of high calibre, completing his training in 1769 as first cadet in his year, for which he received a gold medal from George III. On graduation, he became a practitioner engineer and second lieutenant. After working on civil and military drainage schemes in the Bedford Levels and in Chatham, Page went with his engineer corps to fight in the American War. In 1775, during the early stages of the conflict, while serving as aide-de-camp to General Piggott at the battle of Bunker Hill, Page was badly wounded in the ankle and lost a leg below the knee.

1 I am grateful to Mary Greenacre of the National Trust for allowing photography of the portrait.
2 W Y Carman, 'Sir Thomas Hyde Page, Engineer', *Journal of the Society for Army Historical Research*, XXXIII, 1955, 61–2.
3 Herbert Rix (rev. W Johnson), 'Page, Sir Thomas Hyde (1746–1821)',

Oxford Dictionary of National Biography, 2004, XLII, 333–4.
4 William C Lowe, 'Amherst, Jeffrey, first Baron Amherst (1717–1797)', *Oxford Dictionary of National Biography*, 2004, I, 948–51; Martyn J Powell, 'Townshend, George, first Marquess Townshend (1724–1807)', *Oxford Dictionary of National Biography*, 2004, LV, 155–9.

Pensioned and back in England, in 1778 Page was appointed commanding engineer in the Eastern Coastal District, spending the next five years improving the defences at key installations around the east and south-east coast, notably at Dover, Sheerness, Chatham, along the Thames, and at Landguard Fort opposite Harwich.[5] Harwich had been an important national and international trading and communications port since the 12th century, and contained a naval dockyard from 1700 to 1713.[6] Its strategic importance lay in its vulnerability to capture and use as a bridgehead supplying an invading force, which might then slip through Essex to take London. Landguard Point forms the tip of a long peninsula on the north side of the haven (Fig. 3), where the channel of the River Orwell flows very close to the land, forcing all but light shipping attempting to gain the harbour to pass very close to the point, a strategic value exploited by the positioning of artillery defences there ever since the great scheme of Henry VIII in the late 1530s and 1540s. Moreover, until the 20th century Landguard Point was an isolated location, at times of bad weather and high tides occasionally cut off by seawater flooding across the peninsula along the line of a tidal creek, and inundating the low marshy ground of Landguard Common.[7] These factors made Landguard a strong and easily defended position.

Until the early 19th century, Landguard was, for reasons of economy, usually the location of the principal defences of the haven and there were several successive forts there. An Act of Parliament of 1709 had authorised the purchase of land in Harwich on which to build a new fortification as the main defence for the naval dockyard and port.[8] Although lands were acquired, no fortifications emerged, with the result that only a small garrisoned fort was built on the other side of the estuary at Landguard between 1717 and 1720, replacing one that had been built 1624–30.[9] Such a small fort was plainly inadequate and a new larger structure was completed between 1744 and 1751.[10] This was the one that Page encountered (Fig. 4), a 30-year-old structure comprising a permanent brick-built fort of pentagonal plan with bastions projecting from each salient angle. There was a dry ditch, a covered way, with infantry step,

traverses and ravelins, and a glacis beyond. The seaward face had an additional battery on the glacis to cover the deep water channel.

THE ENTRENCHED CAMP AT LANDGUARD

Page's appointment came during a difficult time for the nation. Britain was embroiled in a costly war with the American colonies, and in 1777 General Burgoyne's army was decisively defeated by the Americans at Saratoga. This was the rebels' first major victory of the war and it emboldened France, in July 1778, openly to take the American side. In the following year, the Spanish joined the French and planned to invade; 40,000 French troops and their transports were assembled at Le Havre and St Malo, waiting for the Franco-Spanish fleet to defeat the British Home Fleet before crossing the Channel to capture Portsmouth and march on London. Weather, sickness, bad planning and lack of co-operation resulted in disaster for the invading fleet and after revised plans to take Plymouth failed, the whole enterprise was abandoned. Nevertheless, the year 1779 was one of acute crisis in Britain and a major revision of defences was undertaken. The crisis deepened in 1780 when Holland joined the alliance against Britain.

It was against this background that Page began to transform Landguard into a much larger defensive work with the fort forming a small citadel at its heart. At this time, the principal threat to Landguard Fort and to Harwich Haven lay in a combined operation comprising naval bombardment and landing of a substantial force to take the fort by infantry assault. Although a flotilla of warships carried many more guns than were mounted in the fort, their accuracy could not be relied upon in the shallow and rolling waters of the estuary and certainly could not match that from guns on a stable platform. Land assault, therefore, was the chief threat to the fort and thereby the haven. British and French forces were in the early stages of developing effective combined operations and in the Seven Years War had occasionally deployed them successfully in Canada and North America, most spectacularly in the capture of Quebec.[11] Moreover, Page himself had a permanent and painful reminder of the cost of a frontal assault on even

5 Rix, *loc. cit.*

6 M R Eddy and M R Petchey, *Historic Towns in Essex*, Chelmsford, 1983; Jonathan G Coad, *The Royal Dockyards 1690–1850*, Aldershot, 1989, 2, 10.

7 F Hussey, *Suffolk Invasion*, Lavenham, 1983, 10.

8 Andrew Saunders, *Fortress Britain*, Liphook, 1989, 115, 117.

9 *Ibid.*, 115–16.

10 P Kent, *Fortifications of East Anglia*, Lavenham, 1988, 109.

11 T Hayter, 'The army and the first British empire', in D G Chandler and I Beckett (eds), *The Oxford History of the British Army*, Oxford, 2003, 120–2.

Fig. 4: Thomas Gainsborough, *A View of Harwich from the Cliffs above Landguard Fort*, c.1743–53, detail

hastily prepared land defences, as the British losses sustained in taking Bunker Hill were appalling.[12] Page's device at Landguard, as it was also on Dover Western Heights, was the entrenched camp.[13] This was a large enclosed fortification defined by a defensible perimeter, covered by artillery and infantry fire from several mutually supporting but independent strongpoints, the whole sheltering a larger

garrison and, if required, one capable of engaging the enemy outside the fort in a field action. It was estimated that the camp which Page built at Landguard could hold between 1,000 and 2,000 men.[14]

One of Page's early designs for Landguard, signed by him and possibly his earliest, is dated June 1778 and shows his proposals to improve the defences for the battery on the glacis facing the

12 *Ibid.*, 127.
13 J G Coad and P N Lewis, 'The Later Fortifications of Dover', *Post-* *Medieval Archaeology*, XVI, 1982, 111–200.
14 Saunders, *op. cit.*, 123.

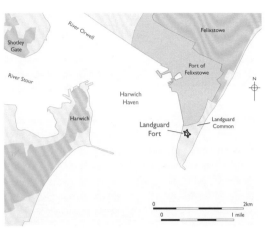

Fig. 3: Plan of Harwich Haven

completion in January 1784 (Fig. 6, see page 92).[17] All of them reveal that the entrenched camp was not to be entirely enclosed; there was a gap on the south-east, the least vulnerable side, where a landing could only be forced under full fire from the guns of the fort, in a difficult and fast current. However, all three depict the huge increase in the defended area on the landward approach, where two interlinked lines of rampart, ditch and glacis, the King's Lines and the Prince's Lines, were laid out in a series of salients along the fort side of the creek (Fig. 7). Construction seems to have been largely of local materials, sand and shingle revetted with turf and capped with parapets pierced by embrasures for artillery standing on platforms of imported stone.[18] The low ground alongside the natural line of occasional inundation was to be formed into a broad wet ditch which could be flooded at will through sluices as a defensive barrier, and crossed on a causeway guarded on the outer side by a small sub-triangular *tête de pont*, protected by rampart and ditch, from which access to the road and causeway could be controlled. Behind the entrenched lines, Page proposed a series of buildings for a larger garrison, mostly in brick but some in timber, comprising bomb-proofed gunpowder magazines, storehouses and two guardhouses, incorporating musket loopholes for close defence, for 60 men each.

A second major element in Page's design was the strengthening of the seaward defences. The existing main artillery armament was contained

main shipping channel (Fig. 5).[15] A more developed plan, also signed by Page, records some of the works undertaken between 6 October and 24 November 1781.[16] A third plan, by the draughtsman Thomas Cubitt, shows the state of

---

15 London, British Library, King's Topographical Collection, 39/62, Thomas Hyde Page, Engineer, *A coloured plan of Landguard Fort, with the proposed alterations*, approved by Sir Charles Cocks, clerk to the Ordnance, 12 June 1778.
16 London, National Archives, Public Record Office (hereafter PRO), MR 1/1408, Thomas Hyde Page, Engineer, *Plans and Sections of the King's Wells at Landguard Fort, begun 6th October 1781 and finished 24th November following*.

17 PRO, MR 1/1201, *A New Survey of part of the Peninsula at Landguard Fort showing the Fort and New Works with Sections and References explaining the parts Finished, Unfinished and Proposed. Taken and drawn by Thomas Cubitt, Draftsman, January 1st 1784*.
18 PRO, MR 1/1201; PRO, MR 1/1407/2, *Sections of the New Works at Landguard Fort* [*verso* labelled *Landguard Fort Major Hay 24th April 1794*].

on the south-west glacis of the fort, in Beauclerk's Battery, an open battery of heavy guns named after the fort governor of 1753–68, Lord George Beauclerk. Page proposed to strengthen this battery (Fig. 5) and to add three more, the North, South and Rainham Redoubts, to bring more massive and concentrated firepower to bear on the deep water channel. Each was supplied with a bomb-proofed gunpowder magazine and a defensible guardhouse, the latter with musket loopholes for close defence, and accommodation for 36 men, plus officers, in each one.

The North and South Redoubts were wing batteries extending from the fort to the water's edge. The North Redoubt connected with the Prince's Lines and was intended to hold artillery firing both to seaward and to landward, the latter protecting the rear of the Prince's Lines. The South Redoubt was similar, protecting the rear of the King's Lines and the third new battery, Rainham Redoubt, which was doubtless so named as a compliment to Townshend, whose family were seated at Raynham Hall, Norfolk. Rainham Redoubt was an independent enclosed redoubt positioned on the east side of the peninsula next to the sea. It was almost square but actually had five sides, the two eastern faces forming a shallow salient to seaward. The redoubt comprised a rampart, ditch and broad glacis. It mounted artillery on the north rampart giving covering fire for the King's Lines, and on the east and south firing to seaward. At its centre were a gunpowder magazine and a loopholed guardhouse for 36 men and officers.

Finally, Page designed an advanced work some 550 yards north of the Lines. This was a small redoubt covering access along Felixstowe Beach, the best line of attack from the land, avoiding the low marshy ground of Landguard Common.

One of the most important requirements for the entrenched camp was a reliable water supply. There was in fact a good water supply piped from a source over 1½ miles away but it was not located securely in the defended area. So, in Page's own words,

The Master General of the Ordnance (Lord Townshend) in the beginning of the year 1778, recommended to his Majesty, that the fortifications upon the Eastern Coast, including Dover, Sheerness, Landguard-Fort, and some other places, should be repaired, and new works added, where they might appear necessary towards a proper state of defence, if a war with Holland, or other Northern powers,

was found unavoidable. His lordship foresaw the great objection to fortifications, in the want of fresh water under the command of the guns of our garrisons; and I had directions accordingly to consider the subject, and report to his lordship and the Board of Ordnance any ideas that might be likely to remedy so great a defect.[19]

Page was something of a drainage specialist; his work at Sheerness, perfecting the construction of deep wells in very unstable and dangerous sub-soils, was remarkable and highly acclaimed (and he went on to carry out major drainage and

LANDGUARD FORT,
with the Proposed ALTERATIONS marked in Yellow.

19 Sir T H Page, 'Descriptions of the King's Wells at Sheerness, Landguard Fort, and Harwich', *Philosophical Transactions of the Royal* Society of London, LXXIV, 1784, 7.

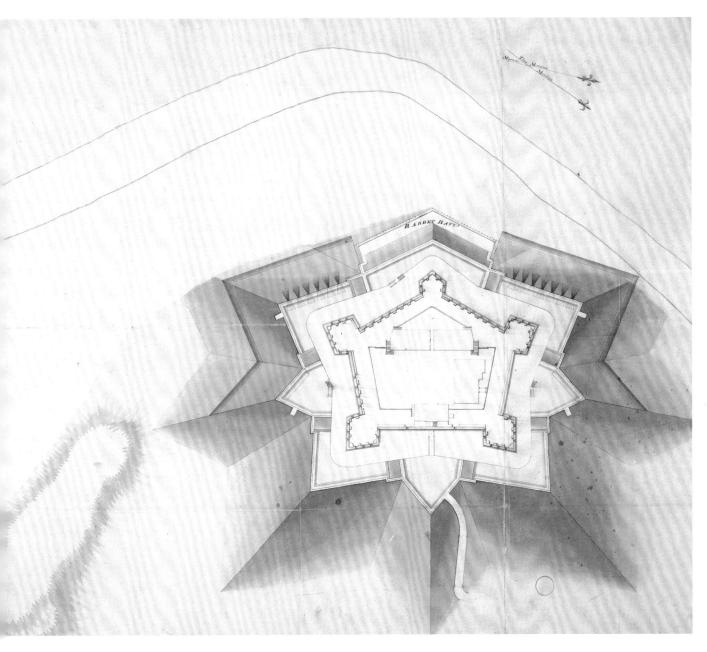

Fig. 5: Thomas Hyde Page, plan of Landguard Fort with proposed alterations to the seaward battery, June 1778

harbour works in Ireland and in the Fens near Kings Lynn).[20] He had new wells sunk on Landguard Common within the entrenched camp in 1781, contemporary with work on the new defences. The source was discovered by accident at only 12ft depth during the digging of a ditch, though an initial attempt to exploit it by sinking a well at first failed because salt water was encountered at a greater depth. The answer to the problem was found by cutting two wells to 12ft depth, above the high water mark to prevent the entry of salt water, and linking them by a 40ft-long brick culvert running almost horizontally (Fig. 8). Holes in the side walls of the culvert allowed fresh water to percolate inwards, perfectly filtered by sand and gravel, and run gently into the slightly deeper wells.[21]

The end of the American War in 1783 brought a rationalisation of the construction of fortifications: the war had stretched the nation and resources were concentrated in securing the defences around the major dockyards in Portsmouth and Plymouth.[22] At this time, the Landguard Fort works were not complete, but in a

20 Rix, *loc. cit*.
21 Page, *op. cit*., 15–18.

22 Saunders, *op. cit*., 124–7.

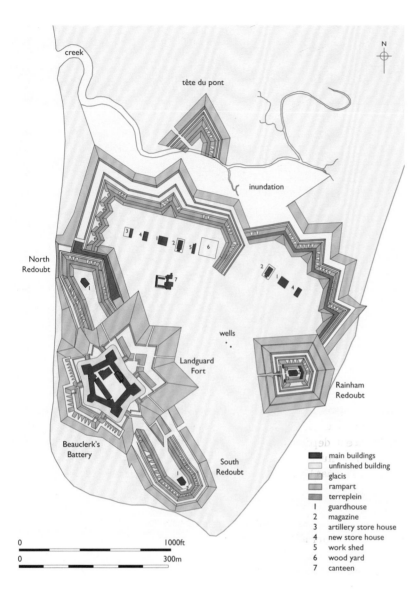

creek

tête du pont

inundation

N

North Redoubt

3 4 1 2 5 6

7

wells

Landguard Fort

Rainham Redoubt

Beauclerk's Battery

South Redoubt

- ■ main buildings
- □ unfinished building
- glacis
- rampart
- terreplein
- 1 guardhouse
- 2 magazine
- 3 artillery store house
- 4 new store house
- 5 work shed
- 6 wood yard
- 7 canteen

| 0 | | 1000ft |
| 0 | | 300m |

Fig. 7: Interpretation of Thomas Cubitt's plan of the entrenched camp at Landguard, 1 January 1784. Redrawn from original in the National Archives

fairly advanced state and are shown as such on Thomas Cubitt's plan of January 1784.[23] Rainham Redoubt was finished and the South Redoubt nearly so, but the North Redoubt and the *tête de pont* were unfinished. The King's Lines were ready, the Prince's Lines not quite; most of the support buildings were up. The huge glacis protecting the north-east face of the fort had not been completed.

It seems that not much was done to further Page's works in the nine years prior to the resumption of war with France in 1793. Early in 1794 another review of coast defences was implemented and Captain Lewis Hay RE was

given the task of assessing and reporting on the state of the Landguard defences. He worked at the fort in 1794 and prepared a 14-page report in April 1795.[24] The report provided a clear assessment of Page's work in terms of strategic issues, state of completion and decay. The main fort was secure and mounted 68 guns firing through embrasures. The North Redoubt was described as unfinished, 'perfectly open to assault' and with no means of communications to the fort. Its guardhouse was finished but there was no magazine or shot furnace. The state of the South Redoubt was similar but it was regarded as a better position; it had embrasures for 15 guns, all in need of repair, and Captain Hay recommended five more to fire over Rainham Redoubt onto what he called the 'ship track'. Rainham Redoubt itself was in a good state of repair, though its palisade and the fraises in the rampart were decayed. The parapet of the King's Lines had 23 gun embrasures, many of which were ruinous; its ditch was incomplete and the rampart had neither palisade nor fraises, though the magazine and guardhouse were in reasonable condition. The Prince's Lines had a considerable part of the rampart unformed. No work at all had been undertaken to make the inundation into a regulated wet ditch.

The defence review of 1794 highlighted the most vulnerable areas, which included a section of the east coast where beaches provided easy landing sites and Harwich a fine potential bridgehead harbour.[25] The nation was in serious danger of invasion and a view was taken that Landguard was in too forward and vulnerable a position to accommodate a mobile field force. By June 1803 another report, by Lieutenant John Thomas Jones RE, reveals that that some small works had followed Captain Hay's report of 1795, as repairs to the gun platforms on the North and South Redoubts were almost complete.[26] But it did not amount to very much. With the exception of Rainham Redoubt, described as a very fine enclosed work of rampart and ditch, with good palisades and fraises and in good working order, Page's entrenched camp was neglected. The lines in particular were described as of more use to the enemy than for defence; there were gaps caused by erosion in the ramparts and the revetments were collapsing. It was probably for this reason

23 PRO, MR 1/1201.
24 PRO, WO 55/733, in particular, report on Landguard Fort, dated 24 April 1795 by Lewis Hay, Captain Royal Engineers; letter to the Board of Ordnance regarding Landguard Fort, written by Lieutenant John Thomas Jones, Royal Engineers, dated 12 June 1803; letter to the

Board of Ordnance regarding Landguard Fort, written by Major Alex Bryce, commanding Royal Engineer, dated 18 October 1803. Plans are PRO, MR 1/1407.
25 Saunders, *op. cit.*, 132.
26 PRO, WO 55/733.

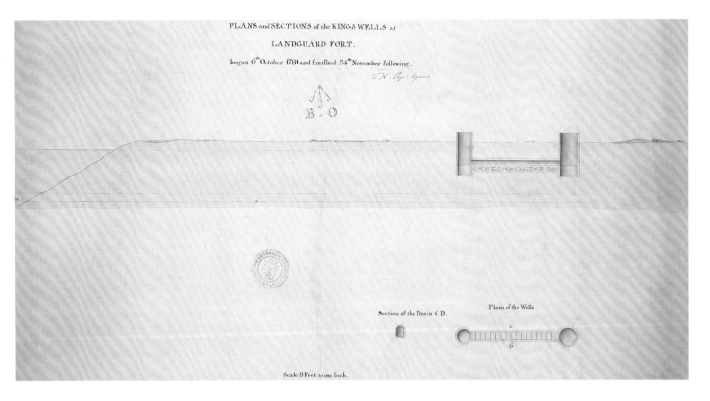

PLANS and SECTIONS of the KINGS WELLS at

LANDGUARD FORT.

begun 6ᵗʰ October 1781 and finished 24ᵗʰ November following.

Section of the Drain C.D.

Plans of the Wells.

Scale 8 Feet to one Inch.

that by October 1803, Major Bryce's letter shows that Landguard Fort had officially reverted to being a strong sea battery rather than an entrenched camp; the Lines had been pulled down to prevent use by an assaulting enemy force, but the outlying buildings were still standing in an exposed position. They were to be pulled down once their functions had been transferred elsewhere. A new infantry camp was to be established in a more sheltered position behind Beacon Hill, between Dovercourt and Harwich,[27] on the south side of the estuary, with much better communications and a better chance of blocking an enemy advance through Essex.

The significance of Page's works both at Landguard and Dover lies in the shift which the entrenched camp represents in military thinking – from a static form of defence around a strategic installation, to one with an element of mobility, from which troops could deploy from a protected place to meet enemy forces which had landed. This was a rarity in 18th-century England and may have its origins in Page's knowledge of the experience gained by British forces in Canada and America, where entrenched camps were built as bases to control key points of communication, and from which to deploy to carry out specific military actions. In the event, the Landguard

example was probably built in the wrong place and it lost its *raison d'être* as new ideas emerged for defence in depth at the end of the 18th and early 19th centuries.

Today, Thomas Hyde Page would still recognise Landguard Fort even though it has been much modified: the outline of most of the mid-18th-century fort survives, complete with four of its bastions. But later military works, coastal erosion and the development of the port of Felixstowe have removed or concealed most of the remains of Page's entrenched camp. The single visible exception is a short section of levelled rampart and ditch of the King's Lines, located some 500 yards north-east of the fort entrance in the only narrow strip of Landguard Common to survive. The rest lies in the realm of archaeology.

Fig. 8: Thomas Hyde Page, *Plans and Sections of the Kings Wells at Landguard Fort, begun 6th October 1781 and finished 24th November following*

---

27 Shown on a plan dated 24 December 1813 in PRO, WO 44/129, Landguard 1812–24.

Calshot Castle: The Later History of a Tudor Fortress, 1793–1945

Jonathan Coad

Calshot Castle, at the end of Southampton Water, was one of Henry VIII's distinctive coastal forts, and its history as such is well known. In the 17th and 18th centuries it became almost obsolete. But from 1793 to the end of the Second World War coastal defence was once more a priority, and Calshot acquired renewed importance. This article describes the ways in which it was adapted to modern tactics, with quick-firing guns, searchlights, a boom across Southampton Water, a flying-boat station and a battery disguised as a seaside bungalow.

Left: RAF seaplanes in the Schneider Trophy race at Calshot Castle in 1931 (detail from Fig. 11)

Henry VIII's chain of coastal artillery defences was built in the late 1530s specifically to protect southern England from a feared invasion by the Catholic powers of Europe (Fig. 1). Since the 16th century, the major forts forming this belt, characterised by their innovative rounded bastions and squat profiles, have had mixed fortunes. Once the immediate threat had gone, there was little money in peacetime for subsequent maintenance, although some of the forts retained small caretaker garrisons, usually a master-gunner and one or two men. Well before the end of the 16th century, their design had become militarily obsolete, overtaken by the development of the Italianate angle-bastion system, best seen in England at Carisbrooke Castle and the defences of Berwick-upon-Tweed. Sandown in Kent has largely vanished, victim of an encroaching sea.[1] The same fate has partly overtaken Sandgate, west of Folkestone,[2] and Sandsfoot on the Dorset coast.[3] Camber in East Sussex was abandoned in 1637, marooned and useless as the coastline shifted and choked the anchorage the castle once protected.[4]

During the Civil War the Henrician castles were frequently garrisoned by one side or the other, and a few, notably Sandown, Deal, Walmer and Pendennis, were hotly contested. After this brief interlude, most relapsed into the torpor of benign neglect. However, in 1708, Walmer was converted

into its present role as the official residence of the lords warden of the Cinque Ports.[5] In the 1730s, Deal was likewise adapted as the residence for the largely titular captain of Deal Castle.[6] Later, Deal was to resume a military role during the Napoleonic Wars, when it was re-armed with nine 36-pounder guns.[7]

The Napoleonic Wars were the first in which major modernisation works were proposed and mostly implemented at a number of the Tudor castles, a reflection of their strategic siting by Henry's commissioners more than 250 years earlier. Sandgate in Kent, and Southsea and Hurst Castles in Hampshire, all had their keeps substantially strengthened and modified to mount heavy artillery.[8] None was to see any action.

By the start of the 20th century, advances in the technology of warfare had had a massive impact on coastal defences. Over the previous 30 years, navies had changed out of all recognition. The introduction of the all-metal armour-plated, steam-driven warship firing explosive shells had had to be countered by equipping coastal defences with equally powerful weapons. Such guns required larger and more sophisticated mountings, new forms of ammunition storage and handling, and better protection. Their far greater range theoretically reduced the number needed, while their sheer size virtually ruled out making use of

1 J G Coad, *Deal Castle*, London, 1998, 22.
2 Edward C Harris, 'Archaeological Investigations at Sandgate Castle, Kent, 1976–79', *Post-Medieval Archaeology*, XIV, 1980, 54.
3 H M Colvin (ed), *The History of the King's Works*, IV (part II), London, 1982, 466.
4 M Biddle, J Hiller, I Scott and A Streeten, *Henry VIII's Coastal Artillery Fort at Camber Castle, Rye, East Sussex*, Oxford, 2001, 40–1.
5 J G Coad and G E Hughes, *Walmer Castle and Gardens*, London, 1992, 11–20.

6 Coad, *Deal Castle, cit.*, 14.
7 *Ibid.*, 34.
8 Harris, *op. cit.*, 54; A D Saunders, 'Hampshire Coastal Defence Since the Introduction of Artillery', *Archaeological Journal*, CXXIII, 1967, 148; J G Coad, 'Hurst Castle: The Evolution of a Tudor Fortress 1790–1945', *Post-Medieval Archaeology*, XIX, 1985, 68–75. A similar scheme was proposed, but never implemented, for the long-derelict Camber Castle [Biddle *et al, op. cit.*, 13].

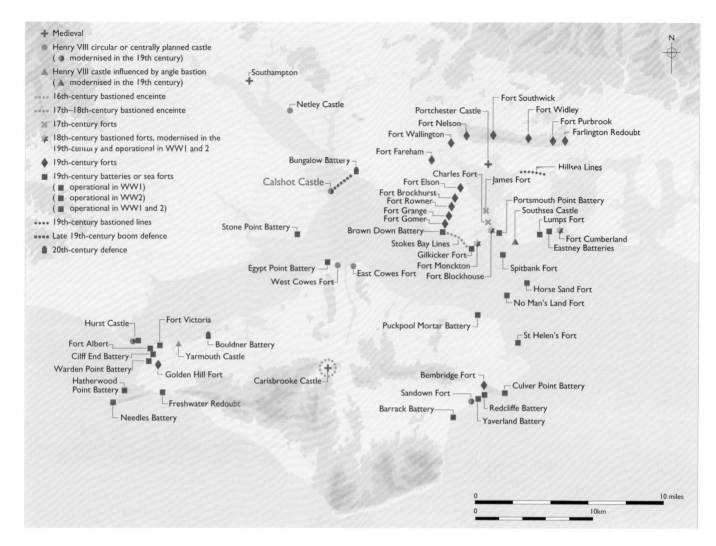

Key symbols:
- ✠ Medieval
- ● Henry VIII circular or centrally planned castle (◑ modernised in the 19th century)
- ▲ Henry VIII castle influenced by angle bastion (◮ modernised in the 19th century)
- ···· 16th-century bastioned enceinte
- ···· 17th–18th-century bastioned enceinte
- ✕ 17th-century forts
- ✸ 18th-century bastioned forts, modernised in the 19th-century and operational in WW1 and 2
- ◆ 19th-century forts
- ■ 19th-century batteries or sea forts (■ operational in WW1) (■ operational in WW2) (■ operational in WW1 and 2)
- ···· 19th-century bastioned lines
- ▬▬ Late 19th-century boom defence
- ⬣ 20th-century defence

Map labels: Southampton, Netley Castle, Portchester Castle, Fort Southwick, Fort Widley, Fort Nelson, Fort Purbrook, Fort Wallington, Farlington Redoubt, Fort Fareham, Bungalow Battery, Calshot Castle, Charles Fort, Hillsea Lines, Fort Elson, James Fort, Fort Brockhurst, Fort Rowner, Portsmouth Point Battery, Fort Grange, Southsea Castle, Fort Gomer, Lumps Fort, Stone Point Battery, Brown Down Battery, Stokes Bay Lines, Fort Cumberland, Eastney Batteries, Gilkicker Fort, Egypt Point Battery, Fort Monckton, Spitbank Fort, East Cowes Fort, Fort Blockhouse, West Cowes Fort, Horse Sand Fort, No Man's Land Fort, Puckpool Mortar Battery, St Helen's Fort, Hurst Castle, Fort Victoria, Fort Albert, Bouldner Battery, Cliff End Battery, Yarmouth Castle, Warden Point Battery, Golden Hill Fort, Bembridge Fort, Culver Point Battery, Hatherwood Point Battery, Carisbrooke Castle, Sandown Fort, Redcliffe Battery, Freshwater Redoubt, Barrack Battery, Yaverland Battery, Needles Battery

Scale: 0 – 10 miles / 0 – 10km

Fig. 1: Defences of the Solent. This map gives a vivid impression of the accumulation here of defences from the 14th to the 20th centuries. Calshot's key position at the entrance to Southampton Water is clearly shown

Fig. 2: Paul Sandby, *Calshot Castle*, 1780, soon after the alterations to the keep parapet and the curtain wall embrasures. The new first-floor screen wall on either side of the Tudor gatehouse partly conceals the extended governor's lodgings

the Tudor fortresses. Where the latter still occupied strategic locations, the War Office was forced to adapt. At Pendennis, guarding Falmouth harbour, there was space to mount the new weapons outside the Henrician castle but largely within the more spacious Elizabethan bastioned defences.[9] At Hurst, overlooking the Needles Passage, engineers had added vast armour-plated granite and brick wings on the eastern and

western sides of the castle in the 1860s to contain the new generation of weapons.[10] Forty years on, their replacements here were much smaller quick-firing (QF) guns, mounted partly in emplacements on the shingle spit outside the castle and partly on the roof of the earlier Victorian western wing.[11] Both Pendennis and Hurst castles were to be fully garrisoned in both World Wars.[12]

Calshot Castle's later history took a somewhat different course. In 1539 the castle had been carefully sited at the end of a shingle spit where its guns could command the deep-water channel at the entrance to Southampton Water. Although one of the smaller of Henry's fortresses, perhaps because it was seen as a secondary defence after Hurst Castle, Calshot nevertheless mounted 36

9 Richard Linzey, *The Castles of Pendennis and St Mawes*, London, 1999, 34–7.
10 Coad, 'Hurst Castle', 63–104.
11 *Ibid.*, 98–100.
12 Linzey, *op. cit.*, 37; Coad, 'Hurst Castle', 100–1.

guns by the later 1540s.[13] Its later history until after the Napoleonic Wars broadly follows the pattern of its sister forts. A peacetime caretaker garrison generally seems to have been in residence, although the fabric was often in poor repair. In the 1580s, the interior of the keep was rebuilt after a serious fire; the reddened stonework may still be seen.[14] In the mid-1770s, the castle underwent a substantial modernisation. A continuous parapet for musketry replaced the Tudor gun embrasures on the top of the keep, and the outer curtain was reduced to its present height, turning the gun ports there into the existing embrasures (Fig. 2). The surviving first floor with its distinctive row of pitched roofs was added to the rear of the gatehouse for the governor or captain of the castle (Fig. 3).[15]

In 1793, at the start of the wars with France, the castle was in the charge of a master-gunner 'so old and infirm that he is past service'.[16] A second report noted that 'the guns … are all bad, but there are three 18-pounders that may be made use of for a short time, with a short allowance of powder, which command the entrance of the river, and three 6-pounders, one of which commands the neck of land south of the castle, and the other two point directly up the river … '.[17] Ten years earlier, another report noted that in the absence of a powder magazine, 'the powder is lodged in a closet belonging to the governor's apartment'.[18] With other more urgent calls on its funds, the Board of Ordnance undertook only limited repairs a few years later. In 1804, the Board decided to use the castle as a depot for ordnance stores 'belonging to

Fig. 3: Calshot Castle in the time of the Napoleonic wars. This clearly shows the governor's new lodgings built to the rear of the gatehouse. On the spit to the right can be seen the master-gunner's house. This view of the castle shows how well it was sited to command the entrance to Southampton Water

13 Colvin, *op. cit.*, 530.
14 *Ibid.*, 405–6.
15 Gillingham, Brompton Barracks, Royal Engineers' Library [hereafter REL], POR/01/1, 30/9/1777. See also Fig. 2.

16 REL, POR/01/12, 28/2/1793.
17 REL, POR/01/15, 28/2/1793.
18 REL, POR/01/5, 25/8/1783.

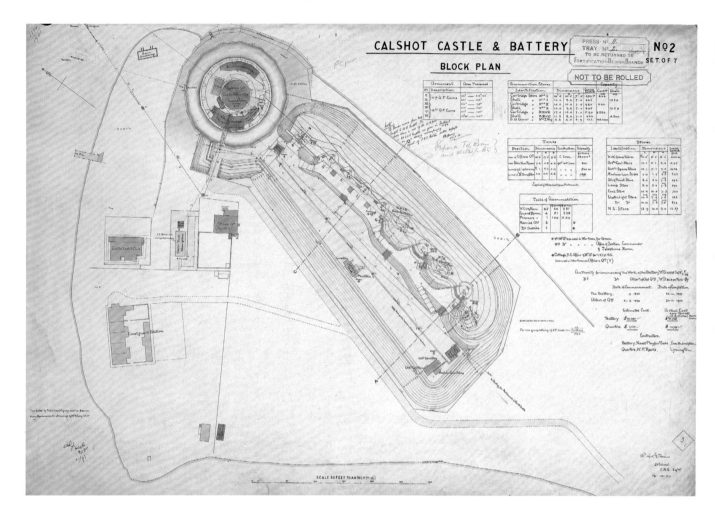

Fig. 4: Calshot Castle and the new six-gun battery begun in 1895. The associated electric light emplacements are clearly shown in the castle's gun embrasures. This plan gives a good impression of the scale of this new defence work, which was totally obliterated after the First World War to make way for seaplane hangars

the fishing vessels armed for the defence of the coast'.[19] These were the boats of the Sea Fencibles, a corps of volunteers raised in 1798 at the suggestion of Captain Home Riggs Popham. Their role was to patrol and keep watch on the coast and to aid British shipping under attack.[20] Calshot Spit was an ideal base for such craft. With the looming threat of a French invasion, a further six 18-pounder guns and one more 6-pounder were also mounted at the castle.[21]

Little is known about garrison life here, but a constant watch would have been kept on shipping approaching Southampton Water. In the latter part of the Napoleonic Wars a spur to garrison efficiency was the presence in the gatehouse of General Sir Harry Burrard. He had maintained an interest in the castle since his appointment as captain, probably as early as 1780, but most of his

army career had been spent abroad. He retired after playing a leading role in agreeing the Convention of Cintra, the 1808 armistice with the French in Portugal, and spent the rest of his life at Calshot, dying there in October 1813.[22]

Well before the Napoleonic Wars, the sheltered water in the lee of Calshot Spit had also been used as a station for revenue cutters in their unending pursuit of smugglers in the Solent. In 1811 the crew of the resident cutter sought accommodation in the castle.[23] It is not known if this request was granted, but it presaged the castle's subsequent use. Soon after 1815 the coastguards took over the castle and were to remain there until 1894, returning again after the Second World War.[24]

The army however, retained an interest in the castle. In 1850, the inspector-general of fortifications, Sir John Burgoyne, recommended

19 REL, POR/01/25, 31/8/1804.
20 Peter Bloomfield, *Kent and the Napoleonic Wars*, Maidstone, 1987, 22.
21 K W Maurice-Jones, *The History of Coast Artillery in the British Army*, London, 1959, 87.

22 J G Coad, *Calshot Castle*, London, 1986, 16.
23 London, The National Archives, Public Record Office (hereafter PRO), WO 55/787, 17 December 1811.
24 From 1856, control of the coastguards passed to the Admiralty [Coad, *Calshot Castle, cit.*, 18].

that Calshot should mount nine 18-pounders on 'the lower battery', the space within the outer curtain wall. However, he added as a rider that 'it [the castle] is as it were an interior or secondary defensive position, and the battery at best is defective in being immediately under a tower [the keep], the splinters from which would be a great impediment to the service of the guns, if not silence them'.[25]

Two years later in 1852, a joint report by a group of Royal Engineer and Royal Artillery officers suggested more radical and ambitious surgery to modernise the castle. The courtyard was to be filled by casemates for six heavy guns with a further five mounted en-barbette on the roof or terreplein above. The gatehouse and immediately adjacent outer curtain were to be demolished and replaced with two wing batteries with a total of three traversing guns. Each wing battery was to be flanked by a circular tower, each with one tier of guns in casemates and a further gun mounted above en-barbette. Had this scheme been implemented, Calshot would have bristled with four 68-pounder guns, fifteen 8-inch shell guns, eleven 32-pounders and two 24-pounder howitzers for high-angle fire.[26] These proposals were vastly over-ambitious and nothing was done. However, elements of just such a scheme – wing batteries, casemates in the courtyard and new barbette gun positions – were then being provided at Hurst Castle, whose location at the Needles Passage gave it the strategic edge over Calshot.[27]

The 1850s were the start of a period of rapid developments in heavy ordnance. New rifled guns firing explosive shells accurately over hitherto undreamed-of distances were to make most existing fortifications obsolete. When such weapons were mounted in the new ironclad steam warships which entered service at the end of that decade, the potential threat to national security led the British government hastily to set up a royal commission to examine the defence of the United Kingdom. The subsequent report was to lead to one of the most extensive and sustained programmes of fortifications ever undertaken in this country. The prime need, to protect the great naval bases, saw a massive concentration of new defence works in the Solent area, the Isle of Wight and around the landward side of Portsmouth.[28]

Calshot, however, remained untouched by all this. An 1859 report, which could have been written at any time over the next few years, noted that the ground floor of the Tudor keep was a kitchen for the coastguard officers, while the two floors above were occupied by 'an officer of the coastguard'. The gatehouse was used as married quarters for the men. In total, the coastguard here numbered two officers and 42 NCOs and privates. Keeping an eye on what was still Board of Ordnance property was a master-gunner who lived in a small house outside the castle.[29]

Technical developments in ordnance and warship design and capability in the latter part of the 19th century were, however, to have a dramatic impact on Calshot. The great coastal fortresses of the 1860s had been designed to counter contemporary warships. Both fortresses

Fig. 5 (below): The former gun-boats HMS *Marina* and *Reindeer* adapted as boom defence vessels, photographed at Devonport c.1904–9. A sister ship, HMS *Melita*, was one of a number of similar vessels based at Southampton Water by 1910

Fig. 6 (bottom): The 1907 alterations to the top of the keep to allow the mounting there of two 12-pounder QF guns. This was the last significant work to the castle's fabric for armament purposes

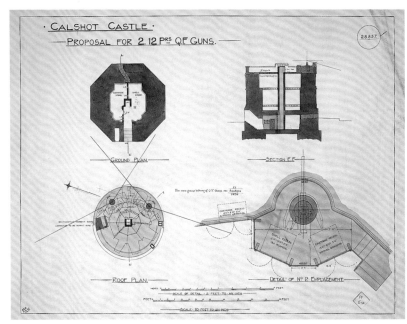

25 PRO, WO 44/285, 12 June 1850.
26 PRO, WO 55/796, 24 September 1852.
27 Coad, 'Hurst Castle', *cit*., 76–84.
28 Saunders, *op. cit.*, 151–68.
29 PRO, MPH/568.

Ground plan

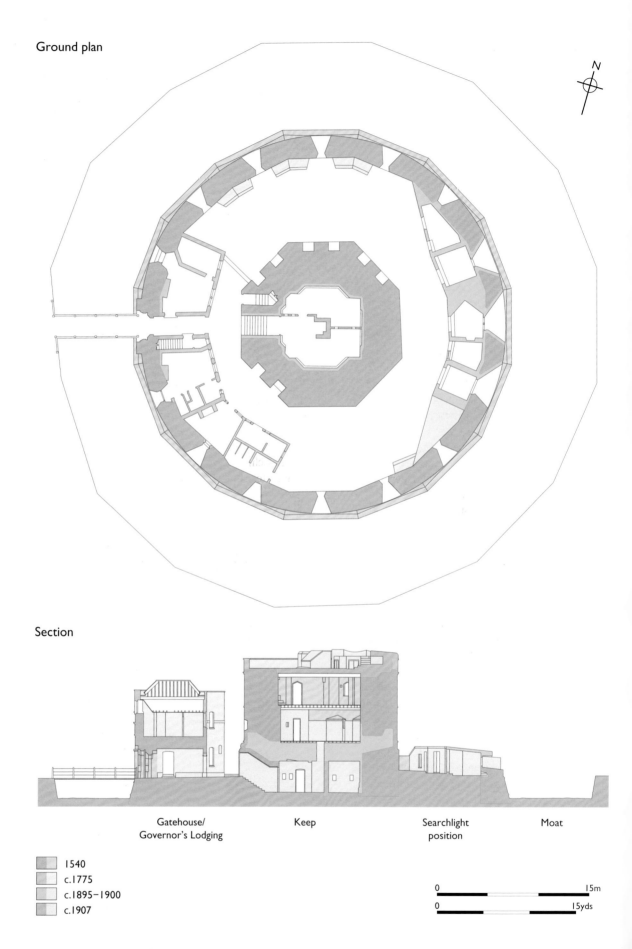

Section

Gatehouse/   Keep   Searchlight   Moat
Governor's Lodging   position

1540
c.1775
c.1895–1900
c.1907

0   15m

0   15yds

and warships were then armed with much the same heavy weapons, generally only capable of firing a round every two or three minutes. These leisurely rates were matched by warships' speeds of around 12–14 knots, which in favourable circumstances could allow time for coastal gunners to fire several rounds at a ship from each gun. But in the 1870s and 1880s European navies were experimenting with small fast craft armed with the torpedoes invented by Robert Whitehead in the 1860s.[30] By the 1880s, although only capable of steaming in sheltered waters, such craft could reach speeds of 22 knots and were being built in large numbers by the French navy. Alarmed that existing guns on warships were too slow and cumbersome to be sure of sinking such craft, the Admiralty asked gun manufacturers to design a weapon that could fire at least 12 aimed rounds a minute. The resultant quick-firing (QF) weapons were first mounted as secondary armament on board the Royal Navy's warships. But by the end of the 1880s, torpedo craft had increased in size and seaworthiness to a point where they were capable of crossing the Channel. This raised fears that raids by flotillas of such craft, perhaps under cover of darkness, could cause havoc among shipping in commercial ports and naval bases and would be very difficult for the Royal Navy to counter.[31]

The solution adopted was to mount QF guns and searchlights on existing coastal forts or on new gun batteries. Where the importance of the target and geography permitted, movable booms were to be installed to block the seaward approaches. Defending the great port of Southampton was seen as just such a priority. Initially, works concentrated on installing QF guns on the outer ring of Solent defences, at locations such as Hurst Castle and the Needles Battery, but fears remained that torpedo craft might still manage to elude these and steam unopposed up Southampton Water.[32] Calshot Castle was the obvious location for a second line of defences. In July 1894, the Admiralty handed over the castle to the War Office for modernisation.[33]

In 1895, a substantial new gun battery was begun to the south of the castle facing the Solent, and completed in 1897 (Fig. 4). This mounted two 4.7-inch and four 12-pounder QF weapons.

Fig. 7 (facing page): A plan and cross-section of the castle as it stands today, showing the main building phases

Fig. 8 (left): The interior of the first floor of the keep, displayed as it would have appeared c.1910 in use as barracks for the gunners

Reinforced concrete shell and cartridge stores were incorporated below the rampart. Within the castle itself, the gun embrasures on the north-eastern curtain were adapted for three searchlights, or defence electric lights, as they were then known. Power for the lights came from generators driven by oil engines located in the keep basement; fuel oil tanks were installed in the courtyard. The upper floors of the keep and the gatehouse became barracks for the gunners. A single-storey cook-house and latrines were added to the east side of the gatehouse; these remain, along with the concrete searchlight housings. The latter works were completed by November 1896.[34]

An important element of the scheme here was the provision of a boom to close the entrance to Southampton Water. Along with Portsmouth Harbour, Sheerness and Portland, Southampton was selected as a location for these new defences. The submarine threat had yet to materialise and booms then were simply designed to stop fast surface raiders. They were constructed using substantial baulks of timber wired together and apparently stiffened at intervals by rafts. A section could be drawn aside to allow ships to pass through. For practical reasons, the booms were kept ashore until needed; at Calshot, the boom was stored to the south-west of the castle. When required, it was winched into the water, towed into position by tugs and boom defence vessels, and secured to 'dolphins', lattice metal and timber towers fixed to the seabed. The Calshot boom had two of these dolphins, one adjacent to the castle,

---

30 A Wolstencroft, 'The Whitehead Story', *The Mariner's Mirror*, LIX, 1973, No. 3, 345.
31 A D Saunders, *Fortress Britain, Artillery Fortification in the British Isles and Ireland*, Liphook, 1989, 191–2; D K Brown, *Warrior to Dreadnought: Warship Development 1860–1905*, London, 1997, 115–17; David Lyon, *The Ship: Steam, Steel and Torpedoes*, London 1980, 48–54.
32 Coad, 'Hurst Castle', *cit.*, 98. In the 1880s the technical and practical problems associated with booms and submarine minefields

were to exercise the Royal Navy [Matthew Allen, 'The Origins, Conduct and Outcome of the British Naval Exercises of 1885', *The Mariner's Mirror*, XLI, August 2005, 421–35].
33 PRO, MPHH/611.
34 PRO, WORK 78/4954, parts 2 and 5. It has not so far proved possible to establish if this new battery retained its armament at the start of the First World War.

Fig. 9 (right): One of the original buildings of Calshot Royal Naval Air Station, photographed in November 1916. Apart from their hangars, air stations had yet to evolve a distinctive style of architecture. The number of doors in this building suggests some sort of office use, with the first-floor balcony and 'gazebo' used for observing flying activities

Fig. 10 (facing page top): Calshot Spit in 1917. This remarkable air photograph shows the Royal Naval Air Station at one of its busiest periods in the First World War. The castle lies to the right, dwarfed by the 1895 battery. By then, the guns had been removed from the latter and it was filled with storage and accommodation huts. Beyond the battery are seaplanes, their wings folded, the launching rails and seaplane hangars. On the foreshore to the left is a twin-hulled flying boat. This was the *AD 1000*, built by J Samuel White of Cowes and mounting a 12-pounder recoilless cannon. The hapless crew was expected to fire this at the un-armoured decks of German warships. In 1917, this was the largest seaplane built in this country. It never entered service

Received in Drawing Office. 15·11·

the other close to the shore at Warsash on the far side of Southampton Water. Each dolphin had a platform with two 12-pounder QF guns and a machine gun. The boom and boom defence vessels were provided by the navy.[35]

In 1907 permission was sought and obtained to convert the existing boom to a ladder boom.[36] As its name suggests, this was formed from longitudinal spars connected by shorter cross-spars. Its advantage may have lain in its manoeuvrability, although later that year it was suggested that five rather than three boom defence vessels were needed to operate it. The ladder boom appears to have had a short life, for by 1909 it was recorded that the boom consisted of 'several hulks' that would take 'from five to seven days to place … in position and remove'.[37] Given the amount of shipping using Southampton Water, there cannot have been many practices of this operation. The boom may have been modified again in 1910 and apparently remained in use until superseded early in the First World War by submarine nets across the Solent and at Spithead.[38]

The boom defence vessels (Fig. 5), elderly former gunboats, were berthed initially on the Hamble River and at Netley. The latter location proved unsatisfactory, in part due to the 'too handy public house'. By January 1908, the vessels had all been removed to the Hamble River and the senior officer was happy to report that with the provision of proper facilities such as a mess room and a billiard table, 'sobriety has improved to a

marked degree – to the great advantage of the work carried on'.[39]

In 1907 the keep roof at Calshot was extensively reconstructed to mount two of the existing 12-pounder guns from the adjacent battery, giving them better command of the boom (Fig. 6). A new reinforced concrete roof was inserted and a brick-lined ammunition hoist linked this to the basement, which now became a cartridge and shell store (Fig. 7). The two floors above remained in use as barrack rooms (Fig. 8). A new generator house was built outside the keep. These were the last major military modifications to the Henrician keep.[40]

Some idea of the numbers of men required to operate the defences of Southampton Water can be gained from the 1910 mobilisation plan. This envisaged that the three officers and 85 other ranks in the castle would be augmented by a further seven officers and 69 other ranks, who would be accommodated in private houses and tents. The Alexandra Hospital at Cosham would provide one civilian surgeon and an orderly.[41] To this number must be added the naval crews of the boom defence vessels.

These new arrangements, which followed the Owen Committee report of 1905 on the future structure of Britain's coastal artillery, were to be short-lived.[42] Defences at the entrance to Southampton Water were increasingly seen as of secondary value to the major 9.2-inch batteries protecting the Needles Passage and Spithead. By early 1914 the castle's armament had been downgraded to 'reserve' status. A year later, with the country at war with Germany, two of Calshot's guns were relocated to new batteries at Egypt Point and Stone Point where they could protect the new anti-submarine net across the Solent.[43]

In 1912 Calshot Spit entered a completely new military phase when the Admiralty had authorised the establishment of a chain of flying-boat stations around the coast from Scapa Flow to Pembroke Dock.[44] These were to serve as bases for naval seaplanes operating with the fleet. The comparatively sheltered Southampton Water

35 PRO, WO78/3908 shows the proposed Calshot boom line, the dolphins and shore anchors, and is dated 26 January 1897. See also PRO, WO33/383, fol 261, for the scheme as in 1905. PRO, WORK 31/4955, fol 2, has details of two dolphins dated 11 June 1910. PRO, ADM 179/130, 1 January 1909, mentions four dolphins at Southampton. *Ibid.*,18 May 1907, mentions one '20 horsepower hauling engine' costing £1,000. This was presumably the winch used to drag the boom to and from the water.
36 PRO, ADM 179/130, 18 May 1907 and 4 September 1907.
37 *Ibid.*, 7 November 1907 and 15 July 1909.
38 C S Dobinson, *Twentieth Century Fortifications in England, VI, Coast Artillery. England's Fixed Defences against the Warship 1900–1956*, York,

2000, 1.174–5; PRO, WO 192/307, fol 18; PRO, WO 192/306. Elements of the Spithead submarine defences remain in place today.
39 PRO, ADM179/130, 10 January 1908.
40 PRO, AIR 28/120, 4 and 28 September 1940; PRO, WO 192/307, fol 18.
41 PRO, WO33/551, 1910 Mobilisation Plan. It is difficult to see where 85 men could have been accommodated in the castle. Perhaps the adjacent coastguard cottages were also used.
42 Dobinson, *op. cit.*, 1.20.
43 *Ibid.*, 1.173–4.
44 PRO, AIR 28/120, 29 March 1913.

Fig. 11 (left): The 1931 RAF team photographed alongside Calshot Castle after winning the Schneider Trophy outright for Great Britain. Flight Lieutenant Boothman's S 6B S1595 is on the right; in the centre is the S6AN 248 of Flying Officer Snaith; to the left is the S6B S1596 of Flight Lieutenant Long

Fig. 12 (left): Calshot Castle in 1972 with the now-demolished coastguard station on the roof

Fig. 13 (right): Calshot Castle in 1984, during the re-excavation of the moat. The south-eastern part of the latter had been concreted over, probably in the late 1930s, as a hard-standing for flying boats. In the foreground are the wheels of seaplane trolleys recovered from the fill. These are now in Southampton Museum

and the relative isolation of Calshot Spit made this the most suitable location in Portsmouth Command. On 29 March 1913 a Royal Naval Air Station opened here. Three hangars were provided for 12 seaplanes and the naval personnel were split between the adjacent coastguard cottages and accommodation in Warsash. Up until August 1914 the base was used for experimental flying (Fig. 9). On the outbreak of the First World War it became a training base for seaplane pilots, but by the autumn of 1916 German submarine activity in the Channel had become so serious that Calshot became an operational base, mounting regular patrols. Satellite stations were established at Bembridge, Portland and Newhaven, together with an airship base at Polegate in East Sussex. On 1 April 1918 RNAS Calshot was transferred to the Royal Air Force, later that year becoming the School for Naval Co-operation and Aerial Navigation, RAF Calshot.[45]

The effect of all this activity is well shown in an aerial photograph of 1917 (Fig. 10). The Spit is crowded with hangars, workshops and seaplanes. Wooden huts fill all vacant spaces in the 1895 battery, stripped of its guns, some possibly to be used on the Western Front in France. A similar fate was to overtake the guns mounted on the castle roof, which by then had a small glass-sided cabin, presumably for seaplane observation purposes.[46]

After the First World War, RAF Calshot continued to expand. The 1895 battery was demolished to make space for additional hangars

and on 1 October 1931 a seaplane training squadron was established here. However, Calshot was probably best known between the wars for its association with the Schneider Trophy races. To encourage the development of aviation, the French engineer Jacques Schneider in 1913 had donated a trophy valued at 25,000 French francs to be awarded to the fastest national team. By the mid-1920s, these races attracted huge interest and the support of national governments. In July 1927, the RAF's High Speed Flight had trained at Calshot before going on to win the trophy that year in Italy. As a result, the 1929 races were held on a course over the Solent from Cowes to Hayling Island, with all the competitors based at Calshot. The RAF retained the trophy, won by Flying Officer H R D Waghorn in a Supermarine 6, flying at a speed of 328mph.[47] Two years later, the RAF team won the trophy outright (Fig. 11), with Flight Lieutenant J N Boothman attaining a speed of 340.08mph, a record broken later that September by G H Stainforth who achieved a speed of 407.5mph.[48] As Jacques Schneider had anticipated, these races forced the pace of aviation development. In Britain's case, the lessons learnt over the Solent were to be applied a few years later to the direct descendant of the Supermarine 6 and 6B, with the creation of the Supermarine Spitfire that played such a crucial role in the Battle of Britain and was the only Allied fighter aircraft to remain in production throughout the Second World War.

In 1938, with war seemingly inevitable, the Air Ministry purchased Calshot Spit and by Easter 1939 had cleared it of all beach huts.[49] The month after the outbreak of the Second World War, RAF Calshot's duties were defined as training and flying boat repairs.[50] For the moment, the castle itself remained unarmed and the greatest threat was thought to come from the air. By early December 1939, a barge mounting two 3-inch anti-aircraft guns and a Bofors gun had been moored alongside. Air-raid shelters were provided in the north-western part of the moat and a very substantial reinforced concrete generator house was built just outside the gatehouse, partly in the moat.[51]

Calshot Castle's importance was to change with the fall of France in May and June 1940. In May

45 PRO, AIR 28/120. This is the Station Record Book that has provided most of the information on the flying-boat history of Calshot.
46 By February 1916 only the two 4.7-inch QF guns remained in position [Dobinson, *op. cit.*, 2.264]. These must have been removed that year. The roof-top cabin can be seen in a number of inter-war photographs of Calshot.

47 *The Times*, 7 September 1929.
48 *Ibid.*, 14 September 1931. The Station Record Book records that the speed on 29 September was 408.8mph [PRO, AIR 28/120].
49 PRO, AIR 28/120, 20 May 1939.
50 *Ibid.*, 11 October 1939.
51 These were removed in the 1980s.

plans were hastily drawn up to sink a line of block-ships, culled from available merchant ships, across Southampton Water from just south of Calshot to the Hook Beacon.[52] This scheme would have required such a large number of vessels that in June a shorter line from Hythe Pier to Southampton was substituted but never implemented.[53] In September 1940 new defences were planned to protect Southampton Water from surface raiders. The gun mountings on the roof of the castle were checked and shortly afterwards two 12-pounder guns were remounted here. A little later, these were given concrete roofs as some protection against air attack. Works were also undertaken to update and increase the number of searchlights to six, with new housings formed in part on girders laid across the castle moat. Concurrently, a new battery to work in conjunction with Calshot was established on the north side of Southampton Water. Bungalow Battery, so named from its disguise as a seaside home, became operational on 30 January 1941. This too mounted two 12-pounder guns and had six searchlights. Firepower was further augmented by the re-activation of Stone Point Battery on the mainland south-west of Calshot Castle where three 6-inch mark VII guns were fixed on old naval mountings.[54] The re-arming of the castle in the autumn of 1940 was the last military alteration to be made to it. By late 1943, the tide of war had turned sufficiently for all the defences at the entrance to Southampton Water to be reduced to a 'care and maintenance' basis.[55]

After the end of the war, the keep roof housed a coastguard station until the completion of the nearby coastguard tower in the late 1970s (Fig. 12). Calshot had closed as an air base on 1 April 1961 when the RAF ceased to use flying boats. In the early 1980s, English Heritage undertook conservation of the castle's fabric and it is now displayed as it would have appeared just before the First World War (Figs 13 and 14). The nearby hangars, witness to the Spit's long aviation connections, are a recreation centre run by Hampshire County Council, while 'Douglas', one of the narrow gauge locomotives that once hauled trains of servicemen along the Spit between 1921 and 1945 (Fig. 15), is still at work in the Welsh mountains on the Talyllyn Railway.[56]

THE CALSHOT EXPRESS.

ACKNOWLEDGEMENTS

I am very grateful to Maldwin Drummond, a great source of support and advice over the years. Mrs Murley, President of the Fawley Historians, kindly supplied the photograph of the 'Calshot Express' and identified the people in the photograph of the Schneider Trophy flight. Mark Fenton has redrawn the maps and plans used in the article, which has been prepared for publication with great skill and efficiency by Jen Nelson.

Fig. 14 (top): Calshot Castle in 1985 after restoration. The tower in the right distance is the replacement coastguard tower, constructed in 1972

Fig. 15 (above): The 'Calshot Express' passing one of the flying-boat hangars on the Spit, between the wars. This narrow gauge train ran the length of the Spit carrying personnel and stores

52 PRO, ADM 179/142, 24 May 1940.
53 PRO, AIR 28/120, 3 December 1939; PRO, ADM 174/142, 24 May and 11 June 1940.
54 PRO, AIR 28/120, 4 and 28 September 1940; PRO, WO 192/307, fol 18; PRO, WO 192/306; Dobinson, *cp. cit.*, 1.170–2.
55 Dobinson, *op. cit.*, 2.329.

56 NA, AIR 28/120, 13 June 1932 (the light railway ran from the camp at Eaglehurst to the end of the Spit); NA, AIR 28/999 17 October 1953. Calshot Air Station was transferred to Maintenance Command in 1953, becoming 238 Maintenance Unit.

Glossary of technical terms used in this volume

ROMAN

Arena, -ae Sand

Canaba, -ae Civilian settlement outside a fortress

Cavea, -ae Auditorium

Colonia, -ae Settlement of veteran soldiers established by the military authority

Gladius, -i Sword

Municipium, -a Self-governing town

Retiarius, -i Gladiator armed with a net

Samian ware Fine reddish-brown pottery from Gaul

Sestertius, -i Small silver coin

Vomitorium,- a Entrance and exit passage of an amphitheatre

MEDIEVAL

Burh Defensible settlement established by royal authority

Collegiate church Church of a college of secular priests

Cloister-garth Uncovered part of a cloister, surrounded by covered passages

Honour Lordship of a group of manors

Porticus, -us (in medieval Latin) Large room or gallery

Purveyor Domestic officer responsible for provisioning, lodging and transport

Refectory Communal dining room

CARPENTRY & CONSTRUCTION

Architrave Ornamental border of an opening

Cambered Arched very slightly

Carriage piece Raking beam carrying timber steps

Closed string Raking beam holding the outer ends of timber steps

Crease Tiles or slates covering or throwing water off a joint

Dado Wainscot covering the lower part of a wall

Dado rail Ornamental upper framing member of a dado

Dogleg stair Stair without a well

Mitre Diagonal abutment of two timbers at right angles to each other

Mortice Socket cut in a timber to form a joint by clasping a tenon

Mullion Post dividing a window opening

Newel Post to which steps and balustrades are joined at the landings of a staircase with straight flights; or, axis of a spiral stair

Nogging Infill of the openings in a frame

Packing piece Timber block or wedge inserted in joints to stabilise a frame

Post Vertically aligned structural timber

On the quarter/quartered Tree trunk sawn radially into quadrants

Radial conversion Tree trunk split into tapering boards of equal breadth, each board extending from the centre of the tree to the bark

Rail Horizontally aligned timber

Riser Vertical component of a step

Sash Movable frame holding part of the glazing of a sash window

Soffit Under-surface

Strut Structural timber in compression, usually aligned diagonally

Tangential conversion Tree trunk split into parallel-sided boards of diminishing breadth

Task work/piece work Work paid for by the amount done

Tenon Projection cut out of a timber, to form a joint with another by insertion into a mortice

Through-and-through Tree trunk sawn into parallel-sided boards of diminishing breadth

Tie/tie beam Beam at eaves level, holding together the feet of a pair of rafters

Transom Rail dividing an opening

Truss Jointed frame supporting a weight, usually that of a roof

Wainscot Fine board used in lining walls or in cabinet-making

ARCHITECTURAL

Arcade Sequence of arches, side by side

Arch Opening with a curved span

Architrave Lowest horizontal division of an entablature

Balusters Small posts supporting a handrail

Balustrade Sequence of balusters, forming an open parapet

Blind Without any openings

Bolection moulding Run of moulded ornament of triple-curved profile

Capital Ornamented head of a column or pilaster

Colonnade Sequence of columns supporting horizontal spans

Column Almost cylindrical pillar with a capital

Composite One of the 'orders' (systems of decoration) of Greek temples and the buildings which emulated them

Cove Quadrant-sectioned border to a ceiling

Crenellation Parapet alternately high and low, the low parts being (or resembling) embrasures from which to fire missiles

Cusping Ornament formed by two intersecting arcs pojecting from the frame of an opening

Dado Area between the base and the cornice of the pedestal of an order of antique columns or pilasters

Donjon Principal tower of a castle

Engaged column Column abutting a wall behind it

Entablature Horizontal span of a colonnade (or an implied colonnade), ornamented in three horizontal divisions – architrave, frieze and cornice

Finial Ornamental termination of a post, pinnacle or gable

Foliate Ornamented by the representation of foliage

Frieze Central horizontal division of an entablature

Half-column Engaged columns of semicircular plan

Hood mould Ornamental moulding over an opening to throw off rain

Impost Horizontally aligned block, usually moulded, at the foot of an arch

Ionic One of the 'orders' (systems of decoration) of Greek temples and the buildings which emulated them

Jamb Side of an opening

Keystone Wedge-shaped stone (or representation of a stone) at the apex of an arch

Mask Carved representation of a face

Merlon High parts of a crenellated parapet, affording (or appearing to afford) protection for soldiers

Metope Space between the triglyphs in a frieze of the Doric order

Middle Pointed Phrase used in the 19th century to categorise 14th-century English architecture, usually synonymous with 'Decorated'

Murder hole Hole in the vault of a fortified gatehouse, through which the defenders could aim missiles

Obelisk Free-standing pillar of square plan, tapering upwards, with a shallow pyramidal termination

Pendant drop/pendant finial Ornamental termination of the lower end of a post

Pilaster Engaged column of rectangular plan

Pilastrade Sequence of pilasters supporting horizontal spans

Portico Forebuilding which is roofed, but has open sides

Pulvinated/pulvino Convex surface of a frieze

Rusticated/rustication Illusion of extra-wide joints in a masonry surface, to give the impression of crude but particularly solid masonry

Spandrel Space above and to the sides of an arch, but below a horizontal line level with its apex, and within the vertical alignment of the jambs of the opening

Voussoirs Tapering stones or bricks forming an arch

MILITARY

Bandolier Shoulder belt to hold ammunition

Barbette Platform with parapet low enough for artillery to fire over

Bastion Projecting part of a rampart, with flanks to allow defensive fire along the outside of the line

Battery Emplacement for a number of pieces of artillery

Block-ship Ship deliberately sunk to block a channel

Bofors gun Type of light anti-aircraft gun, originally manufactured in Sweden

Boom Barrier stretched across a channel to block it

Cartridge Case containing explosive and propellant charge

Casemate Bomb-proof vaulted chamber within a rampart

Corps Body of troops assigned to a special duty

Covered way Passage along the outer side of a ditch, protected by a rampart

Embrasure Opening with angled sides in parapet or rampart, through which guns are fired

Fraises Sharp stakes set horizontally in the front face of a rampart to discourage infantry assault

Glacis Regular man-made slope outside a fortification, to deflect artillery upwards and to expose attackers to fire

Hangar Shelter to house aircraft

Infantry step Ledge behind a parapet on which infantry stand to fire

Latrine Communal lavatories

Magazine Store for explosive and ammunition

Musketry Troops armed with muskets; or, fire from muskets

Ravelin Detached triangular rampart in advance of the main defensible line, in or beyond the ditch

Redoubt Small enclosed fortification without flanking defences

Round Single artillery or small arms discharge; or, an assembly of explosive propellant and projectile sufficient for one discharge

Salient Angle formed by two defensible lines projecting outward towards the field

Shot furnace Furnace for heating shot to fire at ships, to set them alight

Terreplein Level surface for mounting guns on top of rampart, behind parapet

Tête de pont Defensible work on the outer side of a ditch, protecting a bridge or causeway

Torpedo Self-propelled submarine missile, carrying a charge which explodes on impact

Traverse Lengths of rampart within and at right angles to the main line, protecting troops from flanking fire

Traversing gun Artillery piece which can be turned sideways

COSTUME

Lappets Hanging flaps of material

Mob cap Cap covering all the hair, generally worn indoors

Ruffles Strips of material of which one edge is gathered and attached to a garment

Stomacher Triangular panel in the front of a woman's dress

OFFICIAL

Board of Ordnance Senior officers of the crown responsible for munitions and fortifications

Board of Works Senior officers of the crown responsible for its buildings

Board of Treasury/Treasury Board Senior officers of the crown responsible for the management of its revenue

Clerk of chancery Officer of the Lord Chancellor's Court

Closet keeper Senior officer of the king's or queen's chamber, with responsibility for their private closet

Coastguard Officer responsible for the prevention of smuggling

Gentleman of the bedchamber High officer, usually a nobleman, attending the monarch in his or her private apartments

Lord lieutenant Head of the magistracy in each county

Lord warden of the Cinque Ports Senior officer of the crown responsible for coastal defence and administration of maritime law in Kent and Sussex

Master of the horse Third highest officer of the royal household, attending the king out of doors

Master of the robes High officer of the royal household responsible for royal clothing

Maid of honour Unmarried senior officer of gentle status, attending the queen or a royal princess

Poet laureate Senior officer of the royal household responsible for writing poems on state occasions

Sergeant painter Senior officer of the Board of Works, responsible for the painted decoration of the crown buildings

Syndic Member of a university committee responsible for a particular business

Vice-admiral Senior officer of the Admiralty appointed to administer maritime law in a particular county

Vice-chancellor Acting head of a university, representing the chancellor

Visitor Official inspector and occasional supervisor of an institution or corporation

SCIENTIFIC/TECHNICAL

Graticule Grid of fine lines in the telescope of a measuring instrument

Palynology Study of pollen grains

English Heritage Historical Review is commissioned by the Properties Presentation Department, Research and Standards Group

Copyright © English Heritage 2006
First published by English Heritage 2006
1 Waterhouse Square
138–142 Holborn
London
EC1N 2ST

Editor: Richard Hewlings
Project Editor: Jennifer Nelson
Drawings and maps: Richard Lea,
Mark Fenton and Allan Adams
Printed by: Hawthornes

Printed in England
C10 09/06 11984
ISBN 1 905624 33 6 (978 1 905624 33 1)
ISSN 1752-0169

English Heritage Historical Review publishes articles on the history of English Heritage's properties and collections.
Articles should be submitted to the editor, Richard Hewlings, at
   English Heritage
   24 Brooklands Avenue
   Cambridge
   England
   CB2 2BU

English Heritage Historical Review is published annually and is available as a single copy or on subscription from
   English Heritage Mail Order Sales
   Gillards Worldwide
   Trident Works
   Temple Cloud
   Bristol BS39 5AZ
   Tel: 01761 452 966
   Email: ehsales@gillards.com
   www.english-heritage.org.uk/EHHR

English Heritage Historical Review costs £20.00 plus post and packaging for individuals, or £45.00 plus post and packaging for institutions.